P9-DNZ-105

Street Survival

Preparation, not paranoia, is the name of the game.

Deputy Chief R. "Zip" Zbinden
Pomona, California
shooting survivor

Street Survival

TACTICS for ARMED ENCOUNTERS

Special Agent
Ronald J. Adams

Lieutenant
Thomas M. McTernan

Charles Remsberg

CALIBRE PRESS • NORTHBROOK, ILLINOIS

Published by:
CALIBRE PRESS, INC.
666 Dundee Road
Suite 1607
Northbrook, Illinois 60062
(312) 328-4411

Library of Congress Catalog Card Number: 79-57196
ISBN Number: 0-935878-00-9

*The authors, advisors and publisher accept no liability whatsoever for
any injuries to person or property resulting from the application or
adoption of any of the procedures, tactics or considerations presented
or implied in this book.*

Printed in the United States of America

To those
officers whose deaths
have taught us
the most important
survival procedures

CONTENTS

II. BASICS THAT STRENGTHEN TACTICS

ACKNOWLEDGMENTS

This book deals with *positive* tactics officers can employ on the street to effectively use their own firearms to defeat those of assailants. It is devoted exclusively to understanding and mastering techniques that work for survival in *real life situations*—not what works in range competition against paper targets or what some academician in a classroom speculates might work in some hypothetical encounter.

Unfortunately, most of the current literature on so-called "combat shooting" falls into these latter categories. Few street-wise experts or truly contemporary articles have emerged on street survival, although deadly assaults on the police continue to occur year after year, with alarming frequency. While officers are dying, well-meaning training authorities too often seem obsessed with discussing such firearms esoterica as customized grips, ribbed barrels, fancy leather gear and other irrelevant subjects, rather than the real issues of tactics to help officers survive in armed confrontations.

We began our research by analyzing more than 400 detailed reports of officer-involved shootings and by surveying some 50 law enforcement agencies about the firearms instructions they offer...the major problems their officers encounter on the street...and what their greatest survival needs appear to be. For more than a year, our research team then searched coast to coast to identify practical, realistic tactics to meet those needs. More than 30 street-wise authorities who have devoted their careers to officer survival and nearly a dozen police departments on the cutting edge of survival training were consulted for their best tactical procedures. Their contribution, plus the authors' cumulative 26 years' experience, most of it in high-risk or survival-oriented assignments, have formed the basis of what you will read here.

Without the help and knowledge of many people, this book could not have become what it is: the most comprehensive compilation of street-relevant survival methods ever available. For their special assistance, we want to acknowledge: Lieutenant Francis J. McGee of the Firearms and Tactics Section of the New York City Police Department, considered by many to be the "father" of the street survival movement; Pierce R. Brooks, chief investigator in California's infamous "Onion Field" case; Officer John S. Farnam of the Elroy (WI) Police Department, a combat veteran and leading on-site consultant on weapons training programs for law enforcement agencies, and Lieutenant Thad C. Curtis, Commander of Technical Services for the Pima County (AZ) Sheriff's Department, an enthusiastic proselytizer and practitioner of survival awareness. These officers reviewed the manuscript in draft form and offered innumerable constructive comments.

Those to whom we are grateful for help with research include: James Daugherty, Senior Police Firearms Instructor, and Herb Chambers, Education and Training Division, National Rifle Association of America; Inspector Robert W. Martin, Supervisor of Firearms Training, Philadelphia Police Academy; Sergeant Ray King, Rangemaster (ret.), and Sergeant Donald E. Smith, Chief Firearms Examiner, Chicago Police Department; W. Fred Pickler, specialist in high risk patrol tactics and chemical munitions and President of Fred Pickler & Associates; Lieutenant W.L. Dickey, Commander of the Ordnance Division, Memphis Police Department; Al Burnett and Len Ross, Firearms Trainers, Department of the Treasury, Federal Law Enforcement Training Center; James Whitmore, Assistant Professor, University of Illinois, Police Training Institute; Chief Eugene Ferrara, University of Cincinnati Police Department; Robert L. Monroe, former Instructor, FBI National Academy; Joseph H. Chernicoff, Director of Training, U.S. Association of Firearms Instructors and Coaches; Ed Lovette, Director of Training, New Mexico Law Enforcement Academy; Sergeant Robert Givan, Instructor, Advanced Combat Training, Indianapolis Police Department; Paul A. Zolbe, Chief, Uniform Crime Reports Section, F.B.I.; and Sergeant Dick Newell, Officer-in-Charge, Ordnance Unit, Los Angeles Police Academy.

We are also appreciative of the candor with which certain officers shared their memories and emotions about personal armed encounters. These include: Deputy Chief R. "Zip" Zbinden, Pomona (CA) Police Department; Detective Jack Fisher, San Bernardino County (CA) Sheriff's Office, and Sergeant Jerry Dunn and Detective Jim Rowe, Riverside (CA) Police Department. Valuable insights into officers' psychological reactions to shooting situations were gained from interviews with Walter Gorski, a psychological consultant to Pennsylvania law enforcement agencies, and Dr. Nahman Greenberg, a Chicago psychoanalyst and authority on stress behavior.

Finally, we want to thank Dennis Anderson, who conceived, produced and directed the award-winning instructional films, **Survival Shooting Techniques** and **Handling Firearms** for MTI Tele-programs Inc., of Schiller Park, Illinois. His unique motion pictures have pioneered in communicating the state of the art of survival training. Without his tireless collaboration, constant support, astute insights and high professional standards, this book would not have been written.

INTRODUCTION

```
13 05 04.10/78 00396 CA
TXT AP.
ML01K21707

TO        APB RELAY TO LOCAL AGENCIES

   MONTANA HIGHWAY PATROL ADVISES OFFICER, AGED
30, SHOT AND KILLED APPROXIMATELY 3 00 P.M., 4/8.
VICTIM, WORKING WITH LINCOLN COUNTY DEPUTY
ATTEMPTED TO STOP SUBJECT WANTED ON FELONY CHARGE.
AFTER HIGH-SPEED CHASE, SUBJECT EXITED HIS VEHICLE
AND BEGAN FIRING AT PATROL CAR.

   VICTIM STRUCK IN CHEST WITH .308-CALIBER RIFLE.
DEPUTY RETURNED FIRE AND SUBJECT FLED TO NEARBY
RESIDENCE WHERE HE HELD TWO HOSTAGES FOR SEVERAL
HOURS BEFORE SURRENDERING.

AUTHORITY-P. ZOLBE
        FBI-UCR WASH DC    BKR
```

```
13 56 04/17/78 00551 CA
TXT AP.
ML01K23413

TO        APB - RELAY TO LOCAL AGENCIES

   CATOOSA COUNTY, GEORGIA, S.O. ADVISES DEPUTY
WM AGED 24, SHOT AND KILLED APPROXIMATELY 1 50
P.M., 4/14.  VICTIM HAD STOPPED TO ASSIST ANOTHER
OFFICER WHO HAD JUST DETAINED ARMED ROBBERY SUS-
PECT.  WHILE BEING SEARCHED BY FIRST OFFICER,
SUBJECT GAINED CONTROL OF VICTIM'S .357 MAGNUM
HANDGUN.  VICTIM SHOT IN NECK AND ABDOMEN.  FIRST
OFFICER, ALSO WOUNDED, RETURNED GUNFIRE AS SUSPECT
FLED SCENE.

AUTHORITY-P. ZOLBE
        FBI-UCR WASH DC    ACA
```

```
07 55 08/9/77 00487 CA
TXT AP.
ML01J54099

TO          APB - RELAY TO LOCAL AGENCIES

  SAN PABLO, CALIFORNIA, PD ADVISES OFFICER, AGED
42, SHOT AND KILLED APPROXIMATELY 11 48 AM, 8/4.
VICTIM OFFICER RESPONDED TO SILENT ALARM AT LOCAL
JEWELRY STORE, THE SITE OF PREVIOUS UNFOUNDED
ALARMS.  UPON ENTERING THE STORE HE DISCOVERED
ROBBERY BEING COMMITTED BY TWO NM S.  ONE ROBBER
FIRED A SHOT FROM A .38-CALIBER REVOLVER STRIKING
OFFICER IN HEAD, KILLING HIM INSTANTLY.  ONE SUB-
JECT APPREHENDED IN IMMEDIATE NEIGHBORHOOD. SECOND
SUBJECT ESCAPED.

AUTHORITY-P. ZOLBE
        FBI-UCR WASH DC    JRR
```

```
12 49 11/28/77 01030 CA
TXT AP.
ML01J68923

TO          APB-RELAY TO LOCAL AGENCIES

  MILWAUKEE, WISCONSIN, PD ADVISES PATROLMAN,
AGED 27, SHOT AND KILLED APPROXIMATELY 5 00 PM,
11/25.  VICTIM OFFICER AND PARTNER RESPONDED TO
FAMILY DISTURBANCE CALL AT LOCAL RESIDENCE.  AS
VICTIM APPROACHED DOOR TO KNOCK, SUBJECT APPEARED
IN DOORWAY AND FIRED RIFLE STRIKING OFFICER IN
CHEST.  SUBJECT, NM 38, BARRICADED SELF IN HOUSE,
BUT SHORTLY THEREAFTER SURRENDERED.

AUTHORITY-P. ZOLBE
        FBI-UCR WASH DC    RMR
```

Every three to four days, on the average, notification clatters across the teletypes of the National Law Enforcement Telecommunications System that the life of another law enforcement officer has been taken. And after the official regrets are spoken, the taps sounded, the badge retired to a place of honor, an unfortunate, brutal truth too often remains: more effort is likely to have gone into planning the funeral for the slain officer than he or his department devoted to his survival.

In some cases, the fault lies with the officer failing to practice what he has been taught. Other times, a department is culpable for sending its officers into the street with little appreciation or concern for what it takes to stay alive.

Usually, it's a combination. The survival training of the classroom, the gym and the range, however earnest, fails in crucial ways to reflect the challenges of the real world. And the officer, complacent in the knowledge that most people in law enforcement reach retirement without ever confronting or using deadly force, makes no effort on his own to compensate for these shortcomings. Day in and day out, he answers so many calls where nothing happens that he comes to assume, insidiously, that nothing *can* happen.

And then it does.

In the last decade alone, more than 1,100 city, county, state and federal officers have been feloniously slain in the performance of their duties. During one typical year in that period, 19,000 officers besides those killed were injured in nearly 50,000 assaults on police. The deaths and injuries have included both sexes, have come from all sizes and types of communities and have run the gamut of officer rank, experience and assignment.

Ninety-five per cent of those killed were attacked with guns. Some victim officers were excellent target shooters. But in nearly 60 per cent of the cases, the officers involved were so unprepared to react that they *did not even get their guns drawn* before violence erupted. Only 27 per cent managed to shoot back. Only 15 per cent were able to wound or kill their assailants.[1]

There's no denying that an officer faces critical disadvantages in a shooting situation. His uniform, his marked vehicle, his spoken commands make him highly visible and easily identifiable to any would-be assailant—while a potential assailant may be difficult or impossible for an officer to sense or see in advance.

Despite the ceremony attached to an officer's funeral, how many officers have an interest in finding out what really happened during that fatal mistake?

Those close to the victim officer express grief in different ways. The officer in this case died from a "routine" traffic stop.

---

1. FBI "Law Enforcement Officers Killed" Summaries.

3

An assailant can decide when, where and whom to shoot, on grounds that are purely selfish or totally irrational and indiscriminate; if his gun is aimed and cocked it takes him only half a second to get off accurate fire.[2] An officer is usually influenced by moral and psychological considerations that inhibit instant, impulsive action. Even if he has no personal qualms about killing, he must evaluate whether the circumstances legally justify his using deadly force and whether innocent bystanders might be harmed. If his gun is holstered, he needs a minimum of 1 to 1.2 seconds to draw and fire, assuming he is *extremely* skilled. However, he may not be thoroughly familiar or comfortable with the firearm that could save his life. The myth persists that officers tend to be ''gun nuts,'' both before and after they join law enforcement. In truth, an estimated 70 per cent of law enforcement recruits have *no* previous experience with firearms, and even after instruction, many are not proficient enough with their guns to adequately defend themselves. In one major city, until recently, recruits were assigned to the field after limited target practice and only four hours of orientation.[3] In many smaller communities, officers receive no training at all; they are expected to pick up whatever they need to know on the job.

2. ''**Some Comments on the Hostage Situation**,'' by J.C. Muirhead, *The Police Chief*, February, 1978.

3. *Police Use of Deadly Force*, Catherine Milton, et al., Police Foundation, 1977.

Tribute to a comrade. Highway patrolmen fill church pews during services for a veteran officer, killed with his own revolver during a traffic stop.

Rescue workers try in vain to save the life of a highway patrolman shot while stopping a driver for running a toll booth.

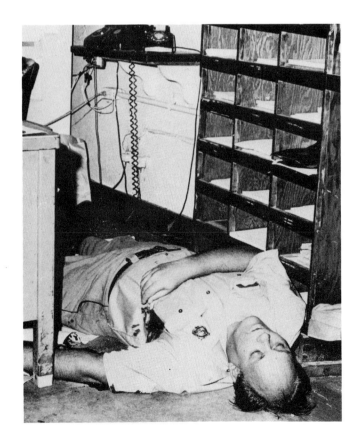

This officer was talking on the phone at his precinct when an armed assailant entered and fired three times. The officer died unarmed.

A .357 Magnum round was fired at this officer after he and his partner responded to a domestic disturbance call. The bullet hit the officer's nameplate [held in his right hand], twisting the metal and ripping two holes in his leather jacket. His only injury was a bruise on one arm.

Among officers who have managed to survive shooting attacks, more than one has admitted, "I was just lucky." With equal candor, many concede that despite a close call with death, they still would not know what to do differently the next time around.

Luck is a frail reed on which to hang your life—especially if other alternatives are available. And dismal as the police position may appear, there *are* alternatives for handling most violent encounters. Indeed, with the knowledge of survival methods now available, your opportunities for staying alive on the street have never been greater.

Some studies of confrontations have revealed that in as few as 1 per cent of shootings are officers genuinely ambushed without warning or fired at for no apparent reason.[4] Most times, they have prior knowledge of prospective danger. Even when violence does explode suddenly, their fate is not always innately hopeless. *The overwhelming majority of officers killed in gunfights most likely could have emerged alive*—if:

    1) they had understood the dynamics of armed confrontations;

    2) they had properly evaluated the risks they were facing;

    3) they had planned what to do in the event of a deadly threat, and

    4) they had known and, through practice, had mastered appropriate survival tactics.

4. "Analysis of Police Combat Situations," New York City Police Department, 1974.

This book can help make you *survival sensitive.* The techniques it emphasizes are designed to affect the way you prepare, plan and react, to keep you alive in *real* situations. They are not hypotheses, but proven procedures, based on the insights of officers who have experienced gun battles and survived— and on the lessons left behind by those who have died.

These tactics fall into two broad categories: 1) those that will help you *prevent* risky situations from escalating into life-threatening encounters, and 2) those that can help you *survive* if, despite your best efforts, violence does erupt. Procedures from both categories are integrated throughout, so that while each chapter relates to firearms, the emphasis is not always on actual shooting performance.

Among other things, you will come to understand the common attitudes that lead suspects to engage the police in gunfights...officer attitudes that hamper response...the circumstances likely to influence confrontations...safe methods for approaching high-risk situations...ways to use light, verbal commands, surprise, movement and protective cover, concealment and equipment to reduce or overcome a suspect's advantage...as well as procedures to assure that your gun will work when you need it...and the latest, practical techniques for delivering swift, accurate, deadly fire. By *studying* the table of contents you can review, in summary form, the elements of any armed confrontation, from the things you need to know and do before firearms are used to the psychological pressures you may feel afterward. In effect, the chapter headings encapsulate the factors you should be continually concerned about, for these most likely will determine your ability to survive, whether you acknowledge that to be the case or not.

The circumstances in which the use of deadly force is permitted vary considerably with state laws and departmental policies. However, *all* jurisdictions permit an officer to shoot to protect his own life or the lives of other innocent persons from imminent danger. Where shooting is called for in the tactics presented here, we have considered those to be the circumstances. This helps underscore the fact that law enforcement firearms are *defensive* tools, not to be used offensively.

The use and handling of revolvers, semiautomatic pistols and shotguns are referenced throughout because they are the most common law enforcement firearms. If you're like the vast majority of officers, you carry a .38 cal. revolver as your regulation on-duty weapon. But you may use a semiautomatic off-duty or as a back-up gun, and if you're assigned to street patrol you may have a shotgun in your patrol car. The more proficient you become with both the mechanical and tactical use of these firearms, the higher your survival quotient, for you can never be certain which you will have at hand at the crucial moment.

Your firearm, of course, is always the tool of last resort. Survival should begin long *before* the moment you need to fire, and if you wait until then to think about it, you are depending on luck, whether you realize it or not.

True survival readiness is like an equilateral triangle involving:

Mental/Physical Conditioning

Tactics   Shooting Skill

All corners are of equal importance to the whole, and the omission of any element leaves a potentially lethal gap. For a defense structure that will enable you to control the outcome of most life-or-death encounters, your mind, your body and your gun must be molded into a combined, coordinated "weapons system."

The system approach is the core of this book. It requires that you develop skill at a variety of distinct but related procedures of anticipation and response. Some involve shooting, the instant delivery and accurate placement of rounds. Some concern forestalling or avoiding an assailant's shots, making yourself a hard target. *All can be learned.*

Some survival principles may appear harsh. Survival is not community relations, concerned with courtesy and codes of fair conduct; there are no "gentlemen's rules" in a gunfight. Some of the estimated one to four million people carrying concealed guns illegally in this country (and some who own them legally, as well) are willing to take on the police on incredibly brutal terms. To save your life or someone else's, you may sometimes need the **ultimate** responses.

The ability to use decisive tactics successfully, however, does not equate with recklessness. Actually, it is the *un*skilled officer who is likeliest to be reckless, and thus a danger not only to himself and fellow officers, but to the public he is sworn to protect. Because of his lack of confidence in his ability to protect himself in risky situations, he will react to threats of violence with panic born of desperation. A trained officer, on the other hand, is confident because he is ready, and his controlled skills can help him keep violence to a minimum or stop it instantly. Realistic tactics can reduce the number of incidents that escalate to the point of gunfire, reduce the number of suspects shot or killed by police, reduce the number of tragedies where innocent parties are shot because of mistaken identity, as well as substantially reduce the number of officers wounded or slain—even though the number of contacts between police and criminals remains undiminished.

Nothing set forth in the pages that follow should be regarded as The Absolute Answer to all survival problems. *There are no absolutes in tactics.* No two situations are ever exactly alike, no set of procedures always effective. What's offered are *options* that are valuable for your repertoire of skills because they will work for most officers in most situations most of the time.

Most survival techniques are simple, based on common sense. But they require *extensive practice* to be used successfully. You need to know what works for you, and the tactics you favor need to be honed until they become natural and reflexive. FOR, UNDER STRESS, IN A CRISIS, YOU WILL INSTINCTIVELY REVERT TO THE WAY YOU HAVE TRAINED.

Training to face reality takes extra time, extra energy, extra creativity. It requires that *you* accept the responsibility for assuring your survival education. You need to work constantly at refining, adapting and supplementing your survival capabilities, not only in formal and informal training sessions, but, most important, on a daily basis in the course of your patrol duties.

It's easier, of course, to play the odds that you will be among the fortunate majority whose lives are never challenged. But that's a game of Russian roulette that too many officers have lost.

There are no guarantees in law enforcement. The only predictable is the unpredictable. Your next call could be another "routine" run...or it could be the one that tests everything you've got.

If you wonder whether you're ready, ask yourself: "How many people could have had me today if they'd really wanted me?"

And then ask: "What would I have done if they'd tried?"

The body of a man who moments earlier killed one officer, seriously wounded two others, and wounded his wife and a neighbor. The gun in the foreground belonged to one of the officers.

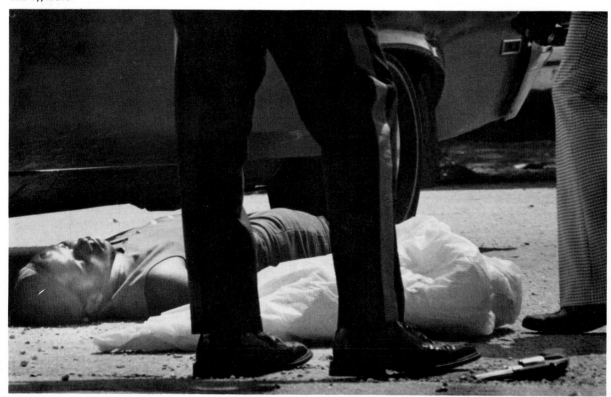

I. TACTICS

...for Survival

THEM AND US 1

Most Americans think they know about gun fights. They've seen thousands on TV. During the average hour's action show, nine handweapons are displayed, guns mostly, and they're used with dramatic derring-do. Policemen with handguns successfully blast away at adversaries several hundred yards distant...a detective with a two-inch barrel revolver outshoots a criminal with a scoped rifle... an agent fires a derringer into the air and brings an airplane crashing down...

People believe it's possible, including some cops. Many officers truly believe they are carrying guns and ammunition which will literally blow people away—even though it's nearly impossible to move a human body with a bullet from a handgun.

At the same time the distortions of this cultural saturation endow guns with super capabilities, they generally sanitize their effect. Eighty-four per cent of the bullets fired on TV miss their targets entirely, according to one foundation study. Only eight per cent or less cause injury or death, and even then, they induce "little bloodletting or suffering."

To the men and women who've been there, real-life gun fights are altogether different. What the movie or TV screen fantasizes as extended, exotic, antiseptic episodes, they know in fact to be fast, banal, brutal encounters, played for keeps, often with pain and much blood.

Indeed, officers suddenly thrust into armed confrontations often are startled to discover just how different they really are.

In interviews excerpted below, eight veterans of officer-involved shootings share their perceptions of what the experience was like. Four of these men have been convicted of killing law enforcement officers and are serving time in Illinois correctional

13

facilities. The other four **are law enforcement** officers in California who have been critically wounded—and *survived*.

In many respects, these individuals typify Them and Us, the two sides of any confrontation.

Their comments about their respective tactics, presented in their exact words, are a fitting prelude to realistic survival education. Their insights regarding attitude, preparedness and mistakes made are particularly important.

No factors are more pivotal to the outbreak and outcome of shooting incidents. Few are less well understood on both sides of the law.

INMATE 1:

There was a stick-up that morning. I walked into the store, armed with a .38 revolver. I drew down on the cashier and took $3,500 cash money. Then there was a shrill whistle throughout the store, a warning that police were coming. I started out, running the length of the store, about 100 feet, at which time the police officer stepped in the doorway with his revolver drawn, I guess to assess the situation inside. It scared the hell out of me. And I shot him.

Q. *When you fired, how did you do it?*

A. Instinctively. I was about 15 feet from the door. My pistol was at my side, and when I saw him standing in the doorway, well, my gun came up and one shot went off. Reflex. Nothing that was aimed.

Q. *Would you perceive yourself as being a good marksman?*

A. No, I wouldn't. I never really had much practice. I think that anyone can point a revolver and shoot it at a subject and hit. You just do like this (quickly points finger)—BOOM—and shoot to kill.

Q. *At the moment you squeezed the trigger, what thought was going through your mind?*

A. Escape. The officer was a threat to my freedom and to my greed for the money. He was in the way.

Q. *What mistakes do you think he made?*

A. He should have waited for a back-up force. He could have hidden and issued a verbal challenge: "Drop your weapon, I've got you covered!"... "Come out!" Anything. He should have never stepped into that doorway, putting his body in jeopardy.

Q. *Now, you're a weightlifter, you keep yourself in good shape. How would you compare your physical and mental fitness for dealing with a shooting situation versus the officers you knew when you were out on the street?*

14

A. Most police officers are not conditioned. They're overweight, they drink a lot of beer, they stay up at night and they don't sleep very well. I think most have got ulcers, heart trouble, premature illnesses. But a person that keeps himself conditioned, his mind is steady, his eyes are clear, his aim is good. He's got more stamina, more patience, a sharper perspective on things.

Q. *Mentally, what kind of preparation do you think most guys on the street have, so far as being ready to take on a cop if they have to?*

A. I think that most people who come from high crime areas, they view the police as the enemy, a threat. Obviously, a person who carries a concealed weapon, he's not ready to submit because he has the audacity to possess a firearm in the first place. Therefore, it's a matter of who gets the drop on who. Once I pull my pistol, well, yours is counterfeit. That's the way it's played.

DEPUTY CHIEF R. ''ZIP'' ZBINDEN:

The call was a ''family peace disturbance,'' and my approach was rather ignorant. I went right up and knocked on the door of the house. The mother of the man causing the trouble let me in and said he was down the hallway off the living room. I obediently started down the hallway. He came out of one of the bedrooms at the end.

In his right hand, he held what appeared to be a 9-shot, .22 target pistol, pointed directly at my sternum. It was very steady in his hand. He had a blank stare on his face, and he was looking just directly at me. I knew I was in a bad position...this long hallway, and my weapon not drawn.

I tried to inch up on him very slowly without any sudden movements, speaking about the weather, anything that could come to my mind and keep him from becoming frightened or disturbed. That was about all I had going for me. He was in control of the situation. I had no idea what he was going to do. I could predict a lot of alternatives, but I couldn't predict exactly what or when.

When I got within about four or five feet of him, I thought he had relented. His hand with the gun dropped to his side, his head dropped. I started patting myself on the back so hard I about broke my arms. I thought I'd silver-tongue-deviled him right out of his original intention.

I extended my hand to grab his gun.

The weapon came up from his side. It was an extremely rapid movement. It immediately discharged, and I was struck right here below where the pens are in my pocket.

A weird feeling went through me. It wasn't like I'd seen on TV. I felt like someone had punched me with a closed fist and then run a hot poker through my chest. I knew it was bad.

I grasped his weapon with my left hand and when I took it away from him, he had no control at all over his movement, action or anything. He was just a vegetable standing there. I walked outside to wait for my back-up and an ambulance.

Before this happened, I used to think I could stop off in a phone booth and change clothes and there'd be a big red "S" underneath my shirt. I found out that I was subject to human frailties and human errors and I hurt just like everybody else.

INMATE 2:

The killing occurred over a traffic ticket. One word led to another and the officer hit me. When he hit me, he went for his gun and I went for mine. I just beat him to the shot. He died and I wounded his partner.

Q. *What kind of a gun did you have?*

A. I had a .380 Browning automatic. I wasn't a marksman, so I just held it and pulled the trigger, and the gun took care of itself.

Q. *Prior to that incident, had you given any thought to how you would deal with a police officer if you ever became involved with one?*

A. Oh, yes sir. At the time, I was influenced by the teachings of the Black Muslims, the rhetoric of the Black Panthers and other black revolutionaries. So I'd given some thought to an encounter with the pigs. I had an idea of what I'd do if I was confronted with a belligerent cop.

Q. *How did you feel the moment you shot the officer?*

A. I didn't have any feelings at all.

Q. *From your experience, how well do you think officers are prepared in shooting situations?*

A. Mentally, I don't think they are prepared that well. A policeman's job isn't for everyone. It takes ability, it takes courage, it takes patience, a feeling for humanity. But most officers, they're scared, they're nervous, they're prejudiced. They shoot, and then ask questions later.

Q. *In most shooting situations, where do you think officers are looking just before everything explodes?*

A. Well, I would say most police, they're trying to view the whole body, which I don't think is correct. The whole body is not going to harm you. The most dangerous part is a man's hands. If you can try to get the general view of his hands, especially his right hand, even if he's got his back turned to you, you're pretty safe.

SERGEANT JERRY DUNN:

The post office called and said a guy we wanted for bank robbery was there picking up a package. As I drove up, I saw him walk down the post office steps and head around toward the back of the building. I confronted him and told him he was under arrest. He started saying, ''Not me. I didn't do anything.'' I felt I had the right guy. But I'd only seen a picture of him and there was still that doubt. I kept saying, ''You're under arrest,'' and he started fumbling with his belt, with his back somewhat towards me.

He came up with a gun, turned around and started firing. I tried to shoot back twice as fast. We hit each other. I went down first. He stood over me with his gun in both hands, pointing at me. Then he fell.

Q. *What kind of impact do you think TV and films have had on the way officers perceive themselves in a shooting?*

A. Well, in the movies, an officer gets shot, stuffs a bandana in the wound, goes on and catches the bad guy, and then he's home in the next scene having a drink with a little blonde. It doesn't happen that way.

Q. *What's different?*

A. Well, in my case I got shot in the thigh. At the time I didn't feel that was a serious wound. But I understand if I hadn't been close to a hospital I would have died within four minutes.

Q. *How accurate is an officer likely to be in a shooting?*

A. I think we actually hit the target we're shooting at only about 20 per cent of the time. Suspects have a much better average, probably 40 per cent. The suspect knows what he's doing, but the cop can't take any action until the suspect does. Then it may be too late.

Q. *What did you do wrong?*

A. I didn't wait for a back-up officer. I felt that time was of the essence. With hindsight, I can see that the situation could have been resolved better had I kept my suspect under surveillance and had officers surround the building with me.

Q. *Based on your situation, what would you say is the difference between target shooting on a range and being in the real thing on the street?*

A. They're as different as night and day. Shooting targets, there's no pressure as such. But firing at an individual who's returning fire is just an unbelievable experience. No matter how much practicing you do on the range, you're never prepared to have to fire and be fired upon by another individual.

Q. *What was going through your mind at that point?*

A. Disbelief. I couldn't believe that anyone would want to shoot me. Here I am, just an ordinary guy doing his job. Why would an individual try and kill me just because I wanted to apprehend him? I've done it dozens and dozens of times. I was under the impression that nothing would ever happen to me. I believe officers, as a rule, feel that they're invincible, that they're going to do their job, go home and start over the next day. Then all of a sudden I found someone who'd rather die than be incarcerated. I couldn't believe it.

Q. *At the moment the first round went into the suspect, what was your reaction?*

A. I don't know to this day which round struck him. I never saw any look on his face, any reaction at all from any of my rounds. I had no idea whether I'd shot him. In fact, I didn't even know that I had been shot, except that I had a pain in my leg that knocked my feet out from under me.

Q. *How much of your surviving do you think was luck versus your being ready to come out on top?*

A. A large portion of it was luck. The bad guy didn't get me in a vital spot and I did him. It could have been just the other way around.

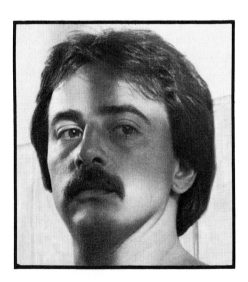

INMATE 3:

My uncle and I pulled up in front of the liquor store, and he handed me the gun. He said, ''Now's as good a time as any.'' I walked past the place once, then came through the door and pulled out his Rossi snub-nose .38. A guy was standing to my right I hadn't seen. He just ducked his head down and started toward me running, trying to get his gun out at the same time. I realized he was a cop. The next thing I knew, we both went flying up against the wall and he was shot. The bullet went right in the top of the center of his head and came out the back.

Q. *Had you had very much experience with guns?*

A. No, I'd never shot a gun in my life, not even a rifle. I had absolutely no experience at all.

Q. *How prepared do you think he was to fire on you?*

A. I don't think he was prepared to fire at all. I don't think he really wanted to shoot me, or he probably would have from the beginning.

Q. *Do you think guys on the street are more prepared than police?*

A. Probably. The stick-up man realizes when he goes in that the situation might come down to where he has to shoot, whereas if an officer's caught in there, he's caught by surprise.

Q. *What do you think the officer should have done?*

A. What I wanted him to do, like lay down on the floor. He could have tried to get a good description of me, perhaps waited til I turned around, then shot me. Anything but try to draw his gun on a gun that was already drawn.

Q. *What was your reaction to him when he started coming toward you? Did you feel that you were going to win?*

A. No, because I wasn't trying to shoot him. That's the point. I didn't have any time to think. I mean, before I realized it, the man was on me and the gun was shot.

Q. *Just one round?*

A. Yeah. One Shot.

Q. *Now, your brother wants to be a cop. What would be your hope for him if he ever got involved in a shooting situation?*

A. I would hope he was better trained. Like, I think it would have been no problem for the officer in my situation to even say a word to me and he could have disarmed me. If he'd known what to do, he wouldn't have been killed. It's that simple.

DETECTIVE JACK FISHER:

Earlier in the day a prisoner had escaped from a sheriff's sub-station. He'd asked to go to the toilet, and an officer had unlocked one of his handcuffs. He jumped the officer, wrestled him to the floor, took his .357 Magnum and stole a patrol car. During a chase, he lost control of the car and skidded off the road. He then grabbed the shotgun from the car and took off up a mountainside.

A sergeant and I were on the point of a search party, tracking his footprints. We were coming up on a little clearing when the sergeant saw him, crouched way down low under a large bush, holding the shotgun.

My first reaction was to dive for a bush, take cover. The suspect brought the shotgun up on the sergeant, and when he wouldn't throw it down like we commanded, I fired my first round. I missed. He spun around and fired at me. The blast went over my right shoulder and one or two of the pellets hit me on the forehead. I fired, I think, six rounds until he finally went down and didn't get up, hit in the knee and the heart.

Q.   *What's the difference between shooting paper targets and shooting live people?*

A.   The primary difference, of course, is the paper targets don't shoot back. Also they don't move very often, you usually have good background, the light's good—so it's easy, it becomes routine. And, of course it's different in the movies, too. There the officer can drop anybody at 200 or 300 yards with a revolver, his gun never empties, he doesn't have to worry about reloading at critical times. It's just not that way.

Q.   *What's it like to get shot at by someone?*

A.   Very frightening, scary, all the words for that. But you don't realize that at the time, when you're instinctively reacting. The scariness comes later, when you sit back and critique yourself. Then you get scared, because there's usually something you didn't do that you should have.

Q.   *What did you do wrong?*

A.   The biggest thing, I think, was to miss with my first shot, thereby affording him the opportunity to crank one off at me. Had he been successful, I would have been out of the picture, and who knows what would have happened.

Q.   *Say I've been an officer for about six months. What kind of advice could you give me in a shooting situation?*

A.   If you don't remember another thing, remember to do *something* immediately. Move, run, jump up and down, fall down on the ground, yell, scream—just *react* so you're not standing there giving the suspect a perfect target. Anything might give you an edge, because he may be amazed at what you're doing and therefore not pull the trigger. That could give you the opportunity to draw your weapon, if you don't already have it out, and get him before he gets you.

Q.   *What does it feel like to shoot somebody?*

A.   You think about it later. To take a human life is never a pleasure and I don't ever expect it to be one. I've had some uncomfortable moments as the result, but I did what I had to do.

INMATE 4:

Fifty-eight police officers were staked out around a plant where they'd been informed we were gonna rob an armored car. We came and waited for an hour or two, but the truck was late, so we proceeded to leave. A gunshot was fired, and we returned fire. Five or ten minutes later, after the shooting had ceased, a police officer was found dead, along with two of my co-defendants.

Q. *Was the officer out in the open when he fired?*

A. He was positioned directly in front of the vehicle I was occupying and 15 to 20 feet directly in front of six officers who were shooting over his shoulder. Testimony later revealed he was shot by them due to the fact they was blind from the bright light.

Q. *What kind of gun did you have?*

A. I had an AR-15, a semi-automatic high-powered rifle. It's the civilian version of the M-16. Very powerful and very damaging weapon.

Q. *Are you a good shot?*

A. Well, at a distance of 25 to 30 feet, I would hit a moving target of moderate size eight out of ten times. I knew the most successful criminal would be the one who had the most experience in handling a gun, so I studied guns. I used to go hunting and to a rifle range and shoot shotguns, AR-15 rifles, M-16s, Army .45s, .357 Magnums with six-inch barrels, police specials and P-38s.

Q. *How proficient do you think most officers are with a handgun?*

A. I don't think my vocabulary contains the words to describe the lousiness of the way police use their handguns. When they dismount their handgun from its holster, they're not fixed firmly, they don't tense themselves up. They're very loose and casual. That indicates poor accuracy, poor efficiency. Anyone who's fired a handgun knows that you should be as sturdy as possible when you're in a firing position.

Q. *To your knowledge of the way things are on the street, what do you think the easiest way would be to take out a cop?*

A. To watch his movement. A good armed robber or a good burglar, he have one thing in his mind: to pull off a successful caper. In order to do that, he must have his eyes on the door. And coming through the door, he always expects the police. He anticipates. In my experience, officers just come through the door with their gun unholstered, not knowing where the criminal is located. They leave themselves vulnerable...no protection. I think it's an emotional reaction, because a great deal of your officers is actually afraid, so the thing that mostly runs through their mind is I have to get in here, make this arrest and that's it. They never look at the possibility of being killed in the process.

Q. *What odds do you give an officer in that kind of situation?*

A. If I sought out to commit a robbery, I would give the police a 30 per cent chance of living, once he walked through the door. As soon as I hear a noise, I'm automatically turning and shooting. I want what I've come for and I want to get away, so my objective is higher than any officer that plan to arrest me.

Q. *And you think you're better prepared?*

A. Than the average guy who goes to the academy maybe once a week, spends 10 or 20 minutes there? Definitely. Criminals study the police. I've studied the way police move, their emotional anticipations. I always watch the officer, not for his eyes or his hands—his chest part. I have his chest part in visual sight.

Q. *And you can shoot him without reservation?*

A. I'll put it in this perspective: where there's $2,000 or more involved, the average guy have no reservations whatsoever about who he kills. In fact, he'd be more inclined to kill a police officer rather than anyone else. He expects the worst to happen.

DETECTIVE JIM ROWE:

I was a patrolman when the shooting occurred. I was on my motorcycle checking out a lower parking level for a guy who'd stolen two guns from a pawnshop when I noticed someone who looked like him walk by on the sidewalk above. I rode up to within 8 or 9 feet behind him. I had my gun out, pointing at him. I yelled, "Hold it right there!" He kind of looked over his right shoulder and then spun around. Boom! His first shot hit me in the neck. I fired back, but he took off and kept going.

Q. *What effect do you think TV and films have had on officer survival?*

A. Definitely detrimental. In the Clint Eastwood movies, the John Wayne movies, the crooks are lousy shots, the good guys always win. This in itself tends to make policemen feel they're a little more invincible than they really are.

Q. *Where do you think your approach was weak?*

A. Number one, I approached the individual while still on my motorcycle. I came too close to him, I didn't have any cover, and I broke the golden rule of policemen: I did not see his hands. They were in his pockets. I should have known better, because, if he was the suspect I was looking for, I knew he was armed.

Q. *What's it like to get shot by someone who is better prepared than you are?*

A. My personal feeling was one of anger. I felt that with my experience, ten years on the department, I should have been more alert. He was able to just turn and fire and hit me, and I shot nine times at him from a distance of less than ten feet, and I don't know whether I hit him or not.

Q. *Things were a little different than on the range?*

A. Very. Shooting paper targets, you're not pumped up, there's no adrenalin, no danger, nothing to fear. You just have the feeling that that's exactly what they are, paper targets. It's very simple to keep a calm, steady hand when they're not shooting back.

Q. *Where do most officers go wrong, so far as survival is concerned?*

A. Being over-confident, thinking that their blue uniform is going to stop bullets. The more you're in police work, you tend to become involved in situations which are very similar, time and time again. You can become very complacent during those types of incidents, and it can turn bad on you. It did with me.

Q. *Okay, I'm a bad guy and I'm saying I'm better prepared than any cop out on the street. I shoot when I want to, and you don't know what you're doing.*

A. Well, I don't care what you say about being better prepared. I almost lost my life, and I'll guarantee you, *I* won't make the same mistakes again. I'll be better prepared than the typical creep on the street. I practice. I don't become complacent. That's what it's all about. Not becoming complacent, and just practicing at surviving.

2 | CONFRONTATION

The ways and circumstances in which criminals take on officers in gunfights have varied amazingly little since police first began to carry firearms in the middle of the 19th century. The first police killing recorded in New York City, in 1854, occurred after a baker interrupted two ''juvenile delinquents'' burglarizing his establishment. ''The rogues escaped,'' says the official report of the incident, ''and were closely pursued by Patrolman Cahill. He immediately closed in with the rascals and a struggle ensued ...Several pistol shots were discharged...The officer gave a groan, sank to the ground and expired a few minutes later.'' In close sequence in the musty old record books follow reports of plainclothes and uniformed officers—''trusty guardians of the night''—fatally shot upon confronting a shoe store thief who was brandishing ''a large horse pistol''...when called to ''quell a disturbance at an oyster saloon''...while trying to arrest ''a fugitive from justice'' in a liquor store...during the pursuit of ''a gang of vagabonds'' who had ''debauched a wretched female against her will''...and while attempting to seize ''a mad man'' who had vowed to shoot the first man who came through his hotel room door.

TYPE OF ASSIGNMENT AT TIME OF DEATH	
	Percent
Patrol	66
Detective/Special Assignment	22
Off Duty	11
Total	99

CIRCUMSTANCES AT THE SCENE OF THE INCIDENT	
	Percent
Disturbance Calls	19
Burglary Calls	7
Robbery Calls	18
Attempting Arrest for Crimes other than Robbery or Burglary	21
Civil Disorders	1
Handling Prisoners	4
Investigating Suspicious Persons/ Circumstances	8
Ambush (premeditated and unprovoked)	7
Dealing with Mentally Deranged	2
Traffic Pursuits and Stops	12
Total	99

Today, only the names and some of the language are different, the occupation of law enforcement remains exactly the same. Throughout the country, officers still are killed in bars, stores and homes, on sidewalks and highways, in alleys and gutters, predominantly by guns. *More than 70 per cent of the time, the fatal confrontations erupt during so-called "routine patrol,"* and especially when officers are:

- attempting arrests
- responding to domestic disturbances
- investigating robberies-in-progress, and
- conducting traffic pursuits and stops.

(The degree of danger within these broad categories may vary with circumstances. The danger of domestic disturbances, for example, tends to be heightened when only one officer is on the scene; robbery-in-progress calls are apt to be more dangerous to officers in concentrated urban areas than in rural areas, where the distance an officer must travel in responding often allows the suspect time to flee.)

No assignment can be considered "safe," however. Nor can any time, day, month or location. Officers are killed in daylight, at night, on weekends and weekdays, in winter and summer, inside police stations, jails and judges' chambers and on the porches of their own houses, as well in the heart of hostile ghettos. One in nine of those who die are off-duty at the time they are attacked. Once you carry a badge, you're exposed to the risk of a gunfight at all hours, all places, on all days, in all seasons, and under all circumstances—just as your counterparts were more than a century ago, when the tally of lives lost began.

What's especially disturbing is that officers today still resemble those from the decade before the Civil War in another way: incredibly, *they are making the same tactical errors in regard to armed confrontations.* These persistent mistakes, in most cases, are directly responsible for the toll of officer injuries and deaths.

After more than 100 years of consistency in the circumstances and outcomes of officer-involved shootings, many departments are finally beginning to recognize the core problem: a large gap exists between the training most officers receive in how to defend their lives and the kinds of challenges to their defense they actually confront on the job. In short, *the patterns of instructions don't match the patterns of encounter.*

This is nowhere more evident—or more important—than in the area of firearms.

An officer who misjudged the intent of two men stopped for cashing stolen money orders. The officer's revolver lies next to his body.

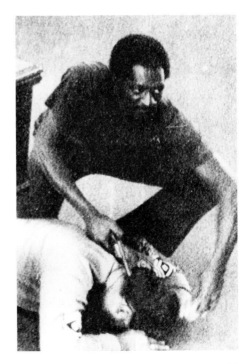

A close call. A 23-year-old suspect holds a sergeant at gunpoint during a bank robbery. This robber plus two associates fled with $21,000.

Most initial recruit range training and subsequent qualification requirements, for example, focus overwhelmingly on shooting stationary paper or metal targets at a distance of 21 to 150 feet. The action is slow and deliberate. The rangemaster hollers out a measured countdown: "Ready on the right! ...Ready on the left!...Ready on the firing line...Fire!" You concentrate on grip, stance, breath control, sight alignment, trigger squeeze and proper follow-through. After shooting each round, you may be told to re-holster your gun, and when you reload, you're cautioned to dump your brass in a bucket or put it in your pocket to keep the range tidy. There's usually little pressure...the light's good...and if your gun or ammunition malfunction, you just stick your hand in the air and call time-out.

But, real life-or-death episodes, as survivors are quick to point out, are drastically different. Shoot-outs tend to be at close quarters, quick and dark. Your target shoots at *you*...and moves. While you're trying to duck bullets, see him and fire back, you may be scrambling for footing on ice, trying to keep your balance on a rickety fire escape, or fending off stones and bottles hurled from an angry crowd. Your gun may be wobbling, because you're panting and trembling from the exertion of a chase. To reach cover, you may have to roll through a patch of cactus or over broken glass. You may run out of ammunition before your assailant does, and while you're struggling to reload, he may rush you. You may face multiple suspects in different locations and with more powerful guns than yours, all firing at once. You may become wounded and start pumping blood. Or at the split-second you need to shoot to save your life, your gun may malfunction.

For certain, when you are under sudden stress and fear, your pupils dilating, your heart thumping, your lungs heaving, your adrenalin surging, your stomach and bowels in turmoil, your ability to distinguish time, colors and distance diminished, *you revert without thinking to the habits you have learned in training*. Unless you have trained realistically, this alone may cost you your life. In a notorious highway patrol incident, four officers were killed in a gunfight that broke out during a felony stop. After the shooting was over, one of the dead officers, who had reloaded during the shoot-out, reportedly was found with spent cartridges in his pants pockets. Under fire, he had unconsciously taken precious seconds to do what he had learned on the range: eject his empties into his palm and stuff them into his pocket before reloading live rounds.

The officer who has had little or no training or has not recently undergone re-training is likely under stress simply to panic. His behavior can be just as threatening to himself and to other innocent parties as that of the officer who is improperly trained.

No one should underestimate the importance that the basic fundamentals of marksmanship can play in armed encounters. But they should be regarded as the foundation, not the finished product, of survival expertise. And they should be utterly free of the practices that may be convenient to the range staff, but jeopardizing to the officers in whom they have become ingrained (such as putting empty shell cases in your pocket to avoid cluttering up the grass).

Some agencies have modernized their firearms training to include instinct shooting, dim-light firing, stress courses and close, multiple and moving targets in simulated street situations. Some, in doing so, have been startled to discover that officers who have been winning target shooting trophies often are unable to hit "combat" targets at 8 to 10 feet, particularly when the targets are moving. In most jurisdictions, however, range facilities remain inadequate, instruction minimal and the techniques conveyed too outmoded or unrealistic for practical application.

As a beginning for your survival awareness, you need to know just what factors you are likely to have to deal with in a real shooting situation. You may find it sobering to compare the training you have received to date with these statistical probabilities of the street. You may agree with one officer who assessed his formal instruction this way: "It seems like they give you a bow and arrow and send you out there to do your job."

Patterns of Encounter

No two shooting confrontations are ever exactly alike, but over the years records have been kept, certain recurring patterns have been identified. Of course, one should always train for the exception as well as the rule. But where traditional firearms instruction falls short is in preparing its trainees *only* for the exceptions—as some of these realities indicate:

Distance: While most range practice involves targets set at 7 to 50 yards, spans of *less than 7 yards* exist between officers and suspects in almost 85 *per cent* of actual shoot-outs. When officers are killed, they are only 0 to 10 feet from their assailants in the vast majority of cases;[1] half are 5 feet or less, close enough many times to touch each other. Of the more than 250 officer deaths recorded in New York City since 1854, in only *one* did the suspect shoot from more than 20 feet away. Yet, 21 feet is the distance at which most range training starts and it lengthens from there. That conditions you to think in terms of relatively vast spatial relationships, when you should be thinking—and preparing—for *close* quarters. The suspect who shoots at you is likely to be less than half the length of your patrol car, or the length of your arm, away.

Light: In contrast to the typical sunny or brightly lighted range, more than two out of three fatal officer shootings occur during the hours of

---

[1] FBI "Law Enforcement Officers Killed" Summaries.

darkness or in locations where the light is very dim, like hallways, bars, warehouses and basements. Outside you may have only the light of stars or the moon, or a street lamp half a block away. The light may be so poor that you won't be able to see the sights on your gun when you need to return fire.

Time: The time you take to position yourself on the range is probably longer than most gunfights last. Confrontations are sudden affairs, over in *2 to 3 seconds*, in the majority of cases. Almost never is there time to cock your gun, stand in profile, and take careful aim at your target. You and the suspect together are not likely to fire more than a total of 3 shots, whether the situation is an ambush, an armed robbery or a family fight.[2] In the majority of cases, the initial exchange of fire will determine the outcome. The speed with which you can react to danger, therefore, is likely to be a more critical commodity than the amount of ammunition you have at your disposal. You probably carry more ammunition than you'll ever need, but time is almost *always* in short supply.

2. "Carrying Duty Ammo for Revolvers," by Ed Lovette, *New Mexico Lawman*, January, 1977.

The scene of a gunfight. Two suspects are dead after wounding a police officer. A short distance away the officer receives assistance from fellow officers. Note the presence of civilians, location, distance between subjects, and the outcome.

Location: Officer-involved shootings occurring outdoors outnumber those inside by 2½ to 1.[3] When the suspect is within a building of some sort, you may have time to contain him and to plan and get assistance. But outside, fast, positive action may be demanded to prevent his escape or to save your life and others. The majority of outdoor confrontations occur on streets and sidewalks or in alleys or yards. That can mean passing motorists, shoppers, kids playing, people leaning from windows...as well as fellow officers or hostages in the immediate vicinity. Rigid safety rules protect everyone on the range, but in real life, your assailant will likely shoot with total disregard for bystanders' welfare. Your return fire, on the other hand, will have to safely accommodate their presence because *you* will be held legally responsible for wherever your bullets impact, even several thousand yards down range.

Assailants: On the range, you typically shoot at one stationary target at a time. At least four out of ten gunfights, however, involve more than one assailant. It's increasingly common these days for armed robbers and other criminals to employ back-up men. Often these individuals are not readily identifiable as suspects and may escape your notice until they open fire. You may find them positioned at different heights than you are, at different distances away, and at different angles to you, and they are quite likely to be moving, thereby complicating your return-fire capabilities.

Weapons: There are no counter-weapons on the average range; the target takes your fire and never responds. On the street, your targets not only fire back, but they generally fire *first*...and their guns may be ballistically superior. One survey indicates that about 15 per cent of the suspects who shoot at police use shotguns or rifles, whereas fewer than 5 per cent of the officers involved have these weapons in hand.[4] Of officers who are killed, however, seven out of ten die from *handgun* wounds. More than 80 per cent of the guns used in these assaults are the same caliber as the officer's or smaller. Many have been stolen, either burglarized or bought from fences. Military and high-quality law enforcement weapons with armor-piercing rounds are easily available to criminals from illegal sources. In some cases, criminal ingenuity can make a standard weapon more hazardous. (In Tennessee, a suspect loaded shotgun shells with dimes to produce a deadlier impact at close range.) From your point of

---

[3] *Target Blue*, Robert Daley, Dell Publishing Company, 1978.

[4] "Analysis of Police Combat Situations," New York City Police Department, 1974.

view, *the most dangerous gun is still the .38 Special revolver.*[5] Suspects favor it, statistically, over all others. Others most commonly involved are .25 cal., .32 cal. and .357 Magnum in that descending order. In about 20 per cent of the cases, the gun used to kill an officer is his *own* service firearm,[6] wrested from his hand or his holster by his would-be target and turned against him—another problem totally foreign from range training. Whatever weapon is used, the suspect in most cases will instinctively fire it double-action. This can give an assailant an additional edge, especially when, as sometimes happens, the victim officer, under stress, reverts to the slower, recruit range-instilled habit of firing single-action.

---

5. FBI "Law Enforcement Officers Killed Summary," 1977.
6. "Revolver Retention for Law Enforcement Officers," Kansas City (MO) Police Department, 1976.

.38 cal. S&W Military and Police Model with a tragic history. The offender disarmed one officer to steal it, then used it months later to kill another officer. Between incidents the barrel was cut down, for better concealment.

Even cap guns have been used to draw down on police. In some cases, toy guns have been made operable and used in robberies.

Guns found in a car which was stopped for having homemade cardboard license plates. Some of these guns were used by the four occupants, who had recently killed an officer in another state.

Long guns confiscated by police after being used in various robberies and assaults in a middle-class suburb of 80,000.

Firearms are often stolen prior to armed confrontations. This collection, plus ammunition, was seized in a "routine" drug raid.

Suspects Who Shoot

Just as punching paper targets fails to reflect the weaponry and most other confrontation parameters, classroom presentations and locker room war stories may, in equal measure, fail to prepare you for the men and women who stand behind the revolvers, the semi-automatics, the rifles, the shotguns, the machine-guns, the pen guns, the pellet guns, the zip guns, and the God-knows-what-you'd-call-'em homemade guns that you may confront on the street. Yet, because they usually dictate the critical factors in a shooting—like time, distance and location—understanding their perspective is crucial.

Once you confront a suspect who has a gun, the odds are better than 40-60 that he will shoot at you and most probably fire the first round. He may do so out of panic, desperation, confusion, anger, fear, derangement, exasperation, revenge, intoxication, hallucination, political zeal or suicidal yearning. But the fact remains that, whatever the motivation, a sizeable proportion of suspects with guns are not intimidated just because you are an officer. Indeed, it may be that very status that impels them to fire—especially when you stand between them and escape.

At some level, of course, even if it's subconscious, an armed suspect faced with your presence must decide whether to run, surrender or shoot; few, if any, are *forced* to fire on police. Again, as with the elements of confrontation, no absolutes can be drawn, and it's risky not to allow for the many exceptions. But certain *patterns* are evident among those who choose to squeeze the trigger.

Of suspects who kill officers, better than 96 per cent are male, nearly half nationwide are black (much higher in some urban areas), most are under 30.[7] (This is not to say, of course, that women and children, Caucasians and the elderly can be ruled out as dangerous suspects. Individuals in these groups attack law enforcement officers, too often with the greatest amount of surprise.) Suspects under 21 and those who are black are likeliest to confront officers while in the company of others, while those over 30 and white tend to act alone.[8] Like you, the average assailant is a pro. Over 60 per cent have been arrested before on criminal charges, about 40 per cent for a violent crime—murder, rape, robbery or assault. A sizeable percentage have been granted leniency on a previous conviction and are on probation or parole at the time of the shooting.

---

[7] FBI "Law Enforcement Officers Killed" Summaries.
[8] *Shots Fired: An Examination of New York City Police Firearms Discharges*, James Fyfe, 1978.

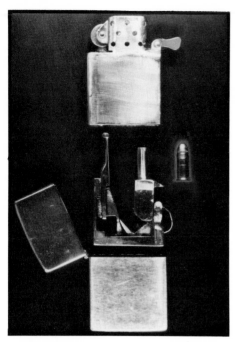

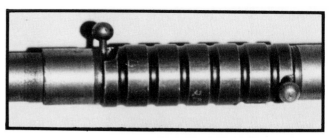

This single-shot [.12 ga.] pipe gun loads with a bolt action mechanism. This 10 inch gun was taken off a juvenile suspect during an arrest.

Concealed lethal weapons are a constant threat to any officer. This converted cigaret lighter can fire either a .22 short or .22 long when breach-loaded.

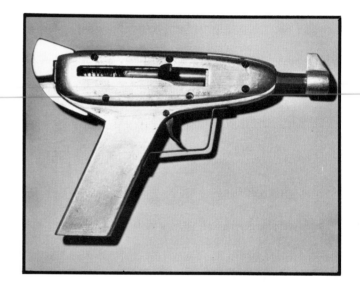

A .22 pistol, custom made from aluminum. Do you think the creator of this gun was capable of shooting an officer?

Most are not trained marksmen, but some have practiced with firearms *much* more than you probably have if you are an average officer. Among the criminal group, especially, many are also astute students of police tactics. In prisons, they may talk police tactics 24 hours a day—and they are surrounded by "experts." It is not uncommon for inmates to hold informal seminars on police maneuvers—how you exit patrol cars, how you approach traffic stops, how you communicate with your partner, how you handle weapons, etc. And in the recreation yard, inmates often practice among themselves ways to disarm and murder officers. Some have been trained in martial arts, such as karate and judo. While "these guys are not Rhodes Scholars" (in the words of a Rhode Island police captain), most do have a pre-arranged plan, however crude, of what they will do if confronted by the police.

Surveillance photos of two convicts practicing disarming techniques during yard time. The convict in the shirt plays the part of the officer.

When they shoot as part of that plan, they are likely to do so without vacillation or remorse. Their attitude mirrors that of an Arizona cop killer: "All I felt was the recoil of the gun." To many officers, especially those with limited experience on the street, this kind of icy savagery is one of the hardest elements of armed confrontations to internalize. It's human nature to expect some rationality and compassion from another human being. But as an Illinois prison official explained after inmates cold-bloodedly murdered three guards at a correctional facility in that state: "The truth is there are a lot of people who are just vicious. They don't have to have any cause to kill."

Often, suspects who will take you on come from elements of society where the cultural norm is to resent and defy authority. From childhood on, in their homes, in their schools, in their gangs, in their fragmented personal relationships, their principal means of communication has been violence.

In a confrontation, most would-be assailants *know* you won't shoot first in all but the rarest situations. Faced with arrest and a possible prison term, the suspect may feel he has nothing to lose by shooting it out. Yet he knows you are armed and usually presumes you are trained. Psychologically, he may expect to get shot, to die, as a natural risk of his lifestyle. And when he makes the decision to pull the trigger, he's thinking only of himself at that moment. He has one objective only: to get on target as fast as possible and blow "that cop" out of his socks.

This man held police at bay for more than three hours. Despondent over domestic problems, he fired at police with this revolver, and was also armed with five other guns and 200 rounds of ammunition.

Officer Attitudes

While the suspect's background and desperation may be bolstering his instinct to shoot, a host of constraints are likely conspiring to *delay* your reaction. As you perceive his threat and begin to react, your mind may flash to your family...to your partner...to bystanders. You may, if only for a split-second, wonder if shooting back will conform to your department's policy on the use of deadly force...whether you can justify it in a report to your superiors...whether your action will be sustained in the judgment of a shooting review board, months later, in a sterile environment where the urgency of the moment can never be recreated.

Nationwide, 92 per cent of shootings by police are later ruled justified, with no reprimand or suspension;[9] usually unbiased witnesses are around and can help clear the officer involved. Only a tiny fraction of suspect shootings are ever referred for criminal prosecution, and in a smaller fraction still do juries convict— only 3 out of 1,500 cases in one survey. But you know that very specific rules exist, by law and department policy, for the use of deadly force, and, if you are like most officers, a doubtful hesitation will affect your reaction.

Rules aside, you may not *want* to shoot. Many officers opt not to even when they have a clear right to do so. In Chicago, an ex-convict, miffed because the police had not recovered a car he claimed was stolen from him, invaded a police station and without warning began firing a gun, seriously wounding two officers. A patrolman in a position to shoot back chose instead to *tackle* the assailant, even though he himself had ducked three of the man's bullets. In one eastern case, a patrolman was disarmed by a man who then shot at him, but missed. The officer wrestled him to the ground, and by kicking him and biting his face, finally got the gun back. ''I really wanted to kill him,'' the officer said later, ''I did, but I couldn't shoot. I smashed him with the butt instead.'' Even with their own lives in jeopardy, a moral repugnance toward killing kept these officers from using their sidearms.

One limited study has suggested that the sex of your partner may influence your reaction. The evidence suggests that male officers with male partners generally are more reluctant to use their guns and are guilty of more mistakes in clearly perceiving danger and reacting to it than are male officers with female partners. Speculation is that male-female teams tend to experience more subconscious emotional

9. *Police Use of Deadly Force*, Catherine Milton, Police Foundation, 1977.

arousal as they work and thus are more attuned to picking up subtle clues to danger in their environment.[10]

In some cases, your decision to shoot may be colored by an acquaintanceship with the suspect. In about 27 per cent of the instances nationally where officers are killed, they know their assailants.[11] In such circumstances, you may be tempted to relax your vigilance and not take cover even if you *see* he is armed. If you've had previous encounters with the suspect that were non-violent or in which you've been able to talk him out of drastic action, you may entertain unwarranted hope for "reasoning" the confrontation to conclusion rather than shooting it out.

Probably your greatest attitudinal enemy in a confrontation, however, is *overconfidence*. You've been successful or lucky enough to avoid injury in so many situations that you begin to believe you will never be unsuccessful. Moreover, through movies, television and an enduring cultural myth, you've been bombarded all your life with the concept of the lawman as an invulnerable super-hero, capable of "walking tall" through any challenge that comes his way, with never a thought even to the possibility he might die. In westerns, the image is that of Dodge City, where "you can't be a marshal until you ride a wild horse bareback with a barbed-wire bridle at full gallop with a tin cup of red whiskey in your left hand, rope a jackrabbit with your right hand, and don't spill a drop." In the cop television shows, the legend is updated with customized Magnums and semi-automatics and an endless supply of back-up guns.

If you buy into this self-image—and plenty of officers do—you're said to suffer the "Superman syndrome." You believe that simply by making a commitment, by putting your body on the line and "hanging tough," you can face down any danger that threatens; it's a matter of will and bravado over all. Of course, to be a "good cop," you must, of necessity, be aggressive; taking chances, playing hunches and so on are all part of the game. But when you add the elements of foolishness or recklessness to your aggressive conduct, then you fall prey to the worst aspect of this unfortunate syndrome.

A real-life—or more appropriately, real-*death*—illustration is provided by the middle-aged Massachusetts detective who responded to a silent alarm at a local club. Two uniformed officers had beaten him to the place, seen that a robbery was in progress

---

10. "The Effect of Female Partners on Male Police Shooting Responses," Christina Johns and Andrew Barclay, Michigan State University, 1978.
11. FBI "Law Enforcement Officers Killed" Summaries.

40

and properly stationed themselves outside to await assistance. When the detective arrived, they warned him that one subject was armed with a .16 ga. shotgun. But he shrugged off their cautioning and brazenly headed into the building. He no sooner set foot inside the club than he was fatally shot in the face.

Such an attitude *invites* hostile fire. And when it comes, the Superman type, who typically has underestimated the adversary, may freeze up, not knowing what to do. Chances are he's under-trained, as well as overconfident. Such officers typically "qualify" in the use of firearms only because of department orders requiring them to do so—not because they feel it necessary for their own protection or to enable them to do a better job. They do virtually no training voluntarily. According to an FBI study, nearly 40 per cent of the officers killed during one review period had not received *any* in-service firearms training at all for at least three years before getting shot.

An armed offender who preys on officer complacency and a bad approach usually wins in a shoot-out. The goal is to make time your asset, not the offender's.

Even if you're relatively free of complacency and of the Superman syndrome, chances are you've been affected enough by these influences to be startled at being shot. In contrast to many suspects, most officers subconsciously *don't* expect ever to get shot; in our mythology, "good" guys rarely do. Wounded, more than one officer has gone into immediate traumatic shock and died. Of those who manage to shoot back and actually hit their assailants, more than 70 per cent fail to inflict neutralizing wounds. Either they don't know where to shoot to inflict wounds capable of stopping their opponents' illegal actions, or they aren't proficient enough to deliver shots to that area.

Statistically, just as assailants tend to reflect certain backgrounds, so do the officers who take their rounds. Overwhelmingly, officers killed are white, male, of patrol status (66 per cent), in uniform, assigned to a patrol car, and working with a partner or back-up in rural or suburban areas or in cities under 250,000 population.

More than 60 per cent are from 25 to 40 years old, and they have a median of five years of service at the time of the confrontation. One might expect the least experienced officers to be the most vulnerable, yet only about 13 per cent have less than a year's service.[12]

Here again, attitude seems to have a bearing. As a new officer, you may not experience so many false alarms that you develop casual patterns for responding to calls within your first year. As you head toward the five-year mark, though, you're likelier to feel you know and have seen everything, you may begin to succumb to peer pressure to be blasé. You may discard or forget or dismiss what you knew about survival and make no effort to learn or practice anything new. To the suspect who's prepared and willing to shoot, you may then be a sitting duck.

The Survival State of Mind

The first step in surviving on the street is to adjust your mental attitudes, in light of the common patterns of encounter and the perspectives both you and the suspect are likely to bring to a confrontation. This involves reminding yourself repeatedly that:

1. law enforcement is a hazardous occupation, demanding your constant vigilance;

---

12. FBI "Law Enforcement Officers Killed" Summaries.

2. a suspect's background, attitudes, motivation, willingness to reason and inclination to shoot may be quite different from your own;

3. there are legal, moral, and psychological implications of shooting that must be anticipated and personally resolved *before* a confrontation;

4. it may be necessary at any time to take a life to save your own or someone else's;

5. practical proficiency with firearms includes learning and practicing new techniques under stress in as realistic an environment as is possible to simulate, and

6. with preparedness, preplanning and proper physical fitness, you can avoid mistakes of less fortunate officers and successfully conclude most suspect encounters.

Now let's look at the tactical procedures—tailored to the realities of confrontation—by which you can project these attitudes into an effective defense system.

Three officers and two priests trying to talk a would-be suicide victim into surrendering the gun in his hand. How would you evaluate their perception of potential danger?

APPROACH TO DANGER

To wait until you need to draw and fire your gun to think about survival tactics is like waiting until you're coughing up blood to think about annual physical checkups. You should have survival in your conscious thoughts the moment you receive an assignment, for the moves you make at the outset may directly affect the outcome. By properly planning your approach to a call, you may be able to *prevent* a shooting from occurring. Or, if that proves impossible, you will have positioned yourself where you are exposed to the least risk and have the best chance of responding safely when danger does erupt.

Where many officers go wrong is in assuming that an assignment is inconsequential and therefore approaching it on what amounts to automatic pilot. They fail to consider that, going in, there is a great deal about *any* situation and the people involved that they do not—cannot—know. Presuming one set of circumstances on the basis of appearances or past experience, they may find themselves confronting quite another, for which they are not prepared. In Oregon, for example, a sergeant who stopped to help a teenage couple in a disabled car did not know the girl was an escapee or that they would kill him because they thought he intended to arrest her. A Milwaukee patrolman responding to a disturbance at a house where police had been fifty previous times without incident did not know that this time the husband beating his wife had picked up a .30-06 rifle on his way home and would shoot the officer for "messin' in." A Georgia officer who walked up to the door of a cocktail lounge that was ajar after normal closing time did not know—until he was shot dead—that an armed burglar was inside.

When you observe a problem on the street or receive an assignment from a dispatcher, all you know for certain is the general direction in which to proceed. What you'll find when you arrive, there's no way of telling.

With a survival orientation, you keep this firmly in mind and *always approach a situation anticipating an armed confrontation*. In many cases, as we know from the common patterns of encounter, an offender has a plan in mind for how he will shoot. So you want to plan ahead, too, but you'll have to let the *circumstances dictate tactics*, not vice versa.

Each step of the way, you consider the opportunities an offender might have for shooting at you and the ways in which you might forestall or respond to an attack. In other words, you make a habit of figuring, "If 'A' happens, I'm going to do 'B,'" adjusting for new developments as you go. It's a habit you practice faithfully, regardless of your assignment. However crude, you discuss your planned movements with your partner and rehearse them mentally, and have a back-up plan in mind in case the first fails. Once the action starts, you won't have time to think things out rationally. *You have to be ready to carry out your plan instinctively*, with a minimum of hesitation, which we call "lag time."

Whenever possible, you want to *cultivate tactics that are unexpected*, to be "systematically unsystematic." Often assailants count on officers responding in predictable, "routine" ways to assignments, and if you are able to depart from stereotyped law enforcement procedures in your approach, you may be able to thwart an assailant's plan while strengthening your own position.

With some calls—"shots fired," "man with a gun," crimes-in-progress and disturbances where a firearm may be available—you have an early warning of possible violence. In other situations, you may have to depend on being observant and applying a "sixth sense" for trouble. Usually there is *some* clue or "danger sign" to violence, something about a scene or a suspect's behavior that isn't quite right. It may involve unusual nervousness on his part or so small a thing as his undue concern with watching you in his rear-view mirror as you approach on a traffic stop. With tactics and a mental attitude that stress anticipation, you'll be in the best position to see the warning...to recognize it...and to pay attention to it.

Many officers get themselves shot at by approaching an assignment carelessly, hastily, sloppily and with overconfidence. Uneventful familiarity breeds complacency. As an armored car driver in Connecticut said after three of his fellow guards were murdered by robbers, "The hard part is that after awhile you become lax. Your're not thinking security." One might argue that there is no one right way to work and no one way to be totally prepared at all times. True. But there are approach tactics that involve right thinking, and it is certainly possible to develop preparedness far beyond that displayed by many officers who become involved in gunfights.

Here are some proven field techniques that can help you *plan, perceive and perform* for survival in a variety of common situations. They are not necessarily blueprints that can be applied arbitrarily to every instance, but guidelines and options that you will want to consider, adapt and expand upon.

Building Approach

A scenario that occurs with haunting frequency in the FBI's annual summary of law enforcement officers killed concerns an officer who answers a disturbance or robbery-in-progress call, hurries toward the front of the residence or business establishment involved and before he can take appropriate action is mortally wounded with a shotgun, rifle or handgun blast fired at him through the door. He answers a call routinely and is routinely shot, as easily as if he had a "ten-ring" pasted on his chest.

Modern communication puts officers on the scene of any complaint call fast. The chances today are greater than ever that you will arrive while the action is still in progress or at least while the suspect is still in the area. Your objective is clear: You have to *locate* the problem that prompted the call...*isolate* the offender(s) from innocent civilians...and *eliminate* the hazard presented by the offender(s). But there's no assurance you'll get a suspect's cooperation in doing all that. Career criminals are always anticipating the imminent arrival of the police and are very often willing to gamble desperately for freedom by committing a greater crime than the one they're involved in—such as your assault or homicide. "Amateurs," like wife-beaters, psychos and drunks, are often more totally absorbed in what they're doing and are often less vigilant. But, in the passion of the moment, they may be just as prepared and determined to shoot.

What you want is an *unexpected* approach that may delay a suspect's awareness of your presence until you have a chance to assess the situation you are confronting.

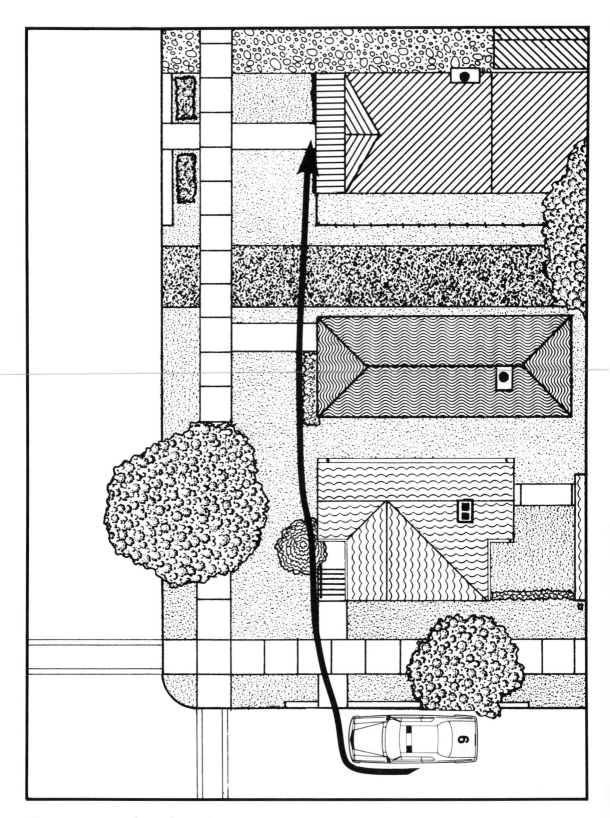

*One proper approach to a domestic
disturbance call involving a residence.*

You're best off to *anticipate* the address you're looking for as you approach the scene and park your patrol car three or four doors away on the same side of the street, *before* you reach it. This forestalls your driving directly into the "kill zone." (Here we're using "kill zone" to mean that area which an armed suspect in a given location can control with hostile weapons fire. The term also means that part of the anatomy where incoming rounds will most likely prove incapacitating.) Make as little disturbance as possible. That means: avoid using your emergency lights and siren in your approach (if department policy permits)...turn your radio down low so it can't be heard outside your patrol car...round corners without squealing your tires...at night, consider turning off your engine and headlights and coasting the last 100 feet or so before you stop, using the emergency brake so as not to activate the brake lights. Some departments permit officers to disconnect the buttons in patrol car doors that turn on interior lights when a door is opened. Having done this will help keep your approach unobtrusive. When you exit your unit, ease your car door shut as quietly as you can or leave it slightly ajar if security allows. At night especially, sound travels far and fast; even at low volume, your radio or a door slamming may be audible a block away. A quiet approach may keep you from attracting neighbors and troublesome onlookers, as well as the suspect.

Certainly, don't just "give" yourself to a suspect, as a new patrolman in Tennessee did. Responding to a complaint of a middle-aged man, a known mental case, beating on an old truck behind his house, the officer stopped his patrol car in the suspect's driveway. As he strode up to the residence, he was easy pickings for his assailant, who killed him with a shot to the chest with a 7.65mm rifle.

Approaching the address of your call, you should survey all vehicles parked or moving in the immediate neighborhood and all pedestrians or loiterers. A lay-off man may be waiting in a car or on the sidewalk as a look-out. A car parked with its motor running is automatically suspicious. In some cases, suspects have been known to hide *under* vehicles. Or, if a crime-in-progress has been reported, the offender(s) may be in the process of fleeing as you arrive.

As you move in on foot, you will want to consider available cover which you can use in the event of serious trouble. Employ an invisible advance to the fullest extent possible. Just the sight of you may be enough to impel an armed suspect to shoot. Where there's reason to believe you may be dealing with a violent situation, invisible deployment is critical. It

Many officers find it hard to resist the temptation to rush in and gain control. Lying dead is a 37-year-old plainclothes officer who rushed in on a burglary suspect.

is usually easier in darkness, but even in daylight or under bright lights by moving behind parked cars, fences, trash cans or shrubbery or by taking an indirect route, you may be able to get close to the building without being observed by anyone inside. Try to blend into backgrounds that match your uniform color where possible, and where colors don't match, try at least to keep your background as dark as your clothing. If you must pass windows, try to go *over* those that are near or below ground level and *under* those that are higher. Try to stay protected by cover when possible and to know always where your nearest cover is. Move rapidly through open areas, trying to move from covered position to covered position.

You want to constantly guard against the "ostrich effect;" that's thinking that because you can't see the suspect, he can't see you. Actually, his perspective on the scene is likely to be entirely different from yours. This was dramatically illustrated to a young Cincinnati patrolman one afternoon when he responded to a silent holdup alarm at a downtown bank. He properly parked around the corner from the entrance and was cautiously approaching on foot along the building's side wall. He was almost to the end when he suddenly realized a major oversight; the wall was of reflective glass, and because its mirrored surface had kept him from seeing through it, he'd forgotten that from the other side that kind of glass is like a normal window. People inside the bank had been able to see him perfectly all along. Fortunately, the call turned out to be a false alarm, or robbers inside could have shot through the glass and killed him any time they chose.

The contemporary design of buildings often works against a safe response for law enforcement.

Stay conscious of your surroundings in another regard, also: before your arrival, a suspect, as part of his plan, may have left the premises you're approaching and moved to another vantage point from which he can shoot. In another Ohio case, two sheriff's deputies one afternoon were simultaneously approaching the front and rear of a house where a rape had been reported in progress. Their attention was so focused on the residence and what they would encounter there that they ignored a garage beside it. The alleged rapist had hidden there and from inside was able easily to train a .12 ga. shotgun on one of the deputies. Without warning, he shot the deputy twice and killed him. As you approach, then, *be alert* to possible hiding places, including rooftops and nearby vehicles.

If you need to round a corner on foot in your approach, you may be easy prey to a suspect waiting on the other side if you charge around assuming there is no one there or even if you slowly stick your head around to look. A young sheriff's deputy in Florida, responding to a robbery-in-progress call, hurriedly rounded a corner of a building with his shotgun in hand and ran smack into two suspects and a hostage; one of the robbers shot him fatally in the chest with a .45 semi-automatic, and wounded two other officers as well.

A crucial tactic when making an approach is to always assume the suspect[s] could be anywhere.

1

Applying the quick peek technique. Assume a low position behind cover with your sidearm ready. The suspect will be waiting for you at eye level.

2

Quickly peek out, then pull your head back to your original position. If the suspect shoots, he will probably fire at shoulder height.

3

Now assume a standing position behind cover. The suspect will now assume you're going to come out shooting. But you don't know if he's still there or not.

4

Again apply the quick peek technique. If you have a visual on the suspect with no civilians behind, you now can return fire safely.

5

A profile view of Step 2. Notice the torso and hand positioning relative to the wall barricade.

6

The armed suspect's point of view reveals no more of your head than this as you apply the quick peek technique.

You're safer, of course, to use the "quick peek" technique. For this, you squat on the balls of your feet, facing close to your side of the wall with your legs apart and with your palms against the wall in a balancing brace. Be careful not to expose any of your body past the corner and *stay low*—at or below waist level. Then, shifting your weight onto your foot nearest the corner, suddenly dart your head out beyond the corner and back in one *rapid* motion. You'll get a fast but fairly thorough look at the area around the bend, yet your peek will be so fast that a suspect will not be able to respond effectively. If he does shoot reflexively, your head will be safely back behind the wall before the bullet can hit, probably before he even pulls the trigger. If you want another look, again do the unexpected by quick peeking from a *different* level.

Quick peeking can also be used for seeing around barriers other than walls. Generally, you'll incur the least risk by peeking around the sides rather than over the top of most objects, because at the side you're less likely to silhouette yourself.

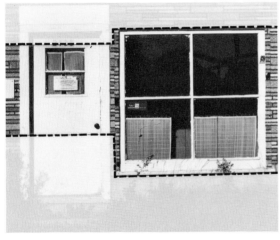

The dotted lines indicate an armed suspect's effective kill zone when you approach the front of a stucco or wood surface residence.

How would you rate the approach tactics of these four troopers? Their mission is to search an "abandoned" house owned by the prime suspect who killed two officers and three civilians hours before.

Throughout your approach, you want to utilize *all your senses* to help evaluate a call. Before entering, you may be able to quick peek at windows to get a visual on the action, its participants and, particularly, on any firearms that may be involved or available. (Don't take slow peeks or long stares through windows, though; it makes you too good a target.) Your sense of smell may suggest whether you will be confronting individuals whose judgment has been impaired by the use of certain drugs. Sometimes what you hear will help you plan. Approaching the rear door of a house where a burglary had been reported one night, an officer heard noises of drawers being yanked out and dumped that led him to believe the burglar was still inside. Instead of attempting an immediate confrontation, the officer tipped over a picnic table in the yard and crouched behind it with his revolver drawn. When the burglar emerged with a gun and his loot a few moments later, the officer announced himself and yelled at him to stop. The burglar fired wildly and ineffectually into the dark, uncertain where the officer was. But the officer, from his protected, clear-view position, was ready to fire back immediately—on target. The old warning is a good one: "*stop, look, listen*" as you approach. *Don't rush.*

A position of cover affords the safest opportunity for maximum observation and control. In this case, a short brick wall provided that advantage.

If you are approaching a scene with a back-up or partner, you want to be able to communicate with each other along the way. Avoid moving in shoulder-to-shoulder or side-by-side, but in staying apart be sure you keep positioned so that you can each return fire if necessary, without placing the other in cross-fire. Maintain visual contact. You should know what each other is going to do. Hand signals can help you maintain a discreet advance. In some cases, flashlights or penlights blinked on and off *rapidly* may be an appropriate signal substitute at night, provided you take care not to illuminate each other. Or prearranged code words can be used where you know the suspect can overhear you. If there is an imminent threat to either of you, shout out abruptly. *Don't assume that your partner sees and hears everything you do*, and vice versa. As with the ostrich effect, your points of view may be significantly different.

If you are alone, you may want to pretend to be communicating with a hidden partner, once you feel your presence is known. You can do this by issuing "commands" or "relaying" information, in a voice audible to any offender. Suspects are not always intimidated by the presence of more than one officer, but if a suspect believes there is an officer out there whom he can't see, he may be less sure of his ability to shoot you and successfully escape.

One of the most dangerous moments in an approach is when you reach a door you can't see through and are dependent on someone else to open, as is typically the case when you respond to a call at a residence. You want to *stay to the side of the door*, so if an assailant inside decides to shoot through it you are not directly in his line of fire.

Narcotics agents about to make entry to the connecting door of a hotel room in search of a suspect. How would you rate their relative safety?

Here the element of surprise lies solely with the subject. The woman holding a semi-automatic in her left hand has just set her house afire and threatened to take her life as well as her daughter's.

Your position may be even more unexpected to him if, rather than stand, you squat down at the side below the normal firing level against the wall, as you reach out with your nightstick in your non-gun hand to rap on the door and announce your presence. This way, if he tries to fire through the wall, his shot is likely to be too high to hit you.

Assuming there are no special cover possibilities, your best position is probably to the right of where the doorknob is located. Here you will be least readily visible to anyone who may be waiting inside the room as the door opens.

Once the door is opened, *don't be too quick to enter.* Your immediate intrusion could precipitate shots from inside. From as protected a position as possible and with your gun side *away* from the person in the door, try to ascertain more information. If the complainant answers, for example, you want to determine immediately: 1) the degree of threat to your own safety; 2) whether the complainant is armed; 3) where the suspect is; 4) whether he is armed; 5) whether there are *any* firearms on the premises; 6) who else is inside and 7) what the interior physical layout is. *Don't dismiss the threat potential of any firearm.* During a shooting incident that grew out of an attempt to serve an arrest warrant, a sheriff's deputy in South Carolina was killed by a suspect wielding an antique rifle.

If there is any indication that the suspect is armed or has access to a gun, try to get the complainant outside with you to a position of cover... call for back-up to help contain the offender...and consider treating the situation as a barricaded suspect incident. The passage of time, negotiation and/or the use of chemical agents are likely to prove far safer alternatives than your barging in in an effort to question or capture him. An unfortunate illustration of this point occurred in Texas where three escaped prisoners were located in a private home. When officers arrived at the scene, several promptly entered the house and started upstairs to flush out the suspects. Before they reached the second floor, one of the escapees suddenly leaned over the railing and shot the lead patrolman dead with a blast to the neck from a .16 ga. shotgun. Only after a gun battle did the surviving officers retreat, station themselves outside the dwelling and finally fire tear gas inside. Even if the suspect(s) escape temporarily, it's better than your getting killed during an ill-conceived capture.

A single officer approach to a door which opens in. The low ground position, use of the baton in your non-gun hand and proper distance from the door add to the element of surprise to any possible armed occupant.

Be alert always to the possibility that *you may not get reliable information* from civilians you encounter during your approach. Be suspicious. Take nothing for granted. In New York, a husband who answered the door when two officers responded to a disturbance call was all smiles and courtesy: "Come on in, officers! Everything is all right here, just a little family squabble." They relaxed and accepted his invitation—without noticing or being wary of one hand held behind his back. It held a revolver with which he momentarily shot and killed them both.

Indeed, in some cases, you may not even be talking to whom you *think* you are. Two officers in Memphis responding to an armed robbery alarm at an all-night grocery store, for example, were met by a male adult who said he was the manager and had set off the alarm accidentally. In fact, as they found out too late, he was the robber.

(Note: We have talked here about approaching a building in the context of your responding to a specific assignment. But anytime you enter a building, especially a place of business, try to view the interior *first*, particularly the cash register area, to determine that everything is normal. A number of officers going after a pack of cigarets or a cup of coffee have been taken by surprise and shot when, without pausing to be observant, they walked right into an armed robbery-in-progress.)

Room Approach

A building search is something no officer should undertake alone. To do so is symptomatic of the Superman syndrome and invites the consequences suffered by a middle-aged constable in West Virginia who went to a suspect's home to arrest him for destroying private property. Receiving no response when he knocked at the door, the constable climbed into the house through a window. To his surprise, the suspect was waiting inside with two strong, young buddies, who easily overpowered the officer, stabbed him once, then shot him four times.

When you have a partner, though, or, better, one or more back-up teams, an assignment may require that you move from room to room in a house, an apartment complex, a store or an office building in search of a suspect who may be armed.

You may not know whether the suspect is, in fact, in the building. You may be responding to a prowler call or complaint of signs of forced entry or to some other crime where the victim or witnesses are not certain whether the offender has fled the premises. If you *know* he's in there, it's safest to try to *isolate and contain* him within the building, then force him to come out to you. In most cases, you're at an advantage to deal with the suspect on your ground (outside) rather than his (inside). If you don't know, you'll have to go in, for what is always a treacherous, tension-charged—and sometimes bloody—game of cat and mouse.

Your disadvantages are legion in this situation: quarters are likely to be close, cover sparse, light poor; you are probably unfamiliar with the layout; there may be myriad obstacles, blind corners, booby-traps and places of concealment along the way—yet you must take the initiative in moving forward to conduct a thorough inspection. The suspect, on the other hand, can secrete himself in a good hiding place, get his gun(s) ready to shoot...and merely wait for your arrival. This makes building searches one of the most difficult and dangerous of your assignments.

With survival in mind, your goals are to approach as quietly as possible and to get a good preview of territory you have to cross while you still are in a protected position. To gain tactical advantage, try to enter where the suspect least expects you to—through a rear door, a second floor window or an opening in the roof. Start at or move to the uppermost section of the building, and conduct your search from top down, if possible. It's easier to fight for your life from a high position moving down than from a low position moving up; you can go downstairs faster than you can go up. Also, if you leave the offender a way to escape—i.e., by going down and out—he may be captured when he exits from the building. If he is trapped on the top floor, he may feel he has no choice but to stand and fight.

Ideally, *all* officers searching a building should be in uniform. This is especially important when many officers are involved and/or when those participating don't know each other. Even when uniforms can help telegraph instant recognition, all officers should be aware of where each will be entering the building, so they can anticipate one another's location and lessen the risk of mistaking each other for the suspect.

Where time permits in a high-risk situation like this, you should attempt to cover any shiny items (like your nameplate) which may reflect light and draw a suspect's attention to your location. Some officers carry a small roll of black electrician's tape for this purpose.

Once officers enter a building, there should be *no firing on the structure* by any fellow officers who remain outside. The only exception to this order would be in a circumstance in which the outside officers could see *all* those inside and determine that they were sufficiently isolated from the suspect that shots aimed at him would in no way jeopardize them.

To adequately guard buildings, at least two officers are required outside, situated at diagonally opposite corners in positions of cover. Such positions permit each officer to watch two sides for a fleeing suspect, yet avoid cross-fire. Don't, however, stay close to the building, for that allows a suspect who is in an upper window or on the roof to get an easy shot at you below. Position yourself a distance away, in your patrol car if no better cover is available, so that you can watch *up* as well as along the sides of the building.

Inside the building to be searched, you want your gun drawn, ready for use. With a firm, two-handed grip, you can move the weapon in a short arc and back as you approach locations where the subject might be. The gun should follow your eyes.

The proper invisible deployment tactic for almost any building approach. This tactic avoids a cross-fire situation and allows officers in both positions to maintain a visual on possible suspect movement.

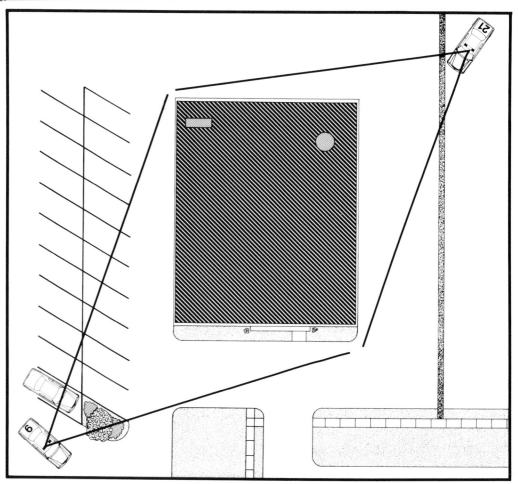

If there are only two of you, *just one should move at a time*. It's extremely difficult to move and shoot accurately at the same time, so while one covers, the other moves to a new position, alternating roles as you advance. Concentrate on moving silently. Noise from your leather belt, from leather-soled and -heeled shoes or boots or from metal jangling against metal, like keys and pocket change, can quickly signal your approach.

As you move down hallways or across large rooms, you may confront numerous doorways that open into closets, storage spaces, bedrooms, offices and other rooms. To bypass *any* without checking the area it leads to is extremely risky. A suspect may be waiting just inside for you to move on past, allowing him the chance then to emerge and shoot you from behind. Community toilets in lower-class apartment buildings and hotels seem to be especially popular places for suspects to hide, but *don't assume that any potential hiding place is safe to ignore*. In a survival course in New York City, based on real-life episodes, trainees sent down a hallway in search of an armed suspect come to one door marked: DANGER! HIGH VOLTAGE! KEEP DOOR CLOSED! Those who obey the sign and go on are usually "killed" by a "psycho" who suddenly flings the door open and pops out behind them. If you carry with you a small roll of electrical or masking tape, you can press a piece across the crack of each door you have checked. Then if you notice the tape broken or pulled off as you retrace your search route later, you'll know someone has backtracked on you.

As you plan your approach to a doorway, keep in mind what's called the "fatal funnel" phenomenon. Because you can't know for sure exactly where the suspect will be, you have to be concerned with every part of the room beyond that doorway entry. But from the point of view of one or more suspects inside the room, all sensory concentration can be funneled down to just that small opening. It's *your* only way in, all *they* need to watch. Framed by it, you'd make an obvious target.

Using an approach that minimizes your funnel framing, then, you advance silently toward the doorway by moving *low* along a wall, utilizing whatever cover you can along the way—recesses, hallway trash cans, furniture, etc. It's usually best if you and your partner can approach the doorway from opposite sides. But if that's not possible, one of you should quickly move across the closed doorway at a level *below* the doorknob so you are on opposite sides before attempting entry. (Even if the door is open, a low, fast jump is likely to get you across quickly enough that you won't be hit by someone shooting from inside.)

Without exposing any vital portions of your body, reach with your weak hand and try the knob. In numerous instances, officers have forced entry through doors that they later discovered were unlocked. So always try the sensible and quiet method of least resistance first. If the door is unlocked, open it in one continuous motion as you hold your gun ready to fire. If the door is already ajar, you may be able to maneuver it fully open by using your nightstick, flashlight, a broom handle or some other probe that allows you to remain in place behind the wall.

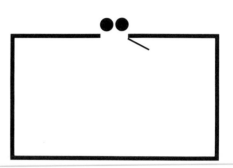

The fatal funnel in action. The two black circles represent you and your back-up standing in front of an open door on a "shots-fired" call.

The problems start when you find your field of vision inside the room is restricted, even while standing in the doorway.

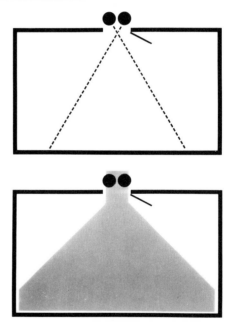

On the other hand, the suspect inside the room has only one place to look to discover your presence. This is why you must always approach a doorway outside and below the kill zone.

Here, you would be standing in the fatal funnel: The only area the suspect has for directing his firepower. Regardless of his position, his visual would be on you at all times.

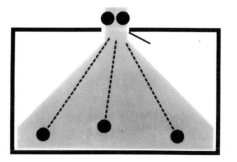

The hinges can tell you whether the door opens out or in. If the hinge pins are on the outside, the door should open out; the officer nearest the door-knob will get the first and widest view of the room. If the hinge pins are inside, the door should open in, and the officer opposite the knob will get the quickest look.

With doors that open in, the officer nearest the knob pushes it in. Be sure to push hard enough that the door bangs back with maximum force *against the wall behind it*. If it fails to do so, that may be a clue that a suspect is hiding in that position. Officers experienced in searching rooms know this is a favored hiding spot of armed offenders. From this vantage point, they can hear officers approaching and note their movements through the crack between the door and the frame.

If the door swings outward, instead of in, the officer nearest the knob or handle gets it open, then pushes it to his partner, so that neither of you has to stand or stretch fully in front of it. Get the door open as fast as you can and work from a *squatting* position. This will put you at a low, unexpected level should a suspect inside decide to shoot.

A proper position for two officers responding to a call at a door which opens in.

Once the door is opened, the officer nearest the hinges asssumes a low position and seeks a visual through the narrow opening between the door and frame. His sidearm is positioned in the direction of the possible location of the suspect.

If the door is locked and manpower permits, post a sentry there to guard it while you proceed with the search, eliminating other less resistant hiding places. When manpower's short or the room seems a very likely hideout or you've checked every place else, try first to get the door open with a pass-key from the building manager...or take the door off its hinges if they are exposed...or possibly telephone the office or apartment beyond the door and see if anyone is inside who'll answer and give you some clues to who's there. If you must force entry, consider using a "slam puller" or "dent puller," a common burglary tool available from most auto body repair shops. This tool has a threaded screw on the end that fits into the keyway of a lock and pops it open when the heavy weight on the handle is slammed back hard. Your last resort is to kick the door in. Many doors will defy the hardest kicks. Your best chance is to stand at an oblique angle to the door, rather than directly in front of it, and kick at the most vulnerable spot: adjacent to the lock system.

Assume the door is opened by one means or another and you and your back-up are positioned as we described earlier on either side of the doorway, below the level at which a suspect is most likely to fire. Now your combined vantage points should give you a visual on most of the room, provided the light is adequate. You won't, however, be able to see to the sides of you immediately on the other side of the wall—among the likeliest spots for a suspect to be waiting. Here, one at a time, you and your partner can use the "quick peek" technique to dart your heads through the doorway and back fast enough to see who or what, if anything, is along the wall you're each standing behind. Remember, you can make this movement in the least expected and safest way by peeking first at a low level, then at a high level...and *never looking from the same level twice.*

Another option for checking around doorways and corners is to use a small mirror on the end of a probe, which you can easily carry in your shirt or hip pocket. Some officers use an auto mechanic's inspection mirror on a telescoping wand or a dentist's mirror taped to an old car aerial, but you'll get better results with a mirror whose reflecting surface is at least two inches in diameter. At a hardware or auto supply store you can buy a parabolic mirror of the type attached to the side view mirrors of trucks and campers. If it has a self-adhesive back, you can attach it directly to the surface of the smaller dental or mechanic's mirror. Or consider simply holding it cupped in your hand. Angled through a doorway or around a corner, the mirror can reflect

Tactical officers making entry to a door which opens out—the mobile home of a man who had opened fire on a parade. A rifle barrel is visible just above the police shotgun. Moments before, a police officer had been killed.

any danger in the room or on the other side of the wall, while you stay back, unexposed.

From the doorway, you may be able to see—but not see into—other obvious potential hiding places, like a closet, for instance. If the suspect is there, you may be able to bluff him out by issuing a verbal challenge from your protected cover position. The idea is to act as if you know he is there so if he is he'll feel it's hopeless to do anything but surrender. If no one emerges from the hiding place, however, you'll still need to check it. And if the suspect is, in fact, waiting there, he'll now be fully alerted to your presence, so proceed with extreme caution.

The auto inspection mirror is held in your non-gun hand and slowly eased around the corner with both hands behind cover.

Your point of view in achieving a safe visual on the suspect. If you turn the book upside down, you will see an armed suspect who's expecting to see your body—not a small mirror.

66

To enter the room, *move in low and fast*, one at a time, while the other covers. Your swiftest entry for *narrow* doorways is the "criss-cross." The officer on the right darts across the threshold to an inside position on the left, and vice versa. Again, keep *low* when moving; some officers, once they start to move, have a tendency to stand up, which makes them easier targets. With wide doorways, consider keeping your back close to the frame and "wrapping around" swiftly to the other side, rather than plunging across the opening. This presents a minimum target. With either maneuver, of course, you want to get out of the doorway as quickly as possible.

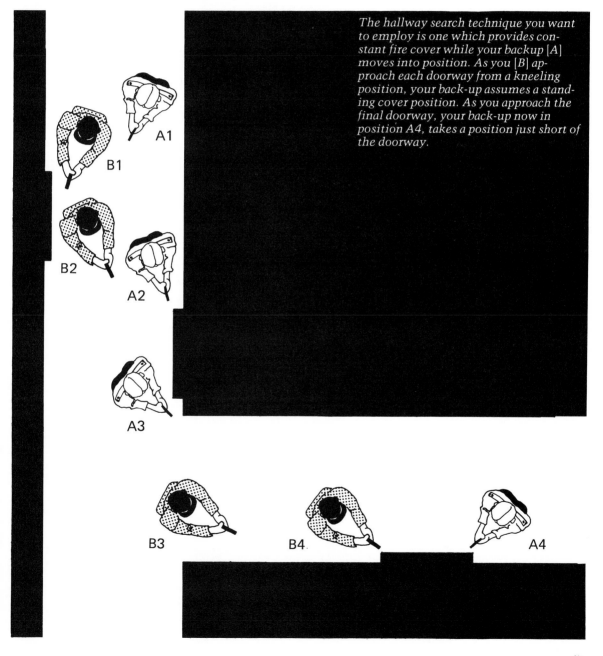

The hallway search technique you want to employ is one which provides constant fire cover while your backup [A] moves into position. As you [B] approach each doorway from a kneeling position, your back-up assumes a standing cover position. As you approach the final doorway, your back-up now in position A4, takes a position just short of the doorway.

Inside, with your back against the wall, kneel in your new position and listen for sounds that may signal the suspect's presence in the vicinity. Use your other senses, too. One pair of officers, pausing in a room that had just been entered, "caught a smell of human fear—the odor of fresh excrement"—coming from beyond another door. Sure enough, that pinpointed the suspect's location!

Once room entry is made where partners are involved, only one officer at a time actively searches, while the other stays still and covers. At night or in low-light situations, it may be hard to see your partner as you move apart. So if you simultaneously try to search different walls, you may lose track of one another's location, increasing the risk of shooting each other by mistake. You're safer having one remain squatted near the door ready to provide defending fire, while the other moves all the way down one wall to the first corner.

If you're the first searching officer, you can use non-verbal communication—like one snap of your fingers—to indicate you have reached the corner. Your partner can then respond with two snaps to indicate he has heard you and that he now is moving along another wall—while you provide cover. By continuing to alternate in this fashion, the covering officer keeps a fix on his partner's location and is free to shoot anywhere in the room except along the wall his partner is searching.

As much as possible, try to stay behind barricades, like pieces of furniture, as you cautiously move along the walls, around the circumference of the room or toward the next door. *Dont forget to always look up in searching the room.* In some places, as in rafters in a home garage or a loft in a warehouse, suspects are able to hide above eye-level, where officers operating in a routine fashion often neglect to check.

Continue trying to keep your exact movement as quiet as possible. But *do not attempt to eliminate noise that is already present.* That can give away your position, too. In an eastern city, an officer turned off a portable radio that was blaring acid rock music when he entered a tenement room in search of a "man with a gun." The suspect, it turned out, was hiding in a closet, unable to see the officer. But he knew exactly where the radio was. The moment it clicked off, he burst out shooting, with deadly accuracy.

Pay close attention to the doorway ahead. Officers in a Detroit narcotics case were completing their search of a living room which appeared empty, when they noticed the knob of a closed bedroom door turn slightly. Seconds later, five shots splintered the door, but because they had been alert, the officers had been able to take cover and escaped injury. (In a situation like this, it would be risky to fire back through the closed door unless you were *certain* the suspect was the *only* person in the room. If a hostage, a child or some other innocent person is there, too, your firing and endangering them could be considered reckless conduct.)

In moving forward, don't get so engrossed that you forget to *watch behind you*. By using other passageways and other rooms, a suspect may be able to circle around behind you and attack. In some cases, you may be able to rig up a warning system against that threat. When you check and pass by a door that swings out into a hallway or room, consider wedging it or moving some sort of barrier in front of it. If anyone tries to come through it to get behind you, he'll either be blocked entirely or at least make racket to alert you.

If it's necessary to move from floor to floor, avoid elevators. Because they telegraph location, confine movement and offer few if any cover options, they can be death traps. Use the stairs—even if the challenge you face is the search of a high-rise building.

Field Interrogation

One of your patrol obligations, aside from responding to specific assignments, is to find...stop... and question suspicious pedestrians you encounter on your beat, according to procedures that legally permit you to do so. These persons may include individuals who fit descriptions of wanted persons or others whose appearance...behavior...and/or location strongly suggests the probability that they are involved in criminal activities. Shootings often occur during such "field interrogations" or "pedestrian stops." Because the officer is in close proximity to the suspect and because the death rate from armed confrontations tends to be inversely related to distance, fatalities are quite likely to result from the gunfire—unless a proper approach has been made first.

When you see a person who bears investigation, try first to observe him for a few moments, whether you are in your patrol car or on foot yourself. These extra moments will allow you time to check his action...reinforce whatever called your attention to him in the first place to provide probable cause to detain...begin forming a plan for how to handle him...call for a back-up if you are working alone...

69

and, possibly, determine whether the suspect is armed. Remember that with an estimated 4½ million people in the U.S. carrying concealed loaded firearms, this is *always* a possibility.

If he's walking toward you when you first see him, let him pass by you as if you are paying him no special attention. You want to approach him from behind, if possible, and from a position where cover is close by if needed. If you seem to ignore him as he passes, you may be able to build an element of surprise into your challenge.

When observing a suspect, scan him from top to bottom for hints of a concealed firearm. A hat that's sitting straight on his head when it's styled to be worn at a jaunty angle may be positioned to help balance a revolver or small semi-automatic underneath. A male adult with one side of his shirttail out may be using it to conceal a loaded gun. If he's walking with his coat open or slung over his arm in cold weather or if he's wearing a jacket when it's hot, consider that he may be armed. Likewise, a bulge at his belt-line or a jacket that hangs heavy on one side may be suspicious. People who are not accustomed to carrying a gun often touch the gun as they walk, for reassurance that it's still there, to practice reaching for it and to enjoy the feel of its presence. This can be a particularly strong clue when potential suspects are approaching people who may be intended robbery victims. Even a limp or stiff-legged walk may be a warning sign. In neighborhoods where street gang fights are common, gang members sometimes carry shotguns to battle, strapped to their legs.

When you believe you are dealing with someone who may be dangerous, try to engineer the stop so it takes place away from crowded places like restaurants, public buildings, movie theaters, bars, and in some more isolated spot where innocent civilians are less likely to be hit by any gunfire, to interfere with your actions or intervene on behalf of the suspect. If it's necessary to follow the suspect on foot, you usually will want to stay to his left rear. He's likely to be right-handed, (about 90 per cent of the population is), and if so, this position will require that he turn the farthest to shoot you, thus affording you slightly more time to react. (An exception to this rule might be when good, quickly accessible cover—such as doorways, trees, parked cars or light poles—is to your right. Then your best option might be to follow to his right rear.) *Maintain peak alertness at all times.* The suspect *knows* who he is and what he has done, while you may not be certain. He may initiate a deadly assault at any time to prevent arrest, without concern for innocent bystanders or the consequences of his actions.

When you know or strongly suspect a person you want to question has a gun, you want to pick a location to stop him where you can be behind cover or at least concealed from view before you issue a command. This is highly desirable even when you have no evidence he is armed. (Cover pertains to obstacles that are difficult or impossible for bullets to penetrate, such as utility poles, mailboxes or fire plugs. Concealment means that you are hidden from view, though not necessarily shielded by a resistant barrier. You may be concealed at night, for example, behind your patrol car's headlights, if the suspect is facing toward them.) In stopping a potentially dangerous suspect, you want to have your gun drawn and pointed at him before you address him. And you want to be in a position where you can respond to and be protected from any sudden threat. Consequently, you avoid an approach like that made by two patrolmen in a southern city who responded to a shooting in a residential area and spotted the suspect walking along the street. With their revolvers still holstered and without taking cover outside their patrol car, they called for him to stop. Instantly, he pulled a .38 from his waistband and began shooting into their patrol car. One officer was wounded in the head and thigh, the other fatally shot in the face. In numerous other officer fatalities, the victims have approached suspects directly and frontally—like the off-duty Maryland police sergeant who walked up and announced himself to a bank robbery suspect sitting at a bus stop, who then drew a gun and shot him in the chest...or the Arkansas patrolman who spotted a subject wanted on warrants at a service station and strode toward him asking for identification; the suspect pulled out a handgun instead and shot the unprotected officer twice in the chest.

Ideally, you want to be close enough when you initiate the stop that you don't have to run and get out of breath to reach the suspect, but not so close that he can lunge for you and start fighting. Also, you want a spot that limits his possible avenues for escape.

Your order to stop, given from a position of cover, should be *explicit...direct...forceful*: "Police! Don't move! I want to talk to you." If his back is not already to you, order him to turn around immediately so he can't watch what you're doing. If his hands are in his pockets or anywhere where you can't see them, you want him to keep them there until after he is facing away from you. If he's going to come out with a firearm, it'll be harder for him to shoot you if he has to turn around first to find you.

If you had responded to this call in which a knife-wielding man is reported to be acting in a bizarre fashion, how would you have approached him?

Keep in mind that your suspect may not be cooperative in the least. Even your pointing a gun at him may not scare him. Then you should call for back-up and, *from a position of cover*, continue to repeat your voice commands until help arrives.

Once he's in a position of relative weakness and you're in position to respond to sudden threat, concentrate on getting his *hands in view*. They are the most dangerous thing about any suspect from your point of view. If they're in his pockets, tell him to remove them "very, very slowly," with his elbows extended away from his body. Even if he has no gun in his hand, order him to raise his hands as high as possible over his head and slowly turn *completely* around, while you check for guns in his waistband. If you see any weapons, immediately order him onto the ground, face-down, head away from you, arms out, palms up. With your partner or back-up providing cover, then approach him as you would an incapacitated suspect.

Where no weapons are visible, have him stand with his back to you and tell him to interlace his fingers behind his head, pushing them together as hard as he can. You can talk to him from a distance in this position, and if you decide to approach for closer inspection and interrogation, you can grasp the top three fingers of one of his hands with your non-gun hand and squeeze them together as a means of controlling him while you handcuff and frisk him. Because of the interlacing, even slight pressure on his fingers will inflict considerable pain and keep him at a disadvantage. You may also want him on his knees with his legs crossed at the ankles to further incapacitate him.

If you are making an arrest, the suspect(s) should be handcuffed at first opportunity and then thoroughly searched. When searching an offender, always hunt in the likeliest place for a gun first. A

The suspect's hands may be in his pockets to conceal a loaded gun, or maybe his hands are just cold. Initially, you have no way of knowing.

Your first step involves a verbal command to extend his elbows outward, then slowly to withdraw his hands. Next he places the gun on the ground with the muzzle pointed away from both of you.

highway patrolman who stopped to investigate a hitchhiker on a turnpike in Kansas ignored this rule and started his search by going through the subject's gear. The hitchhiker was allowed to stand by unhandcuffed and without having been patted down. As it turned out, he was wanted for murder in New York State. While the trooper was probing his luggage, the suspect drew a .32 cal. revolver from his waistband and fatally shot the officer in the head.

In some cases, field interrogation will require less drastic measures than we've outlined here, at least initially. You may, for example, need to approach a witness or complainant for questioning. With any on-foot approach, always stand at an oblique angle to the subject; that is, with your non-gun side turned toward him so that your face, eyes, groin and knee caps—the most easily damaged areas of your body—are protected. *Never stand with your gun side exposed to anyone for conversation or questioning.* Even with a seemingly "harmless" subject, try to position yourself so some cover is between the two of you or nearby, and closer to you than to him. If he suddenly presents a gun, you don't want him to get to the nearest cover first.

You should consider a distance around you of *at least three feet* as your "safety zone." Closer than that, the danger that you will be struck or that an attempt will be made to grab your gun is vastly multiplied. Street-wise suspects may try to penetrate this zone by: feigning deafness in order to draw closer...acting "cool," polite and courteous to blunt your alertness...trying diversionary tactics such as splitting apart when there are two or more suspects...or by holding identification papers close to the body in hopes you'll reach out or step nearer to get them. *Don't permit anyone to move in closer than 36 inches or try to touch you.*

Having begun an interrogation of a suspect or witness, keep him in sight, in your immediate presence. *Never turn your back on a suspect* or permit him to move where you can't see. He may be heading to get a gun from another location. A sheriff in Wyoming encountered a man on a ranch road who had been drinking and reportedly threatening suicide. The sheriff talked with him a bit, then walked with him toward the man's nearby cabin. He allowed the suspect to go inside, out of sight, while he waited in the yard to resume the conversation. Instead of coming back out, though, the suspect fired a .30-.30 cal. rifle through the cabin window, hitting the sheriff in the chest and killing him instantly. The assailant then turned the gun on himself and committed suicide. The keep-in-sight principle applies, of course, when you are questioning someone indoors as well as outdoors. More than one

Any suspect can be armed, especially a man wearing a suit. Here you can see 13 of the 17 firearms which are secreted on this person's body.

75

In conducting a field interview, position yourself at an angle to the subject, and keep your gun side away from his immediate reach.

officer has been slain when the suspect in a domestic disturbance, for example, momentarily ducked into a bedroom during interrogation—and emerged with his trusty deer rifle, ready for action.

Sometimes, it's necessary for you to question suspects in a parked car. Here you can order them out of the vehicle if you are behind cover. Or, if you can approach without being seen, another option is to come up low behind the right rear fender of their car, where you'll be able to see inside, and use that as your protected position. If you are walking toward the suspects when you first spot them, you pass by, faking disinterest, and then quickly whirl and take position behind the back fender. Your partner or back-up should assume another protected position that puts him at a different angle from the car, where he can cover you without exposing you to cross-fire. (You should not attempt to question more than two suspects in a car by yourself.) As you reach the fender, slap it sharply with your non-gun hand to attract the suspects' attention and at the same time firmly direct them to face forward and not move. Get their hands in sight on the steering wheel, on top of the dashboard or behind their heads, or order them to hang their hands out of the windows, before beginning any field interrogation.

There's always the possibility, of course, that the person you've singled out for field interrogation is not guilty of wrongdoing. In that case, apologize and explain what prompted you to detain him: "Your vehicle resembled one wanted on a burglary," or "You're dressed like (or have the same physical characteristics as) someone wanted for homicide," or "We were told you beat up your wife," etc. Most people will accept an explanation and an apology for their inconvenience if you employ an understanding manner, without arrogance.

Don't fail to quiz people who arouse your suspicions merely because you fear embarrassing them. Most civilians on legitimate business can easily prove it. And even if they aren't gracious enough to accept your explanation for acting as you did, it's better to have taken steps that allow you to be around to answer their complaint tomorrow than for there to be no tomorrow.

Traffic Stops

Few patrol events seem more "routine" than vehicle pullovers, yet in an average year 12 per cent of officers killed are shot while detaining motorists.

You may be attacked even before you are out of your patrol car. A young city patrolman in Missouri was killed still behind his steering wheel, when a stopped driver leaped out and fired three shots from a .12 ga. shotgun into the patrol car's windshield. Or violence may occur after you *think* everything is under control—as in the Florida case where a highway patrolman was calmly checking a cooperative driver's identification when a passenger, who had appeared to be asleep, suddenly popped up and opened fire with a .22 pistol.

Dangerous motorists and passengers cannot always be identified in advance. This is why it is so critical to *control* your stop. People you stop may have been involved in a crime you know nothing about and fear you will make the connection. Or the traffic violation alone may kindle an angry, violent reaction. The construction of most vehicles works against you, allowing much to be hidden from your view during your approach, including weapons and some occupants. Consequently, in order to have the advantage should shooting start, your best mental attitude is one that acknowledges, "This time I really could go down"—even if your "suspect" is an 85-year-old woman with blue hair, stopped for having no tail light. Vehicle approaches should be viewed as tactical exercises *regardless* of the motorist involved. Repetition of good tactics forms good tactical habits.

Eight bullet holes in this windshield capture the eeriness of a non-felony stop which became a fatal stop. Two undercover officers died inside this car.

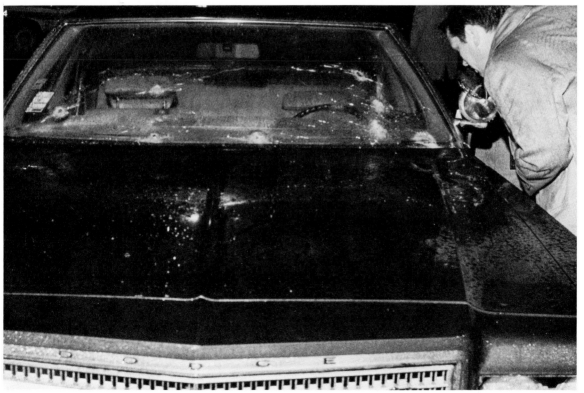

While you are still following the car you intend to stop, relay the license number and description to communications to run a National Crime Information Center (NCIC) computer check. This may give you some warning of trouble. If the vehicle has been reported stolen or involved in a crime or there are wants or warrants on the owner, you want to know it *before* you initiate the stop. The same is true, of course, if you recognize the vehicle or its occupants from a "wanted" description.

NON-FELONY STOP: Even if your preliminary license check comes back "clear" and it appears at the outset that you will be making only a misdemeanor or suspicious vehicle stop rather than a full-fledged felony pullover, there's no assurance, of course, that the vehicle you're halting does not contain guns and people ready to use them. A motorist may give every appearance of being a normal civilian up to the last moment. In Oklahoma, a young truck driver who had done no more than commit a minor traffic infraction ignited a police killing spree when a city marshal stopped him to issue a ticket. Enraged, the driver murdered the marshal with a .12 ga. shotgun, then later killed an auxiliary officer and a sheriff's deputy and critically wounded a police chief who tried to arrest him. Keep in mind that more officers are killed during non-felony pullovers, because their guard is down and they are not anticipating trouble.

When you're pulling over what seems to be an "ordinary driver" for a misdemeanor, give communications your exact location and the car license number and description. *If you're alone, the dispatcher will be your only partner.* You want to keep communications as informed as possible. Be sure he responds to all your inquiries and messages *before* you leave your patrol car.

Don't rush. If the weather is inclement, you may have the tendency to get out of your patrol car and get back as fast as possible. But remember, the time when both vehicles have come to a stop with engines still running is crucial. Errors you make then may backfire a few moments later. Alertness and caution are mandatory. Don't let your concern for your own creature comforts divert you from a good survival attitude.

As you radio in information about the stop, visually examine the vehicle. Make a habit of looking for clues which may indicate something is amiss. Is the license plate properly secured, or is it affixed in a manner or in a condition that may indicate it is stolen? Are passengers revealing undue concern about your presence? This may be indicated by facial expressions, excited conversations, etc.

The outcome of a non-felony stop. The blood in the roadway is from an officer who was shot in the face, then returned fire to the driver who lies dead in front of the patrol car door.

You want to *be sure all doors are closed completely*, to lessen the chance of the driver or a passenger suddenly leaning out and shooting, or setting off a firearm built into the door. The trunk lid, too, should be closed tight, with its lock in place. In some cases, armed suspects have hidden in trunks and then have suddenly thrown the lid up to confront unsuspecting officers, or they've shot at officers through the hole left by a pulled lock. When you're dealing with a van or recreational vehicle, you may want to order the driver out and have him open the rear doors for you so you can see inside, on the chance armed passengers are hiding there, ready to shoot. Here you have your sidearm out, but not in plain view. You open your door slightly and position yourself behind your windshield post so that your head and chest are given some cover protection. With you staying in this somewhat protected position, the driver's body, not yours, is likely to be in the line of any gunfire.

With ordinary vehicles where the driver remains inside, watch his shoulders and those of any passengers for movements that may suggest they are drawing or aiming a firearm. If they reach into the glovebox, under a seat or above a sun visor, they may be going for a gun. If you see any furtive or unusual movement, order the driver and others to remain in the vehicle with their hands in plain view. Immediately call for back-up and get to cover. It may be necessary from that point forward to treat the incident as a *felony* traffic stop.

Do not, as some officers seem prone to do, allow a driver to approach your patrol car to display his license or registration. If he starts toward you, order him to stop and be sure you can see his hands. A driver in Indiana approached a lieutenant during a traffic stop with his hands behind his back—then, at close range, suddenly produced a .45 semi-automatic and fatally shot the lieutenant in the chest.

When you are ready to approach the stopped vehicle, you want his motor turned off before you exit, although you leave *yours on*. Consider having the offender turn his wheels to the right, to inhibit his driving off. Use your exterior speaker to tell him, if you have to. If his motor's running as you approach, he may try to gun the car backwards and crush you between the vehicles or disable your patrol car and then drive off. On some vehicles, when the motor's on, a closed trunk can be opened automatically from the inside.

As you prepare to exit your patrol car, *crank your steering wheel to the left*. If someone tries to shoot you as you step out, you may be able to drop behind the wheel for limited cover. Also, it will offer some protection to your legs from low incoming bullets ricocheting off the pavement. As you exit your car, consider placing your radio microphone outside the window behind your side mirror for fast accessibility.

If you are working with a partner, he should flank out on the passenger side opposite your approach to a protected position where he can look directly into the side and rear windows of the stopped vehicle, perhaps concealed behind a tree or utility pole. He will then be able to see into the vehicle from a different angle than you can. If he's hidden from the occupants, he can unobtrusively draw his sidearm or aim his shotgun and have it ready to defend you at any hint of trouble. Even if they see him, his presence in such an unexpected position can be psychologically unnerving to an armed suspect and may convince him that the odds against him are overwhelming. Your partner should be careful, of course, not to take a position where he would be jeopardized by cross-fire from your sidearm in the event you have to shoot, or vice versa.

As you walk toward the vehicle, consider unsnapping the security strap on your holster and resting your strong hand on your gun butt, in position to draw your weapon without delay if necessary. You can give this hand position a non-threatening appearance by also resting your weak hand on your other hip. You will then seem merely to be approaching in a somewhat sauntering posture, although in fact you are ready for trouble.

An alternative is to carry a double citation book or metal clipboard with a thick sheaf of papers in your non-gun hand. Should an armed offender start shooting while still sitting in his car, these items may stop or deflect some bullets while leaving your gun hand free. Bullet-resistant clipboards are available, which are light and unobtrusive, yet offer protection against many handgun rounds.

During your approach to the driver, watch the interior through the rear window. With your eyes on the vehicle's occupants, touch the trunk crack to be sure the lid is still shut, then glance into the back seat for firearms or hidden passengers. Stay *close* to the vehicle as you move forward. This may make it harder for the driver to see you and certainly more difficult for him to turn and fire at you through his side window.

Statistically, you've entered the zone of greatest danger once you've reached the vehicle. The chances of your sidearm being grabbed or your being confronted by a weapon from inside are greatest from here on. So you want to do what you can to keep the other guy off balance.

As you exit your vehicle, brace the door with your non-gun hand and pause to survey the driver's vehicle for signs of danger. Notice the patrol car's front left tire is turned to provide some protection from ricocheting rounds.

Another approach option is to place your non-gun hand on your belt or waist to draw less attention to your gun hand.

Don't stop directly opposite the driver's window. By standing slightly *behind* his door, you have a visual inside but you make it awkward for him to see or reach you. If he tries to fling his door open, you will not be struck or knocked off balance and you may be able to slam it shut with a hard thrust of your non-gun hand or left knee. Don't be concerned that he has to twist to hand you his driver's license; he'll have to twist to shoot you, too. And in the extra split-second that takes him, you can be reacting to regain control. *Remain watchful.* Hold the license and citation book up in your non-gun hand so that the driver and any other occupants remain within your peripheral vision, and your sidearm hand is free. To help you keep track of the driver's hands, especially if he appears nervous, you may want to instruct him to keep them on the steering wheel. If you want him to step from the vehicle, open the door for him so he keeps his hands in sight. Move backward with the swing of the door so you can maintain a visual on the driver and passengers. Generally, however, you'll have better control if everyone stays inside.

Still another approach option on a suspicious pullover is to unholster your sidearm and keep it in this position as you advance toward the driver. From the driver's point of view, your sidearm is invisible.

As you approach, touch the trunk crack while maintaining a visual on the interior.

...ion yourself close to the driver's ... but back far enough so he can't ... you with his door.

What do you observe on this non-felony stop? If you did not immediately notice the semi-automatic in front of the gear selector, you need to re-evaluate your ability to perceive danger.

Stay alert against distractions. Passengers must be watched, as well as the driver. They are often the gunmen (or women) in traffic stop shootings. Female drivers or passengers can pose a particular threat in this regard, because they may try to divert your attention with sexual maneuvers. Many officers succumb almost instinctively—not so much to sexy *talk*, which may come across as an obvious ploy, but a *show* of sex, which is harder to ignore. During a survival exercise in California, a female volunteer in simulated traffic stops was told to turn in her seat when officers approached her car, so that her skirt hiked up to expose her bikini panties. Officers involved were warned ahead of time that the woman was "armed" and would try to "kill" them. Yet *every* man flashed his eyes from her hands to her thighs the moment her skirt went up. All were "shot" on the spot. Human nature is very predictable.

Whatever the driver is doing, your best visual is with his hands in the steering wheel area.

After completing your contact with the driver, walk back to your patrol car while maintaining a visual on the driver. Then wait until the vehicle has re-entered traffic before you assume the traffic stop is concluded.

You want to return to your patrol car to write any citation. If you remain at the driver's door, you invite a verbal confrontation, you are more easily distracted and you are dangerously close should someone in the suspect vehicle decide to take you on. Write the citation in a position that's to *your* advantage—and *never* while standing directly behind the suspect vehicle.

When for this or any other reason you need to return to your patrol car, walk with your head continually turned back or *walk backwards*, keeping a visual on the occupants. This may seem embarrassing or overreactive to you, but embarrassment is a big killer of officers. Officer slayings during traffic stops often occur as they did to a patrolman in Texas, who made a pullover and talked to the female driver without incident. When he started back to his patrol car to run a radio check on a male passenger, however, he turned his back on the stopped car to walk "normally." Unbeknown to the officer, the passenger was wanted on fraudulent check charges. With the officer unable to see him, the suspect brought a Russian-made automatic rifle up from under the seat, fired through the rear window and dropped his victim with four bullets, leaving him to die as the car sped away.

Even inside your patrol car, don't become so absorbed in what you're doing that you fail to keep an eye on the vehicle ahead. A Minnesota highway trooper who'd brought a tipsy woman's license back to his patrol car, for example, concentrated on it so exclusively that he didn't notice her husband emerge from the stopped car—even though the man carried a rifle. He shot through the windshield and penetrated the trooper's head.

After you've delivered the citation, again walk backwards or look back continually as you return to your patrol car. Maintain a visual on the violator's vehicle until it has safely merged back into traffic.

Throughout your approach, you should *have in mind what you would do* at any instant should you confront a threatening move. Your plan should allow you to capitalize on movement and surprise to buy time for yourself and steal time from your assailant. And you must be ready to execute it *without hesitation*.

FELONY STOP: When you know or suspect you are dealing with individuals who may be criminals, you have a highly dangerous situation on your hands. For your own safety, you should *assume they are armed felons,* who may shoot at any opportunity. Consequently, your tactics will differ in important ways from those for misdemeanor pullovers. *To stop a vehicle occupied by known or suspected felons by yourself is extremely risky.* In circumstances that are all too common, a patrolman in Arkansas stopped a pickup truck fitting the description of a vehicle used in a grocery store robbery. Although he was alone and there were three women in the truck, suspected escapees from a reformatory, he walked up to the vehicle to ask for identification. He was shot in the chest with a .32 cal. revolver, then shot again after he fell, when one of the suspects yanked out the officer's own service revolver and used it against him. Similarly, a highway patrolman in North Carolina, twenty-eight years on the job, tried singlehandedly to apprehend three bank robbery suspects he had stopped in a semi-rural area. As he approached their car, one suspect shot him in the neck and chest with a sawed-off .12 ga. shotgun.

A safer approach is to radio for back-up assistance, even if you have a partner. This is not a sign of cowardice, but only good survival sense. Specify your exact location and direction of travel...why you need the assistance...where you want it...and how many patrol cars you feel are required to safely control the situation. If possible, trail the suspect vehicle at a distance of about 50 feet until your back-up is in view.

Pull the vehicle over at a place of *your* choosing, where the visibility...nearby cover...and minimal amount of vehicular and pedestrian traffic work in your favor. (The more people there are around, the more they may try to interfere, be injured or be taken hostage in the event of trouble. Too much vehicular and/or pedestrian traffic may inhibit use of your firearm should your life become in danger.) If the suspect tries to stop where you don't want him to, use your outside speaker system to direct him on to your choice of stop. *Do not pull abreast* of him to get his attention. This gives him or his passengers an easy target. If he hits his brakes, you will suddenly be in front of him, a very poor tactical position. As you are making the stop, notify communications of your exact location.

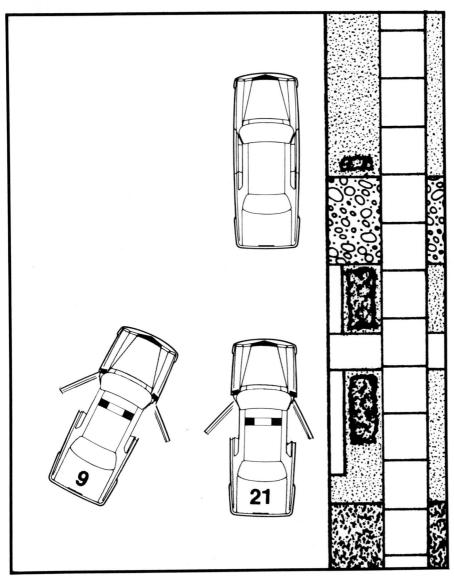

Proper position for primary unit [Car 21] and back-up unit [Car 9] during a felony stop.

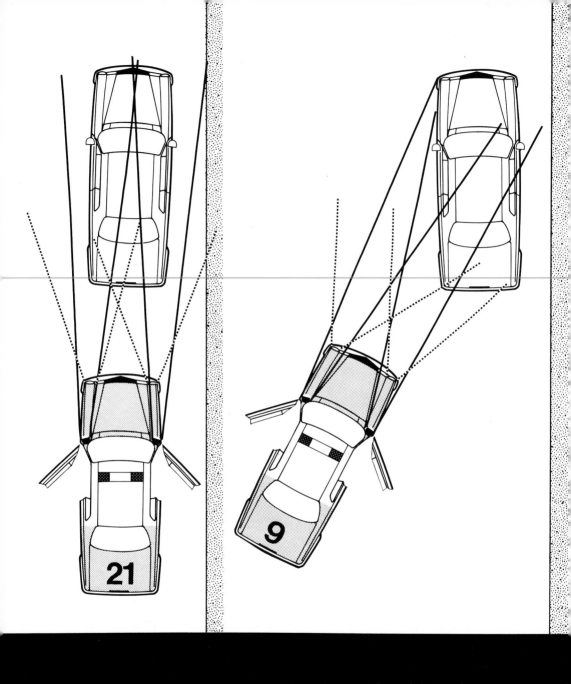

At night, the primary unit [Car 21] uses his high beams for general illumination of the suspect vehicle. Car 21's left spotlight is aimed at the driver's side mirror. The right spotlight is aimed at the right front passenger's side mirror.

The back-up unit [Car 9] during the night felony pullover, also uses his high beams for general blinding illumination. Car 9's left spotlight will blind the driver as he exits. The right spotlight will blind other occupants as they are removed.

On a felony stop where a back-up unit is assisting, consider positioning your patrol car differently than you would for most vehicle pullovers. Depending on the location involved, one alternative might be this: Instead of stopping so your patrol car juts out 3 feet as you ordinarily would to protect yourself from traffic as you walk to the driver's window, park in line with the suspect vehicle and about 30 feet back. At night, this will allow you to use your lights to illuminate the car ahead. Your back-up unit can then pull up directly along the driver's side of your car, blocking traffic in that lane. There should be just enough room between so that you can open your driver's door and the passenger officer in the back-up car can open his door, with space for the offender to walk between them.

You do not want to approach the suspect vehicle on foot. Where there is known danger, all officers open their doors, but *remain inside their patrol cars.* Each positions himself in his seat so his back rests against a door post for support and he is protected at least somewhat behind a windshield post. One foot rests on the floorboard while the other is braced against the door jamb or the open door, *not* resting on the ground where your legs are exposed to low or ricocheting rounds. Assuming you are the driver of the first patrol car, you have your service handgun trained on the driver's side of the suspect vehicle. The passenger officer of the back-up car also aims at that side with his handgun. Your partner covers the passenger side of the suspect vehicle with his shotgun; the driver of the back-up unit covers the suspects inside their vehicle with a shotgun, if one is available.

As the driver of the first responding patrol car, you alone give orders, yelling or using your outside speaker to address suspects and also to order pedestrians to leave the area. Your fellow officers say nothing unless they see a suspect going for a firearm. Yell (or broadcast over your outside speaker): "Everyone! Put your hands up...interlace your fingers...put your hands behind your heads...look straight ahead. Driver! Shut your motor off and take the keys in your hand." (If you have to make the stop before help arrives, you can issue these orders and keep the suspects in this position until you have back-up. Any move you want any occupant to make, incidentally, tell him to make with his *left* hand.)

Now you want to get them out of their vehicle, one at a time, on the *driver's* side. (One of the less desirable methods of maneuvering felony traffic stops involves exits from the passenger side of the suspect vehicle, with the occupants put up against a wall for control, if one is available. Experience has shown that a passenger-side exit is usually less desirable because good cover—like parked cars, trees, utility poles, doorways—is likelier to be on that side and thus readily available to suspects as they emerge. On the driver's side, they'll ordinarily have fewer barricades behind which to escape or shoot. In addition, exiting into the street adds to their disorientation, which will work to your advantage. Also, you cannot be certain at this point just who all the occupants are. One or more may be a hostage. If all are lined up in traditional fashion against a wall and shooting starts, innocent people in the line-up may unknowingly be shot by an officer's bullets. Even where this is not a problem, permitting more than one suspect at a time out of the stopped vehicle and not under physical restraint lessens your ability to control the situation.) Start with getting the driver out. Where several suspects are present, the driver is usually the leader, so you want to isolate him as promptly as possible. You want him to bring the car keys *with him*, so they are not left behind for the other suspects or dropped on the pavement where they're inaccessible to you. If his window is rolled down, order him to reach out with his left hand slowly and open his door from the outside, keeping his other hand behind his head. If the window is up, you'll have to allow him to lower his left (and hopefully weak) hand out of sight long enough to open the door. The spotlight on the first responding patrol car or the back-up unit should be trained on the driver's side at about five feet off the ground so that the driver will face the glare of the light as he steps out and looks toward the patrol cars. As he steps out, have him roll down his window (if it isn't already)...kick the door shut...and get both hands up over his head as high as he can reach, with his fingers spread apart. Remember, the key in this situation is *control*.

As the driver of the first patrol car, you and the passenger officer from the back-up unit concentrate on handling the suspect who has exited. You want him to turn slowly in a full circle while you look for any visible weapons. If you see any, order him to keep his hands interlaced on his head and to walk *backwards* toward you. Advise him that if he moves his hands at any time, you will presume he is going for his weapon and you will take the appropriate action. If he appears weaponless, still assume he is armed. Command him to place his hands behind his head and walk backwards toward you, just as you would an armed suspect.

To his fellow suspects who may be watching from the stopped vehicle, it will appear that he is disappearing into a white void of light as he moves toward you. Suspects who have experienced this illusion concede that it has a strong, inhibiting psychological impact. As the driver backs between the open patrol car doors, the passenger officer from the back-up car will stand behind him and grasp the top three fingers of one of the suspect's hands, as described for field interrogations. This officer takes control of the suspect's car keys. The suspect should be immediately handcuffed...thoroughly searched...questioned about weapons on any of the passengers or in the car and about other passengers who may not be visible...then locked in the back seat of one of the patrol cars.

The key to the felony pullover is control. Here you have the driver exit by opening his door from the outside.

Command the driver to place his hands over his head. Then you can see any gun in his waistband.

Now order the driver to interlace his fingers behind his head and kick his door shut.

Then command him to walk backward with his hands still interlaced behind the head.

Following the same procedures, all visible passengers are removed one at a time from the suspect car, all from the driver's side. Clear the front seat first (after the driver, the most likely leader of a gang is the right front passenger), then concern yourself with getting the suspects out of the back. If the car is a two-door, back seat passengers can push the driver's seat by tripping the locking latch with a foot so they can exit without lowering their hands.

These procedures in emptying a suspect vehicle will work to your advantage at most locations. However, when the stop is being made on a busy freeway or when there are other overwhelming hazards to the left, adjustment in the tactics must be made. It may then be necessary to exit the suspects from the passenger side. If so, the back-up unit should pull up on the right of the first responding patrol car, even if it means jumping a curb to do so. The roles of the officers are reversed, and the exit begins with the right front passenger, who brings the keys. Still, the suspects are brought back one at a time between the two patrol cars.

As the driver reaches the space just in front of the two patrol car doors, place him in the kneeling position.

When the suspect vehicle appears empty, you want to advance and inspect the interior and then the trunk, where additional armed passengers have been known to secrete themselves. There are several tactics for conducting the trunk search. One approach is to take one of the handcuffed prisoners with you to witness your search. Before advancing, make sure you have secured the prisoner's cooperation in bringing him to the trunk, else you are infringing on his rights as a prisoner. When it's time to open the car doors or trunk lid, do so by holding him securely with your non-gun hand and reaching around from behind him. (Don't grip just his handcuffs alone. Experienced felons can twist the cuffs and take off one of your fingers). Your fellow officers, of course, cover you as you make your approach, taking care to avoid cross-fire positions.

After all occupants of the suspect vehicle have been secured, the driver aids in the search of the trunk. As one officer provides cover, you reach around and open the trunk. Notice the officer has hold of both handcuffs and the offender's waistband to maintain control.

Another tactic for the trunk search. As you insert the key from a location low and to the side, your back-up maintains fire cover, while resting the non-gun hand on the trunk lid.

Now you assume a position at an angle to your back-up, who slowly lets the trunk rise to its open position. A visual on the trunk is now possible by both of you.

Firearms Readiness

Obviously, you cannot have your sidearm out and ready to use *every* time you answer a radio call, conduct a field interview or make a traffic stop. Even if department policy and common sense permitted, it would not be wise. Sidearms and shotguns indiscriminately drawn and displayed will frighten and offend civilians and may, in fact, provoke violence in some situations that could otherwise be peacefully resolved.

Many officers, however, do not draw their sidearms when they *should*. Back-up officers arriving at the scene where an officer has been killed often discover to their amazement that the victim's sidearm is still holstered, with no evidence he attempted to draw, shoot or otherwise defend himself. Yet in many of these instances, there was prior warning of danger.

The rule has been: don't draw unless you intend to shoot. That suggests you wait until the last instant to get your sidearm in your hand. The survival approach is: don't draw unless you are *prepared* to shoot, mentally and tactically, if you have to. This allows for the fastest possible "draw": having your sidearm in your hand *before* the fight starts. You should have your firearm ready whenever:

1. you are approaching a situation where you know or reasonably believe someone has physical possession of a deadly weapon;

2. you are involved in a high-risk activity, such as a building search or have responded to a violent crime-in-progress, or

3. you have any reason to fear for your safety or the safety of others.

When in doubt, you may want to go with your gun and risk ruffling a few community relations feathers rather than risk becoming the victim at your own funeral.

Another aspect of firearms readiness is having the most effective gun in hand for a confrontation. The most powerful and intimidating weapon, if made available on patrol by your department, is a .12 ga. shotgun with an 18- or 20-inch barrel; yet its impressive versatility for use in making an approach is often overlooked and misunderstood.

When you take it from your patrol car, a shotgun may make a strong psychological impact. Its appearance and reputation may be enough in themselves to sober a suspect who's considering shooting you. You can induce an additional "pucker factor" with the ominous noise of "racking" the action. Once heard, in the still of the night, it's a sound never forgotten. If you are justified in using deadly force and do have to use it, the shotgun can be even more destructive than a submachine gun, yet, if you are shooting at relatively close range, the pellets are not likely to spread out wide enough to endanger people other than your assailant. For long-distance shooting, rifled slugs can be fired to an effective range of about 100 yards. In addition, the shotgun can be used to fire chemical agents.

The shotgun does have its drawbacks. If you have to run or you get into a physical fight, it may prove cumbersome...if you need to put it aside, it has no holster...if you are using your flashlight it may be awkward to carry. But when you *know* you are facing a possible armed confrontation, these are definitely of secondary importance.

Don't walk into a known dangerous situation with just your handgun. You want *superior* fire power, if possible. So consider employing your shotgun *any time* you are approaching:

1. the scene of a felony-in-progress;
2. a hazardous vehicle stop;
3. a wanted felon, or
4. other situations where the risk of getting shot or killed is high.

Like many officers, you may try to avoid the shotgun in your patrol car because you're unfamiliar with it. Chances are the training you have received with this weapon is minimal. The scope and direction may have been so limited that you feel you have failed to master this weapon. That is ironic because when you need a shotgun the most is when you're on a particularly dangerous assignment, where you may need to draw on maximum training resources to emerge alive. Some range instructors seem to feel that even without sufficient practical experience you can protect your life or other innocent lives with a shotgun simply by virtue of its capability to expel powerful multiple projectiles. Where lives are on the line, that's a poor assumption to make. Part of survival involves becoming familiar and proficient with *all* firearms at your command. Later, we'll examine particularly the procedures for safely transporting and handling the shotgun during your approach to a scene and your subsequent interrogation of individuals you encounter there.

After completing any approach and arresting or releasing the suspect(s) involved, take a few moments to honestly critique what you did. If you have a partner, discuss the actions you both took. Quickly reviewing your job performance and discovering weaknesses that could have worked to a suspect's advantage will help you sharpen your procedures and tactical maneuvers in the future.

LIGHT CONTROL

When the lights go down, your risk goes up, as a rule. Like a camera, your eye needs light to record images, and on night patrol, in darkness or the deep shadows of streets, alleys, yards, rooftops, hallways and rooms, there may be too little illumination for you to quickly perceive images that warn of danger. Even in daytime, when an assignment sends you into low light level locations like bars or basements, you may be temporarily blinded while your eyes adjust to the scene. A suspect already there, cloaked in and adapted to the dark, can present a menace you won't even see.

More than half the times armed suspects take on the police, they do so at dusk...after dark...or where artificial light is limited. More than two-thirds of the shootings in which officers die occur between 6 o'clock at night and 6 in the morning, with the deadliest hours the darkest ones, between 10 PM and 2 AM.

Yet darkness is not always your enemy. Sometimes it can allow you to conceal your movements in responding to crimes. It may provide you with a hiding place. And during potentially dangerous nighttime traffic stops, for example, it may permit you an important tactical edge: taking advantage of the dark, you may be able to draw your gun and hold it unobtrusively above the door frame of a vehicle while questioning the driver. Or—and this is faster because you can raise a gun up faster than you can lower it from an elevated position—you may be able to stand at the vehicle with your gun alongside your leg. In either case, the driver will likely never be aware that you have a firearm in hand.

What's required is that you *control* the double-edged sword of darkness. You want to be constantly aware of the sources of light available to you and the ways you can manipulate light and dark to your advantage and a suspect's disadvantage. Like a proper approach, this control may help you abort a planned shooting or at least put you in the best position should bullets fly.

The lights inside buildings, your flashlight and lights on your patrol car are among those you can control in a number of important ways. In weighing your options with them, you want to plan ahead and to anticipate just how your control will affect your vulnerability to an assailant's shots and your own capability in shooting back.

Try to avoid positioning yourself against any outside background which forces you to become silhouetted.

Building Lights

Where you need to enter a darkened building or a suite of dark offices, there's always the danger that the suspect you're looking for is secreted inside, just waiting for a bad approach by an officer. That proved to be the case in Alaska when a patrolman responded to a burglary-in-progress call at a drug treatment center. To launch a room-by-room search with fellow officers, he crawled into a darkened room through an open window. The suspect was hiding inside that very room—and shot him in the head with a 9mm semi-automatic.

This photo was taken from the general location of an armed hostage-taker. The officer inside this apartment was unaware that lights were setting him up as a target.

As an alternative to moving blindly into an area you can't see, it may be possible to get some or all of the lights turned on ahead of time by master switches. The building janitor, manager or owner will probably know the switches' location and the exact lighting they control. Obviously, having the lights on automatically eliminates many suspect hiding places and improves your view of areas to be crossed and searched. But the lights should *not* be activated until all officers involved in the search are in *protected* positions, since a suspect's field of vision may also be enhanced.

Where general lighting is not possible, it's *usually* safer to turn on lights area by area as you progress, as opposed to moving in the dark and not knowing what is out front. Again, you want to be behind cover—and with your sidearm drawn—before any lighting is turned on. Reach for switches from a low position rather than standing beside them at your normal height, as a waiting suspect may be expecting. Note: If you smell gas, do not turn on any lights. An electrical arc from the switch can easily touch off an explosion.

Control of light inside should be achieved by taking a position below the kill zone. In this incident, an armed offender was standing 6 feet away on the other side of the wall with his gun aimed at normal shoulder height.

If cover is not readily available, you may decide you are better off in the dark, possibly relying on sporadic bursts of lights from your flashlight. You may even want to turn room lights *off* if they are already on, giving yourself at least the concealment benefits of darkness as you move to a safe area. If you have practiced at a range under nighttime conditions, you know it's harder to shoot and hit a target in the dark. A suspect will have the same difficulty. If you are searching an open area like a warehouse and the suspect happens to be hiding in the rafters, having lights on will aid him and jeopardize you. Evaluate the type of building you are in and play off your environment in making decisions.

Remain conscious always of where any light source is in relation to your body. Light coming from behind you, such as street light through a window or lights left on in a room you have just searched, can silhouette you as a perfect target. So can lights over doorways you intend to enter. If, as part of your approach, you can't work a switch to turn off lights above doors or reach up and unscrew the bulbs without outlining yourself in the doorway, consider smashing the bulbs with your nightstick or flashlight. Remember also that light hitting your body from certain angles will cast shadows. If, for example, your shadow extended out beyond a corner, a suspect waiting on the other side could see it and be alerted to your approach.

Flashlight

An important point to remember about this versatile tool is that it does not always have to remain connected to your hand in order to help you detect and defend yourself against potential danger.

With the "flashlight roll" technique, for example, you and your partner or back-up can illuminate a darkened room in search of a suspect without having to leave protected positions on each side of the doorway. With the door open all the way back and the flashlight in your weak hand, squat beside the doorway and hold the flashlight so its lens end is sticking through the entry. Push the slide button "on" and release the flashlight so it rolls off your cupped fingers toward the opposite side of the doorway. The flashlight should roll across the opening almost straight or in a slight arc. Your partner can pick it up without significant exposure and then roll it back from his position of cover.

As the flashlight is rolling, you both should be looking into the room as far as the rolling beam penetrates, with your firearms ready. Between both your vantage points you'll be able to see much of the area and may discover a suspect who otherwise would remain hidden. *Caution: do not enter the doorway while the light is on*; confronted with an unexpected light, a suspect may instinctively fire directly at the source, figuring an officer is behind it. Also, understand that flashlights with certain shapes—notably, large on-off switches— may not work well for this tactic, because they preclude the possibility of a smooth roll. So *know your equipment* and make sure it works properly before you use it.

High angle view of two officers properly positioned behind cover and using the flashlight to avoid becoming a victim of the fatal funnel.

Another room search tactic involves the flashlights of both officers. First, you hold your light around the door frame, while keeping the vital portions of your body behind the wall. From a low or prone position on his side, your partner checks the portion of the room illuminated by your light. Then you reverse roles: he puts his light around his side of the frame, while you check. In both cases, the officer with the light wants to hold it above the level of his head while in a squatting position, to be as deceptive as possible about his true position.

Away from doorways, you still should be behind some kind of cover—a chimney, a garbage can, a store counter, etc.— when trying to search an area with your flashlight. You want to hold the light as far from your body as possible, with as little of yourself exposed as you can manage...use the light as sparingly as possible...and move to a new position immediately after you shine it.

Where cover is not available, probably your best option is the "flash-and-move" technique. With your sidearm drawn and your legs apart and bent, you hold your flashlight at arm's length in your weak hand...higher than the level of your head...and out from your shoulder at about a 45-degree angle. This places the lens to the side, above and somewhat ahead of your body and keeps your vital areas from being brightly illuminated by the aura of light thrown off around the flashlight head. Be sure you stay *behind* the beam of light, not in its periphery, to minimize the risk of being visible in the flashlight's "back-splash." Your flashlight should have a dark and non-reflecting surface of fairly heavy-gauge metal and should be equipped with both slide and button controls. Press the *button* just enough to blink the light on for an instant, allowing you a quick fix on the area, then move immediately to a new location, preferably toward cover. If you leave the light on constantly, then you make yourself a constant target. If you have to shoot, shoot and move with the light off. The number one consideration in such a situation, of course, will be positive identification of your intended target. You don't want to shoot a fellow officer, a private security officer or an innocent homeowner moving in the dark.

If the suspect shoots, he'll probably fire directly at the place he last saw the beam or just to his right of it. If you're holding your light as we've described, you should be clear of the shot. In one case, in which officers entered a darkened house to apprehend a man who had gone berserk and murdered his land-lady, the suspect shot so accurately with a rifle that he shattered the flashlight held in one officer's hand. The bullet kept going, but because the officer had extended the light to his side, his body was clear of the shot entirely and he was able to kill the suspect with return fire. *Do not try to control your flashlight with its slide switch*. The button is faster and there is not the danger, if you drop it, of the light remaining on and highlighting you for an adversary.

If you're moving from one area to another, try to avoid using your flashlight. Often there is enough ambient light from natural (moon, stars) or artificial (street lights, signs) sources to allow you to make your way. Use of the flashlight will destroy your night vision, at least momentarily, and may pinpoint your position for a watching suspect. If you feel you must use your flashlight, angle it toward the ground and partially cover the beam with your hand so the light is just large enough to insure safe footing. Keep the light low...ahead of your body...as far to one side...and turned on as briefly as possible, never for long periods of time. You don't want to silhouette yourself.

During traffic stops, your flashlight and patrol car spotlight can be trained on the driver's side view mirror as you approach. If he's trying to watch you, the beam will blind him temporarily, and he'll likely turn away. Once you reach his door, shine the light directly into his eyes, destroying his night vision. If he turns out to be okay, you can always apologize and make it seem accidental. If not, you may have delayed his getting on target if he has a gun.

Under no circumstances should you use your flashlight in these or other maneuvers *by holding it in the center of your body mass or near your face.* The hazard of doing so was bizarrely illustrated by the fate of a burglar who crawled through the washroom window of a bank one night, a crowbar under one arm, a .45 cal. Thompson submachine gun under the other and a small flashlight in his mouth. A security officer waiting in the darkness inside saw the light bob into the lobby. He did what most officers—or suspects—would do; fired at the only visible portion of his opponent, the flashlight. It was still in the burglar's mouth. The bullet hit the flashlight, drove the battery spring deep into the man's tongue and angled through his mouth and out his neck with fatal results.

When you hold your flashlight extended with your non-gun hand, make sure you stay behind the beam of light, or this is what the suspect will see.

You can avoid the backsplash effect by placing your flashlight on the ground, as you take two steps to your left. Your goal is to remain invisible to the suspect. You are also now free to use your two-hand instinct shooting position.

Vehicle Lights

Recent tests conducted by British authorities[1] show that if you simultaneously blind and distract an armed suspect you can often delay his shooting by an appreciable span of time. You may be able to distract him with a loud noise or by throwing something at him. But even without distraction, blindness alone will cause serious disorientation in some suspects, especially if they are trying to engage more than one officer in a gunfight or if they have to shoot more than once at the same officer.

Among your best tools are the high-beam flashlights and spotlight(s) on your patrol car, particularly during nighttime traffic stops and field interrogations. Using the lights of your car and a back-up car, you're able to control approximately 1 million candlepower to your advantage.

[1.] "Some Comments on the Hostage Situation," by J.C. Muirhead, *The Police Chief*, February, 1978.

Field interrogations at night can be conducted from behind a curtain of light. You and your partner quietly flank out to positions away from your patrol car. From the suspects' viewpoint you are invisible.

If, for example, you want to question a suspect in a darkened alley, you can approach with your patrol car pointed directly at him, high-beams and spotlight on. Stop about 15 to 20 feet from him. Now he and the area around him are clearly lighted, from your perspective. But when *he* looks in *your* direction, he'll see a curtain of bright, white light, and very little if anything beyond it. If he does decide to shoot, he'll probably fire into the lights on the driver's side, where he figures you're most likely to be. To defeat that possibility, you want to move around low to the rear of the car as soon as you stop, or flank out to a position of cover nearby, being careful to stay *behind* the curtain of light created by your headlights.

The tactic is to *put some distance between yourself and your light source* and yet take advantage of the blinding effect it affords. From a protected position behind the lights, you can keep your gun on the suspect while you issue him verbal commands. He won't be able to see your exact location, and if you move occasionally, he'll have a hard time pinpointing just where your voice is coming from. As you move away, you can maintain the impression you're still stationary by speaking slightly louder.

While you keep a suspect distracted with commands, your partner or back-up may be able to keep himself concealed in shadows and move around the perimeter of the lights so that he comes up behind the suspect, assuming the suspect is facing toward your lights. Provided you protect your partner and yourself from cross-fire, your partner then will be in a good position to surprise your suspect if he appears threatening.

Two survival-savvy patrolmen in California showed a police instructor just how effective this technique can be when they were being tested on routine field interrogation tactics. They turned their lights directly on the instructor, who was playing the role of a suspect, and the driver-officer began interrogating him from behind the light curtain. After a few moments of conversation, the instructor called a halt to the exercise and said he was flunking both of them. Why? asked the driver-officer. "Because," the instructor announced, "your partner is so lazy he never even got out of the patrol car!" At that instant, directly behind his head, the instructor heard the click of a semi-automatic being cocked. The second officer was standing inches behind him. While the instructor was blinded by the lights and *assuming* the second officer had remained in the car, he actually had flanked out in darkness around the edge of the headlights and silently crept up behind the "suspect" to a position of strong advantage.

On nighttime traffic stops, you may want to use your external speaker to order the stopped driver to turn on his inside dome light. This ploy tends to unnerve suspects and allows you to get a better visual of the interior before you leave your patrol car. You can then get an even better view and disorient the driver a bit more by flooding the interior through the rear window with your high beams and spotlight(s). If you are alone and have two spotlights on your patrol car, be sure to turn on both and open your passenger door. This may fool a suspect into believing you have a partner whose whereabouts can't be seen from the suspect vehicle.

Be careful during traffic stops not to walk back toward your patrol car and stand directly in front of the headlights to write a ticket, as some officers do. The bright lights will likely destroy your night vision while they clearly silhouette you from the perspective of the stopped driver, thereby turning your headlights to the suspect's advantage.

Similarly, back-up cars responding to a nighttime call must take care that their headlights do not blind or make silhouette targets of officers already on the scene. If possible, back-ups should turn off all their lights as they near the scene, except their parking lights. The cars' rooftop emergency lights should be included in this blackout. They can be distracting, as well as dangerously illuminating. Parking lights will keep the back-up cars minimally visible, but not make them destructive to their own forces.

Improving Night Vision

It usually takes about thirty minutes for your "night vision" to develop to the point that your eyes can distinguish objects in dim light with full acuity. But there are ways you can hasten the process a bit when your assignment demands that you move quickly from light to dark areas.

Say, for example, you are called to a dimly lit bar or restaurant to stop a fight—a situation in which a number of officers have lost their lives. While you are still in the well-lighted outdoors starting your approach to the scene, close one eye, preferably your strong eye. Then, as you step inside, open that eye. Your visual adjustment will already be a step ahead.

In a darkened area, try to utilize off-center vision. In other words, when you focus your attention on an object, don't look directly at it. Direct vision requires the use of eye cells that are least sensitive at night. When you look slightly to the side, above or below an object, the image is formed on the area of the eye with cells most sensitive in darkness. The most sensitive eye area varies with individuals, but usually you can hit it by looking 6 to 10 degrees away from an object, so you see it, in effect, out of the corner of your eye.

Scanning strengthens your off-center vision. If you try to hold an image in the corner of your eye longer than about 4 to 10 seconds, it gradually "bleaches" out. But if you shift your eyes every few seconds in abrupt, irregular movements over and around the object or person you're watching, you can move the image to fresh cells. Colds, headaches, fatigue, narcotics use, heavy smoking and excessive use of alcohol reduce your ability to see at night. In addition, of course, they adversely affect your skills at anticipating and responding to danger, whether the light is good or bad. In short, they work for the suspect...and against your survival.

VERBAL CHALLENGE

"Police! Don't move!"

It's hard to predict what will happen when you voice this command to an armed suspect. He may stop dead in his tracks, throw down his gun and plead with you not to shoot him...he may ignore you or pretend he didn't hear and walk away...he may claim he is a plainclothes officer and order *you* to put away *your* gun...he may consider your words an invitation to a gunfight—and start shooting....

Any way you slice it, the moment of confrontation is a tense one, and those three words—"Police! Don't move!"—often mark the turning point of an armed encounter. You may be accustomed to individuals doing what you say, but when you issue a command to a person who has a loaded gun, you have to be prepared for *anything*.

This much is certain...When the risks and potential benefits are weighed, there is always one persuasive argument for attempting a verbal challenge *before* shots are fired: *situations where you confront armed individuals are not always what they seem.* By clearly announcing your office and giving an order to stop the action, you may be able to buy time in which to better establish the suspect's identity and intentions. The last thing you want is to use deadly force against someone who did not commit a crime.

Two contrasting episodes illustrate the point. One night in Chicago an officer was called to a tavern to put down a fight among the patrons. He got everybody calmed down and was preparing to leave when someone shouted: "They're at it again!" The officer ran the length of the bar, and as he rounded the end, he saw one of the bartenders flat on his back on the floor, a young Latino sitting on his chest. A flash of metal from the young man's hand looked like he had a gun or a knife at the bartender's throat. The officer's revolver was out, ready to shoot...the need for action seemed urgent. But he paused long enough to issue a verbal challenge. It was a decision he has always been grateful for. The bartender turned out to be experiencing an epileptic seizure. The Latino was the cook in the place who was trying to hold the man's tongue in place with a fork to keep him from swallowing it.

For maximum protection, issue verbal commands from behind cover. If this suspect spins around and shoots, the officer [right] is shielded by the wall.

Another night, in Michigan, an off-duty officer heard three shots fired in rapid succession in a hallway outside his bedroom. It sounded as if he were under attack. Without saying a word, he picked up his revolver and shot back in the direction of the noise. His bullet struck the "offender" in the chest—his six-year-old daughter, who was playing with her brother's cap pistol.

A consistent command like "Police! Don't move!" can prevent such tragedies. Commit it to memory right now if your department doesn't specify a different command. Even when used against a genuine suspect, this statement, forcefully delivered from a position of cover either by your direct voice or over your exterior speaker, may be sufficiently intimidating to keep the situation from escalating into violence. It instantly establishes who you are and tells the person challenged exactly what you want him to do. If he follows your order, his safety is protected and you can gain control of the action without gunfire.

Because of the stress and heightened emotion involved in most confrontations, a verbal challenge is rarely a simple, cut-and-dried matter. Your challenging a suspect successfully and making it stick in many cases will heavily depend on your ability to understand and use applied psychology. And like other survival procedures, your tactics can backfire if not properly and confidently employed.

Practice and experience will sharpen your skills. Meanwhile, here are some of the nuances you'll want to keep in mind in using verbal language, depending on whether you're facing a criminal...a fellow officer whose identity is hidden...or an innocent civilian.

Suspect Control

You're safest if you always assume at the outset that the person you're challenging is an offender and will respond violently. Where that proves not to be the case, you've lost nothing with a conservative approach, and where it is so, you may gain everything. Therefore, where possible:

1. *issue your command from behind cover.* This tactic could have saved a state trooper in upstate New York who tried to arrest a young man who was standing in a street with a .22 cal. rifle after having murdered his girlfriend. When the trooper got out of his car and ordered the suspect to drop his rifle, the man instead abruptly raised it. He shot

the unprotected officer in the thigh, then, as he fell to the ground, rushed up and killed him with a shot in the head.

2. *have your gun in hand or have your holster unsnapped and your hand properly positioned, ready to draw.* The suspect may move fast, as in the case above, or, if his back is to you when you issue your command, he may have a gun in *his* hand that you cannot see. If you *know* he's armed, have your firearm on target *before* you open your mouth.

3. *voice your verbal challenge before the suspect makes one of his own.* Sometimes, whoever manages to speak first gains an important psychological, and often physical, edge that may then prevail throughout the incident. Where a challenge has anticipated trouble and was planned ahead, issuing the challenge is likely to coincide with a state of readiness, while the recipient of it may not yet have reached that level of preparedness. In one midwestern case, a man who had been reported acting "suspicious" in an alley watched two officers drive their patrol car up to him and get out to investigate. He looked innocuous enough, but as soon as they stepped away from the car, he whipped a sawed-off shotgun from under his coat and then issued a verbal challenge: "Drop your guns, or I'll blow you away." One-upped, the officers were in no position then to issue him any orders. One was kidnapped and held hostage for several hours with a gun to his head before other officers negotiated an end to the episode. From the outset, you want to maintain an *offensive* position, not a defensive one.

If you follow these procedures and the suspect still ignores what you tell him and keeps moving, you can pursue him...continue issuing the challenge...and, ideally, with the help of back-up officers, try to take physical control of him. There's always the chance that he didn't hear your order (he may have a radio to his ear or turned up loud if he's in a vehicle), didn't understand it (he may speak a foreign language) or didn't think you meant it. In one California case, officers spotted a young man on the street who answered the description of a sniper suspect. As he walked toward them they ordered him to stop—but he kept coming...and reached toward his back. Thinking he was going for a gun, they shot and killed him—to discover that he really was reaching for his wallet to show them a card that identified him as a deaf-mute.

Remember, you're justified in shooting a suspect under most state laws *only* if he holds your life or others in mortal danger, or when you *know* he is fleeing from a violent felony. (Obviously, part of your firearms preparedness involves understanding *precisely* what the law states in your jurisdiction.) The former justification for shooting reasonably applies if a suspect continues to point his gun at you (or shoots) when you tell him to put it down. As to the latter, you need to be very certain in some jurisdictions of what you "know." One officer spotted two suspects standing inside a damaged screen door at a closed grocery store one night. When they ignored his verbal challenge and fled, he shot at them. Another officer did the same when his words were ineffective in halting a man he saw running through an alley carrying a television set and a tape player. Although neither officer hit his target, both were officially reprimanded—the first because subsequent investigation showed no burglary had actually occurred and the other because he couldn't be *sure* a felony had been committed. In other words, just because you're frustrated... can't run any farther...or can't think of another way to stop a suspect is no justification for using deadly force if your verbal challenge fails to work initially. Indeed, even in jurisdictions that permit the shooting of fleeing felons, many departments, to lessen the chance of a tragedy, limit their officers to firing *only* when necessary to defend a life. Legally, that's the safest position.

In some states, officers have the option of telling a suspect, "You're under arrest," immediately after issuing their initial challenge. Any disobedience or aggressive behavior on his part after that is resisting arrest, which is a felony in those jurisdictions. Whether this will work for you, of course, depends on your state laws.

The officer here points his revolver at the driver of a bulldozer [being stopped pending court approval to demolish a hotel]. The officer is reported to have told the driver "move that thing and I'll blow your head off."

Some officers believe they can persuade reluctant suspects to cooperate by underscoring their challenges with verbal threats. They argue that strong talk, à la "Dirty Harry," can overpower an adversary mentally and convince him he has no chance of surviving a confrontation. The idea is to appear utterly menacing, even eager for an excuse to shoot. At the very least, facing a suspect on the street, an officer of this persuasion might yell: "Get up against the fucking car or I'll blow your head off!" Or: "You feel lucky today? You want to die today?" Or, in a tone of lethal sincerity: "Think you can get to that gun? I hope you're stupid enough to try!" "Make him think, if he does, you're gonna put six in the big ten ring," explains a devotee of this approach. "If you're close enough, maybe you stick your gun up against his head and let him hear you cock it. Say, 'Man, if you even *fart* your head's gonna be all over that wall!' You want the crook to think Attila the Hun was a pussy compared to you."

Most departments' brass get apoplexy thinking about such dialog. They point out, quite properly, that its use constitutes unprofessional conduct. And they raise the valid question, What do you do if fear fails to work and the suspect calls your bluff? We know, of course, that verbal threats are used on the street and that they *do* work for *some* suspects. But there are real hazards you should recognize. The chances are overwhelming that you'll be best off to leave this approach to the television cops.

For one thing, it's difficult to *shoot* at the same time you're *talking*: usually your mouth has to stop before your trigger finger can start. Therefore, if you get involved in an extended verbal challenge, you're actually slowing down your own reaction time.

In addition, threatening language can fuel an already volatile situation. Ideally, with a verbal challenge *you want to effect a de-escalation of force*. Your success is confirmed, really, by no one firing a shot. By using aggressive threats, you may provoke violence in a suspect who would otherwise submit. He may get the message that you're taking him on and feel, in desperation, that his only hope is to try to shoot his way out. Or he may interpret your exaggerated language as evidence that you are really terrified—and vulnerable.

Then, too, if you *are* forced to shoot him and a complaint is filed as a result, your defense will undoubtedly be weakened if your verbal challenge has made it appear you were unscrupulously aggressive in the use of firearms.

Unless you're an outstanding actor and an exceptional judge of human response, you're probably better off to draw on some of the basic principles behind threatening challenges and omit the abusive language. That is, in delivering a challenge, you want to sound authoritative...forceful...sincere, so you control and dominate the scene. Bark out your commands, fast...*loud*. Your tone of voice is very important. *You mean business.* It's not: "Don't move," it's DON'T MOVE!"—with your voice conveying that you're on the very brink of action. If you feel you need to underscore your command, keep your words short, plain, uncluttered: "Drop the gun or you're dead...*Now!*" In all cases, you avoid telling a suspect, "I don't want to shoot you," or pleading, "Don't make me shoot you." This conveys a lack of commitment on your part that he may try to exploit. It's best also to avoid stating questions, even rhetorical ones; you're *telling*, not asking.

If you feel you *must* try to reason with a suspect, better than the macho approach might be to tell him: "Put down the gun. You haven't killed anyone yet. If you try to shoot me, I'll still get a shot off." Make it clear that no one is going to escalate violence unless he does—and that he has a vested interest in not doing so.

Whatever you tell him, be sure it's nothing more than you're prepared to back up. Unless it's *true*, you don't say things like, "I'm telling you one last time," etc. If he calls your bluff and you do nothing, you've lost your credibility as well as your offensive position. By the same token, if he does obey you, be careful. The tendency then is to relax, let your guard down. This can be the most dangerous moment for you of the challenge.

Throughout your challenge, watch his hands. *Hands kill.* If he has one in his pocket, order him to turn his back to you if it's daylight or face your spotlight at night. Then have him withdraw his hand...*slowly*. Or, if you are close, pull it out yourself, *slowly* from behind him. You don't want him to bring his hand out unrestricted or uncontrolled. If he has a gun in his hand, order him to drop it or, even safer, to lay it down slowly.

Except for carrying out your orders, you want to hold firm with your command of "Don't move." Tell him if he moves in any way contrary to your orders, you'll be "forced to take appropriate action." That's technically vague, but he'll draw the right conclusion. If you allow a suspect to move of his own volition, you become accustomed to seeing him move. You tend to relax...and then he may make his big move, unexpectedly.

Ordinarily, when you issue a verbal challenge, you have the suspect in sight or know where he is

But sometimes you can use it successfully to determine where he is. You do this by announcing your office and shouting commands at likely hiding places. During a room search, for example, you might address a closet: "Police! Don't move! You in the closet—*slowly* come out with your hands up!" A suspect inside might be bluffed into thinking you really know he's there. But again, issue your challenge from behind cover and be prepared for anything. He might come out meekly and surrender...or he might suddenly burst out...or shoot through the door. And if there's no response from the possible hiding place, you'll still have to check it out before passing on.

Better to try a bluffed challenge than to be left wondering if it would have worked, after it's too late. Like the officers in Louisiana who were searching along an apartment house balcony for a burglar who had killed a civilian and wounded a policeman. As they looked ahead, they spotted a wooden shutter ajar from the wall, not an improbable place to hide. But instead of first shouting a challenge, they walked up on the shutter, cold. The suspect was standing behind it. As the officers got close, he fired on them with a .357 cal. revolver, striking a detective fatally in the chest.

Officer Identification

While you should assume initially that any suspect you're challenging is a criminal, bear in mind if you see that he's armed that he may be a law enforcement officer, out of uniform because he's off duty or assigned to a plainclothes detail. The circumstances may make it hard for you to tell immediately. Say, for example, you're on patrol when someone claims he has just been robbed. You run down an alley in the direction he's pointing and behind a trash dumpster you spot one man facedown on the ground, another bending over him pointing a gun at his head. Both are casually dressed, with no distinguishing insignia. Is the man with the gun a robber, fleecing another victim, or an undercover detective making a pinch?

A case not unlike this occurred on Long Island, New York. An officer working a traffic detail heard a shot near his intersection and when he ran to investigate, he found a man with a gun standing over another man, with blood on the ground around them. When the patrolman yelled, "Drop it!" the armed suspect turned toward the officer. "I saw the barrel of the gun directly at me, and I could see the loaded chambers on both sides," the patrolman said. He fired a single shot. The "suspect" he hit was later identified as a detective— but by then the bullet had ricocheted from a bone in the plainclothesman's shoulder and penetrated several vital organs, causing his death. In another New York case, an officer was told by an excited civilian that two black men were fighting over a gun in front of a store. He cautiously approached and identified himself from behind them. One of the "suspects"— in fact, a plainclothesman trying to subdue a robber—turned toward the challenging officer with a non-regulation revolver in his hand. The officer shot and killed him.

Off-duty officer lies wounded in the abdomen after being shot by another off-duty officer while reaching for identification. The other officer thought he was reaching for a firearm.

As the number of officers has proliferated in recent years and more have been assigned to civilian dress, such risks have mushroomed. Even if you're in a small town where you know all your fellow officers, your not recognizing a suspect with a gun as a lawman may not be conclusive. Suppose he's on assignment from an outside agency...or just an out-of-town officer on vacation who happened to witness the crime-in-progress and responded while passing through. Or suppose it's just too dark for you to see plainly. In large cities, of course, the recognition problem is impossibly magnified. In New York City, besides the police department, there are the FBI, the Secret Service, the Treasury Department, the State's Attorney's Office, the Transit Authority, the Housing Authority, the Corrections Department, Amtrak, the Port Authority...a laundry list of independent agencies with a total of some 41,000 armed officers, in uniform and plainclothes, at work or off-duty in the metropolitan area on any given day. Scaled down appropriately, the same situation exists in other cities coast to coast.

Officers in plainclothes are exceptionally vulnerable. Compared to the percentage of police actions they are involved in, the ratio at which they are killed by gunshots is disproportionately high. And in incidents that are especially tragic, a disturbing number of them are shot by fellow officers who mistake them for armed assailants. Such a case occurred in Louisiana when police responded to a store robbery. The victim reported that a white car sped past his business just after the bandit ran out. Police spotted the car and gave chase. Soon, the vehicle stopped, and the driver emerged with a gun in his hand. He was shot immediately in the chest by approaching officers and died. Unfortunately, he turned out to be a police tow truck operator who had been chasing the real robber in his private automobile.

This risk can be minimized with an appropriate "challenge and reply" procedure and an immediate concern for being understood. In this case, the challenge becomes a two-way street, involving responsible words and actions by both the challenging officer and the challenged "suspect." Realistically

You're a uniformed officer just arriving at this scene. How would you react to the man with the gun?

118

speaking, the officer being challenged has the primary responsibility to give proper responses, but the challenging officer has the obligation to use sound judgment and tactics in his approach.

If you are the challenging officer:

Try to take cover, as always, before voicing your challenge. Positioning yourself behind a "suspect" allows you more time to judge his reactions and gives you a certain tactical advantage over being to his side. But remember, a plainclothes officer surprised by a challenge from behind while he's making an arrest or engaged in other police activity may impulsively whirl and shoot, or at least start to turn in your direction. This possibility is particularly keen should you neglect to announce that you are a police officer at the outset of your command. If you are behind cover, you may not have to shoot at him immediately.

Actually, he's a detective. Here he has taken time to protect himself by exiting the doorway with the badge visible.

Don't become a victim of the "symbolic opponent syndrome;" that is, making assumptions because of a preconceived notion that places a person into a "bad guy" category because of his race, nationality, age, grooming or mode of dress. *Looks can be deceiving* and should not be used as the basis for irreversible police action. Officers in tactical units or on undercover assignments may be deliberately dressed to look like "suspect types" in order to blend in with their work environment. Their handguns, too, may be small, cheap or otherwise unconventional. At one time, an officer's gun was likely to be "factory blued," with a 2- or 4-inch barrel and manufactured by Smith & Wesson or Colt. In recent years, however, there has been a trend toward the stainless steel or nickel/chrome plated revolver, once stereotyped as carried by criminals. Undercover personnel, especially, may carry derringers or small semi-automatics, so a variety of guns are "police guns" nowadays.

If, in response to your challenge, the "suspect" claims he is a police officer, first order him to slowly holster his gun. Then in a firm but courteous manner, tell him to slowly produce his identification card, badge or any other credentials that will identify him. Examine them carefully to determine their validity and, where possible, check to see that any description in the credentials fits the suspect. You might want to pursue his identity by asking him something police officers, but not most civilians, might reasonably know—like the numbered designation for homicide in your state's penal code.

Do not take your gun off the "suspect" until you are 100 per cent certain his story is legit. Even then, remain on guard and attentive. Credentials can be forged...police badges can be lost, stolen or counterfeited.

If you are the challenged officer:

Keep firmly in mind that you are at a strong tactical disadvantage. Remember: to the challenging officer, you are a suspect. *Act as you would have a suspect act* if you were challenging him. Also, remember that the officer may or may not be in uniform and may or may not conform to your stereotype of a law enforcement officer.

As soon as you are challenged verbally, identify yourself as a law enforcement officer in a loud, clear voice, then state your rank...name...and assignment...and the nature of your actions (making arrest, etc.). If your sidearm or shotgun is not drawn or is where he can't see it, inform him you are armed. If you are covering a suspect, ask your challenger's permission to keep your gun on him. If he insists you drop it, place the firearm out of the suspect's reach and try to maintain control over him as best you can.

Follow all your challenger's instructions, without "taking an attitude" about being challenged. *Remain motionless*, even if it means stopping your pursuit of a fleeing suspect. If in doubt about your challenger's directions or questions, ask him to repeat. Don't argue; he's in command.

As soon as possible, try to develop dialog with your challenger, using words and phrases commonly familiar only to police personnel. New York City, for example, advises challenged officers to perhaps begin a response with "I'm on the job!" which constitutes something of a code phrase.

It may be necessary for you to ask your challenger what he wants you to do, in terms of movements. If he does not demand your ID, ask permission to show it. Before reaching for it, inform him of its exact location and get his permission before moving. In anticipation of being challenged, one option is to carry your badge or other credentials in a non-shooting hand pocket when you're in plainclothes. Then you can reach for identification without moving your sidearm, if your challenger has allowed you to retain it. Reach in and withdraw your hand slowly...in a controlled manner...and without unnecessary movement. Another possibility is to hold your badge or credentials in your weak hand with your arm raised when making a plainclothes police intervention. Then if you are challenged, the identification can readily be shown to the challenger. A variation is to hold your badge and firearm together in a two-handed grip, so anyone seeing your gun would *have* to see your badge, too. Remember that in any sustained police action, your shield should be fastened to your outermost garment.

As with other survival tactics, there are few absolutes. You will need to maintain flexibility. However, there are certain guidelines that are always important to keep in mind.

No matter what the circumstances:

> *DO NOT* Simultaneously reach for your identification and tell the challenging officer who you are. If you don't have your gun in hand, reaching for your ID may reveal it and cause the officer to think you are trying to draw.

DO NOT	Turn and face your challenger until he tells you to do so, especially if you have a firearm in hand. The sight of a firearm is most likely to make him react in a manner dangerous to you.
DO NOT	Move your hands in any manner that could be interpreted under the stress of the moment as a hostile or menacing movement.

Some departments try to reduce the likelihood of unwitting encounters between officers by issuing color-coded identification items to plainclothes and undercover units. They are distributed only at roll call and are changed daily.

If such items are not available to you and you are in plainclothes, you may be able to use your radio to gain some protection. When responding to a crime scene where uniformed officers are likely to be present, notify communications that you are going in and give a description of your vehicle and clothing. This information can then be broadcast to alert uniformed officers approaching the scene. If you are not ordered to the scene, you're safest to stay away until things cool off, if possible.

Note: Even if you are in uniform you may be mistaken as a suspect by another officer. This is most likely to happen in dim light when the challenger is behind you and you are wearing a black leather jacket...are in need of a haircut...are not wearing your uniform hat. One way to lessen this risk is to wear your hat whenever you leave your vehicle for any reason, if your department issues hats.

Apologies

Occasionally, you will issue a verbal challenge to a person who turns out to be neither a criminal nor a fellow officer, but an innocent civilian who just happened to be in the wrong place at the wrong time or whose actions you reasonably interpreted as suspicious. He may, for example, be the victim of a crime who has armed himself to pursue his assailant, or he may be carrying a gun for some other good reason. By the time you get the facts straightened out, this person may be confused and resentful about your "unnecessary" display of force.

When you realize further action is unwarranted, *apologize* and give the civilian an *explanation*.

Sometimes, he may verbally abuse you or even file a formal complaint. But in no case should worry about the consequences cause you to be ridiculously cautious when you feel a verbal challenge and quick follow-up action are needed.

Two officers, surprised by a shotgun attack, escaped unharmed because of proper planning.

USE OF SURPRISE

One night in California, two officers on stake-out were sitting in their patrol car, chatting quietly to while away the dragging hours. In the darkness, a man silently crept up from behind, leveled a .30 cal. carbine at their back window and carefully drew a bead on one officer's head. Without a word, he racked a round into the chamber and pulled the trigger. Bullets shattered through the back glass.

To the offender's astonishment, neither officer was hit—because neither was any longer there when the bullets whizzed over the front seat and smashed into the dashboard and windshield.

At the split-second sound of the rifle being racked, without exchanging a word or a glance, each had instantly dived below the line of fire, flung open his door and rolled out of the patrol car to a position of cover—all in one fluid motion. By the time their would-be killer absorbed what had happened, *he* was on the receiving end of *their* fire.

Some confrontations are so heavily weighted in the suspect's favor they seem impossible to survive. Any attempt to shoot your way out as a first reaction may be unrealistic or out of the question. Your offender may have the drop on you cold...or, as in the case of the California officers, he's in the process of shooting before you are even aware of his presence...or, one of the worst predicaments, he has snatched away your gun to use against you.

Whether you emerge alive from such a "no win" situation will probably hinge, as it did with these officers, on your ability to control lag time and confound a suspect's assault through the use of planning and surprise.

Lag time relates to hesitant reaction. Specifically, it's the delay that's involved while: your senses perceive danger...transmit the alarm to your brain...your brain decides what you should do...relays the message to the part of your body it wants to react...and you then actually respond.

This takes longest when you are distracted, unprepared or inattentive at the moment of threat and your brain must first be called back from wherever it has wandered and change gears before it can evaluate the alarm and dispatch a reactive message. Lag time is shortest—and can almost be eliminated, with practice—when your brain is primed to send a ''go'' signal because you have anticipated possible danger and have potential reactions in mind. It doesn't have to think what it will have you do; it already *knows* and is just waiting for your senses to perceive the need.

When you are able to short-circuit your own lag time, you often can turn the tables by inducing it in your adversary. By using sudden, decisive action that he's not expecting—in other words, surprise—you may throw him off balance so he's forced to shift gears mentally in order to grasp and react to what has happened. While he's hesitating, you gain precious seconds in which to re-establish control of the situation.

In some circumstances, you may be able to use noise to create surprise. Sometimes blinding light will work. Some suspects may fall for a realistic bluff. In Tulsa, an intended shooting victim stared wide-eyed at his assailant's gun, gasped for breath, grabbed his chest, went rigid and crumpled over—in a fake heart attack. The suspect was so disconcerted he fled without shooting.

But more times than not—and especially when you are in desperate straits—all you'll have to surprise an offender with will be your ability to move. Executed properly, that may be enough. If you're a hunter, you know that any motion by the animal you hope to bag makes it harder to hit. If the motion is unexpected and then erratic, it compounds the difficulty of getting on target. The same principles apply when *you* are the prey.

The best movements are those that:

1. befuddle or immobilize the suspect;

2. get you out of the line of fire quickly, and

3. carry you to a location or into a posture from which you can shoot or otherwise incapacitate your assailant.

Those discussed here are the likeliest to work in common confrontation situations. But keep in mind that the right move at the right time is hard to pull off. Certain of these techniques require action on your part that is opposite one's normal impulse. That makes them tough to master—but adds immeasurably to their element of surprise.

Exiting the Kill Zone

An important truth to remember where armed confrontations are concerned is that despite certain superficial resemblances, a law enforcement agency is *not* an army. Consequently, police action at a shooting scene should not be regarded the same as a military maneuver. It isn't Pork Chop Hill, where you have to hold the ground at all costs. In fact, your best—and most surprising—response in some shooting situations is to *pull back* and temporarily yield territory to the suspect. In other words, get out of the kill zone, that area the suspect can effectively control with hostile weapons fire. This can work both when you first spot an armed suspect who has not yet started to shoot...and when you are already under fire.

Exiting the kill zone is most practical when there's some distance between you and your assailant and when you are still in your patrol car. It's especially advisable when:

- your adversary has hostages...
- fires on you from a sniper position you can't see...
- has superior fire power, such as a rifle or shotgun...
- is positioned at a higher level, so you'd have to shoot up to reach him, or
- when his shots or your return fire would endanger innocent bystanders.

Most officers in these circumstances stop their patrol cars and try to figure out what's happening. Or they exit with the intention of standing their ground. On an Indian reservation in Arizona, for example, two tribal policemen responding to a call about an individual shooting out street lights were fired upon as they pulled up. The suspect had a .30-.30 cal. rifle. His first shot shattered the windshield and sprayed fragments of glass into one officer's face. He ducked to the floor—but his partner exited the vehicle in the open and started firing his handgun at the suspect, who was well protected behind a parked car. With understandable ease, the assailant killed this patrolman with wounds to the head and chest.

Under circumstances like these, where the odds of hitting your assailant are so heavily against you, quickly leaving the kill zone as your first reaction is not cowardice, but good sense. By avoiding a shoot-out, you may save not only your own life but others in the kill zone, as well. Because once you remove yourself, you probably remove the assailant's motivation for firing.

The direction you exit will depend on the environment around you and the location of the suspect, as near as you can figure it. Your options may include:

1. *making a fast right-angle turn into an alley, driveway or street.* If, by using this movement, you can put buildings or other barriers between yourself and the assailant, you effectively remove yourself from the kill zone and gain excellent cover to maneuver behind. In residential areas, you may be able to drive into a garage, which will afford other cover possibilities.

2. *slamming your car into reverse and peeling backward or doing a "J-turn" or a "U-turn"* (provided there's a clear field behind). Perhaps you've just entered a kill zone (say you've rounded a corner and spotted a suspect with a long-gun ahead) but the suspect has not yet fired. Or you're already taking rounds from the front or side. This maneuver is likely to be your least expected response. Especially if a suspect is "tracking" you with his gun, it'll throw him off.

3. *floorboarding the accelerator and speeding forward.* This response is rarely the most desirable, because it is the one a suspect is most likely to anticipate. Indeed, you may be driving ahead toward a secondary ambush prepared by lay-off men. But if you *must* drive across the kill zone to safety, you want as much protection and speed as possible out of your patrol car. *Get down low, fast.* Your dropping down at the first hint of danger can foil a suspect who's expecting your head and chest level to remain constant. Either scoot far down in your seat to shield as much of your upper body as you can and look ahead through the steering wheel...or lean over onto the seat, steering with your left hand and bobbing up and down erratically to check ahead. Whatever your exit, radio for help as you move. *Do not stop* or consider getting out of your car while under fire, unless it is disabled or better cover is immediately accessible. Once you are out of the kill zone, turn at the first right angle that will put a barrier between you and the assailant.

If hostile weapons fire is coming from the side, get down low and fast as you continue to drive.

To keep driving, lean to your right and peer up and down.

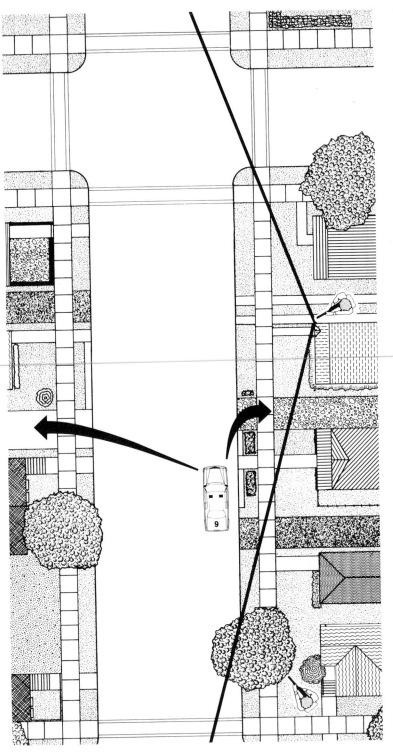

Hostile weapons fire against officers
on patrol can involve a primary ambush
whose arc is indicated by the solid
line. One surprise response for Car 9
is to make a fast right-angle turn.

130

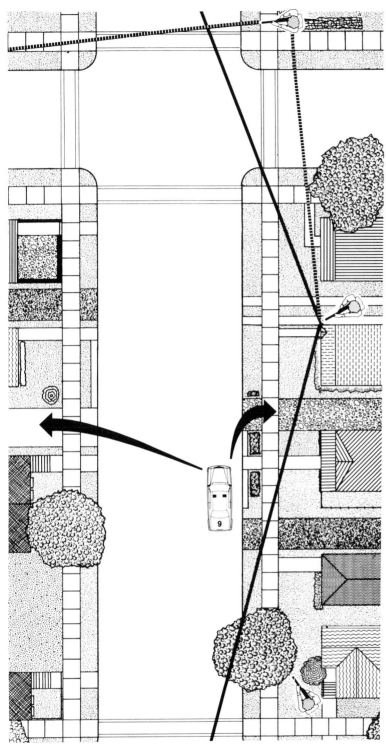

The right-angle turn tactic is also effective if a secondary ambush [indicated by dotted lines] is part of the offenders' assault plan.

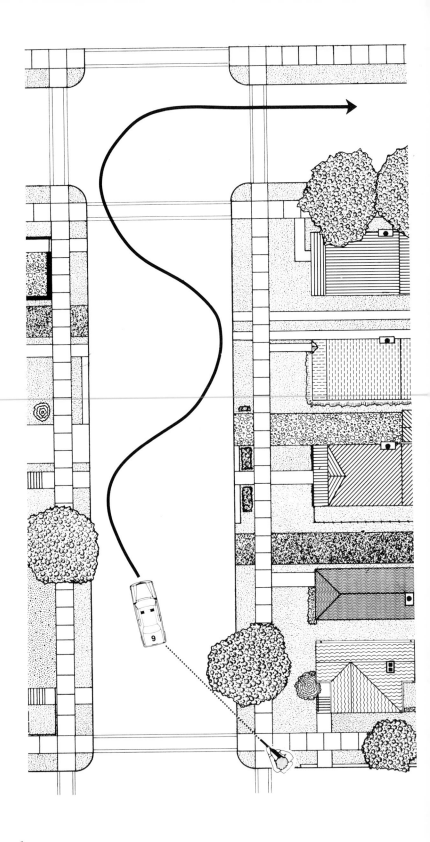

A serpentine movement forward can be effective if you're being fired upon from the rear or side.

In your radio communications, give as much information as possible about the number of assailants, their weapons and positions. Advise responding units about how to approach the area for maximum safety. You have a responsibility to other officers not to draw them into the kill zone.

Because you leave a scene does not mean you abandon it. From your new protected position, you want to lay the ground work for procedures to take control of the suspect. Specialized, tactical teams and hostage negotiators may need to be brought in. But until help arrives, you try to position yourself where you can: observe the suspect's location...keep him contained within it...and work to seal off the area from civilian involvement.

The way two officers handled a shooting episode on a residential street in a suburb of Chicago illustrates good survival procedures. Fired on in their patrol car from an apartment house by a sniper armed with a pistol and rifle, they immediately moved—gunned their patrol car to a position of safety where they could watch the building—rather than stopping abruptly and trying to shoot back. When reinforcements arrived, the assailant was treated as a barricaded suspect. His neighbors were evacuated...tear gas cannisters were lobbed into his rooms...and, eventually, he was shot in the stomach and arm when he emerged and tried to fire at an officer.

In Cleveland, a successful retreat was made at closer range when a beat patrolman unexpectedly interrupted a drugstore robbery. The robber grabbed the druggist as a shield and fired at the officer, who, rather than shooting back, ducked out of the store to a position of safety outside. There he trained his revolver on the doorway. The robber came out with the druggist as a hostage, but in maneuvering through the exit, he turned in such a way that the officer was able to fire three shots into his chest. Both the officer and the hostage escaped the incident uninjured. (Shooting under such circumstances is extremely risky, however, and should not be attempted unless you are *certain* the innocent party will not be harmed.)

Movement Inside the Kill Zone

Sometimes, traffic or other factors may prevent a prompt exit from the scene, and you will be restricted to moving *within* the kill zone. Again, depending on your surroundings and location relative to your assailant, you may have several possibilities for surprising movement.

For purposes of illustration, assume you're cruising a residential street when someone with a rifle suddenly shoots at you from a ground-level position. If you are alone, one option is to turn at a right angle and head toward the suspect's location, using a driveway or bouncing over the curb. This is a basic military tactic—to storm the sniper's nest. Right away you surprise him. By staying low in the seat and driving so your side of the car is away from his hostile fire, you maintain the protection afforded by your vehicle...and quite likely you can drive directly to a tree or barricade in the yard that will provide good cover. If that is not possible, drive straight toward him. Assault his position with your vehicle. Don't touch the brake, don't stop, but try to run right over him.

Another possibility when you are alone is to make a fast U-turn, assuming, of course, that the hostile weapons fire is coming from your side of the vehicle. Depending on the suspect's angle to you, you can whip the turn to the right, to the left, by backing—whatever move gets your side of the car away from him fastest. Now you have the width of the car to shield you while you bail out, stay low, and move to a position of cover behind one of the wheels.

If you have a partner in this illustration, you'd have to move to get and/or keep his side of the patrol car away from the suspect's fire without exposing your own. Here, a possibility is to turn sharply in a direction opposite the suspect's location. Then drive away along a line perpendicular to his position. This puts at least half your patrol car between you and the suspect and prevents him from getting a broadside shot at either of you. This tactic may also work, of course, when you're alone.

Whatever tactic you use with your patrol car, you need to move immediately. If you get pinned down, especially in a well-planned ambush situation, you can be in extremely serious trouble.

In some cases, you may need to move from place to place within the kill zone on foot, to reach better cover. Indeed, that's likely to be the *only* reason you'll move when under fire; you don't want to change from one protected position to another just for the sake of movement. When it's desirable to change location, you're safest if you can stay low and run in short sprints from cover to cover until you reach your ultimate goal. If it's necessary to travel across open space directly toward or directly away from the suspect, run in a zigzag pattern to make yourself a harder target.

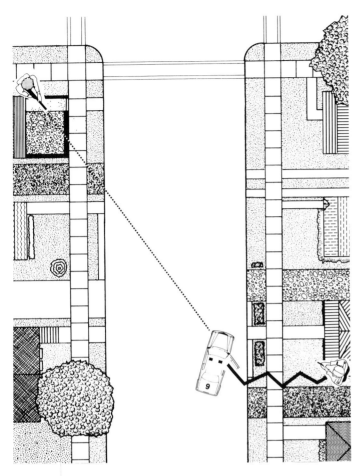

In reaching cover, on foot, try to keep your movement low and erratic.

Under certain circumstances, you may want to roll from place to place, rather than run. This might be true when you are under immediate assault by a suspect in a fortified position, where cover is relatively close yet far enough away that running directly to it seems extremely dangerous, or where you can readily reach the protection of a gutter by rolling. Rolling has its disadvantages; it's slower than running, you lose your ability to change direction rapidly, your view is distorted and you may lose visual contact with the suspect or be unable to watch for additional assailants; if you're on concrete or other hard surface, low rounds may ricochet into your face when you're so close to the ground. On the other hand, being close to the ground, you are likely to appear a smaller target from the suspect's perspective. If he is considerably higher than you, in an upper window or on a rooftop, the effect is even better. Many people, when shooting down, tend to *over-shoot* what they're aiming for. By rolling, you may exaggerate this tendency because you are so much lower than any height an assailant is normally conditioned to expect.

With one tactic, rolling allows you to lay down

fire cover as you move. This is most effective with a shotgun. As you begin your roll, you hold the shotgun in a shooting grip, lengthwise against your body, with the barrel extending over the shoulder of your shooting side. You rack the gun (or reload it) while you are on your back. When you roll around on your chest, you're ready to shoot with a slight bracing of your elbows. By repeating this pattern, you can continue shooting as you move, without losing momentum. Your shots coming in fast from a low position will probably be something your assailant is not expecting and will likely throw him off guard and delay his reaction time. This tactic can be one of your best uses of surprise, but there's no doubt that it requires *extensive* practice to master.

Of course, you should also use a rolling movement to get over walls and other obstacles. That is, you hug the top of the barricade and "wrap" yourself over to the other side, presenting as small a target as possible. If you jump or go over upright, you attract more attention and make yourself a larger target, by silhouetting yourself against the background.

As you move over a wall, you want to create the smallest possible target. Assume the low crawl position, rolling over, rather than standing up or jumping over.

Close-Up Surprise

From the statistics about officer killings, you know that your danger increases markedly when an armed confrontation erupts suddenly and the suspect is close to you. If anything, the time you have to react will be even shorter (the encounter is likely to be over, start to finish, in less than three seconds) and the space in which you can maneuver will probably be restricted. Your moves must be scaled down to reflect the armed suspect's proximity. And with the use of surprise, you can realistically expect to buy only milliseconds.

You're likely to be best off, of course, if you have your sidearm out and ready when a suspect suddenly tries to draw his gun or you suddenly confront a suspect with a gun already drawn. When an offender is as surprised by your armed presence as you are by his, your ready fire-power may permit a standoff where you can negotiate a resolution, if for some reason you feel immediate shooting on your part is undesirable. A New York City police sergeant chasing an armed robber through a tenement, for instance, rounded a corner to find the robber waiting, gun in hand, five feet away. Because the sergeant had his revolver ready to shoot, too, the suspect hesitated—and the sergeant managed to persuade him he was wiser to surrender and take a fall for robbery than to risk a first-degree murder charge or being killed himself, by firing.

Where the suspect is committed to shooting, you may, with your sidearm ready, be able to move swiftly into an "instinct shooting" position and fire on him before he can shoot you. Instinct shooting, which we'll discuss in detail later, basically involves point-and-shoot maneuvering. You can adapt it to maximize surprise. Had the New York sergeant encountered a determined suspect when he rounded the tenement corner, his least expected action probably would have been to drop backwards to the floor and shoot from a sitting position. For this tactic, you cross your ankles, flex your knees and bring your hands together as you are falling. The force of the landing will rock you back, and as your crossed ankles come up, you quickly lay the barrel of your gun between them and fire with a two-handed grip. The suspect undoubtedly is anticipating a target at normal head or chest level; if he fires reflexively, the bullet will go through thin air. By the time he registers where you actually are, you should be able to return fire effectively. (As with other unusual tactics, this requires extensive practice so that it is executed as a reflexive reaction when circumstances are appropriate. If you take two seconds to think about doing it, the advantage is lost.)

If you *don't* have your sidearm unholstered for a confrontation, your chances for survival diminish. A fast draw *may* work. In Cincinnati, an officer checking a bar in search of a robbery suspect asked one patron to get up out of a booth for questioning.

One effective method for safe, return fire is to drop to a lower position to shoot. The armed suspect at close range assumes you will shoot at shoulder height. With practice, you will be able to apply this tactic as an instinctive move.

The man came out with a .25 cal. semi-automatic, which he jammed into the officer's stomach. As fast as he could, the officer drew his revolver and pumped five shots into the suspect's stomach. The suspect did not fire once. He evidently was so startled that the officer would draw against him under the circumstances that he developed monumental lag time.

Fast-draw successes, however, are *extremely* rare. More often than win the confrontation for you, they'll prove suicidal if your adversary is close to or already on target. After all, you're not fast-drawing against his fast draw—he's got a head start and can, if he's psychologically prepared to kill, shoot in about one-third the time it takes you to get on target. Moreover, the type of holster that most readily facilitates fast drawing is poorly designed for street use. In order to accommodate speed, this style holster sacrifices security. Its design increases the risk of your sidearm falling out during a fight or other exertion and permits dangerously easy access to a suspect grabbing for your gun. In a large proportion of cases where officers are shot with their own firearms, the initial loss of the gun can be directly attributed to the holster.

Assuming fast draws to be inappropriate, then, in the overwhelming preponderance of situations, other, more surprising movement may still be used to derail a suspect's intention and stretch out the action enough for you to bring your gun into play. During your questioning of a driver in a traffic stop, for example, the clipboard, citation book or flashlight you've carried in your *non-gun hand* during your approach can make a powerful distraction if he suddenly reaches for or comes out with a gun at close range before you have a chance to draw yours. As soon as you perceive the threat, hurl the object in his face with your weak hand, while simultaneously drawing your gun with your strong hand. As his eyeball is threatened, his body alarm reaction will force an involuntary response on his part that may delay his shooting or at least throw him off target. Meanwhile, you can fire and/or drop below window level and roll to the rear of his vehicle, out of the kill zone, where you'll have better cover. In Detroit, a narcotics addict who had just made a buy from an undercover detective sitting in an unmarked vehicle suddenly drew a semi-automatic, stuck it in the window at the officer and cocked the hammer. *Without hesitation*, the detective swung the door open with all his strength and knocked the suspect backwards, as he drew his own semi-automatic and fired.

If you're working with a partner, he may be able to cause distraction. A shout or other loud noise to the side may cause the suspect to turn his head long enough for you to draw and shoot. Noise from behind—a window being smashed, for instance—is especially effective. It's corny, but sometimes just shifting your glance to look behind a suspect as if someone else is approaching will be enough to induce lag time. Remember, *any* unexpected movement, no matter how minute, is better than just standing there waiting to be shot.

Sometimes you can capitalize on distractions that are surprising to *you*, as well as to the suspect. Noises or movement may occur around you, independent of any action by you or a partner, and if you are alert you can instantly exploit them. In a midwestern city, an off-duty officer was waiting at a bus stop when a car pulled up and a man inside asked directions. As the officer was responding, a passenger in the back seat suddenly pointed a revolver at him and snapped, "Throw all your money in the car!" At that moment, a passing car backfired with a loud bang, and the offenders ducked. The officer immediately dropped down and circled the rear of their vehicle, coming up to their surprise on the other side, his revolver ready.

In a Chicago case, an officer was chatting with an employee of a drugstore when an apparent customer approached and joined in the conversation. The stranger said he was a policeman, too, and showed a star and identification from a suburban police department. Then, suddenly, he drew a .22 cal. revolver and announced a holdup. Understandably, the officer did not have his revolver in hand. But as the store's employees followed the robber's orders to get money, get watches, and get barbiturates, one of them made some movement that caused the offender momentarily to look away. In that split-second, the officer drew his revolver.

Being part of a hostage incident involving a fellow officer required a plan and firearm discipline. Would you try to shoot this offender? Did you consider the lives of civilians sitting in the restaurant behind them?

When the suspect spun back, the odds were suddenly changed. The officer fired one shot, and the robber fell to the floor, hit by the officer's bullet.

A special circumstance that may demand close-up use of surprise for survival is when you, your partner or a fellow officer are taken hostage by one or more suspects. Here, as in other danger situations, a *pre-arranged* plan and quick action will aid an effective response.

In California, a back-up officer responding to a robbery-in-progress at a pawn shop was greeted by two suspects walking out of the place with the first responding officer at gunpoint. They had taken his gun, and they intended to escape in his car. They demanded the second officer's gun, too. Fortunately, the back-up officer had positioned himself behind cover during his approach, with his sidearm drawn. He fired one shot over the suspects' heads. At that instant, the hostage officer dropped down, leaving the startled suspects momentarily unshielded. The back-up officer was able to kill them both.

In other instances, hostage officers have faked heart attacks and gone limp as dead weight in their captor's arms. In the split-second confusion that followed, fellow officers were able to take effective action. *Whatever you do, it must be instantaneous and believable, with complete follow through.* Don't try half-hearted measures, or you or some other officer may wind up in an even worse predicament.

In this incident, the officer on the right was led out of a bar as a hostage. He faked a heart attack. The offender was so surprised, his reaction was to drop his gaze. This gave the partner officer the opportunity to disarm the offender.

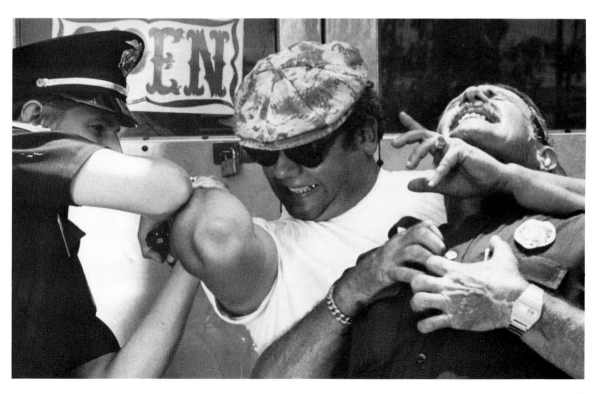

Just how unprepared most officers are to react is demonstrated by an exercise used at one survival school. Two officers who have been partners for several years are called to the front of the room. When they are close, the instructor suddenly grabs one officer and puts a gun loaded with blanks to his head. "I'm going to count to ten," the "hostage-taker" tells the officer's partner, "then I'm going to shoot. One...two...three...."

The free officer usually sputters something like, "Hey, wait! I wasn't ready...."

"...Five...six...seven...."

"Wait! Wait!"

"...Nine...ten!" BANG! The gun goes off. The hostage officer is "dead" with a shot to his head before his partner does anything to help him.

Officers on whom this exercise is pulled often admit afterwards that in five years or more of riding together they had day after day or night after night discussed great broads, great restaurants, great fishing holes, great places to buy clothes and a hundred other time-killing subjects. But not once had they discussed options for action should one or both of them find themselves at the mercy of desperate individuals.

Firearm Retention

In some close encounters, a suspect may grab for your sidearm in an effort to disarm you. Then your equipment, your stance and your ability to react may literally decide your fate. Lose your gun and you quite likely will lose your life. A notoriously high percentage—some estimates say *90 per cent—of suspects who succeed in disarming police officers, end up attempting to kill them.* More than 20 per cent of officer deaths each year are caused by the officer's own sidearms, in the hands of suspects.[1]

Your first line of defense is to prevent a suspect from seizing control of your sidearm. That's far preferable to trying to get it back once he has taken it. Your leather gear should be chosen with this in mind. A good holster hides and protects as much of your sidearm as possible, balancing your access to it with security against someone else yanking it out. Faulty leather gear—specifically fast-draw-type holsters—proves to be a major contributing factor every year to officers losing their firearms.

A study in Kansas City has revealed that

---

[1] *Revolver Retention,* Marvin Van Kirk, Kansas City (MO) Police Department, 1976.

another common factor in officer disarmings is leaving the holster unsnapped or snapped improperly in the suspect's presence. If you do release your holster, at least keep your hand protectively on the butt of your gun. Or if you have a thumb-break holster, you can leave the safety strap in place until you are ready to draw.

Even with these precautions, some suspects may be drunk, drugged, mentally disturbed, cocky

Many trainers won't teach firearm retention because they feel it takes too much time to perfect.
What odds do you give this deputy for survival, knowing he wasn't prepared to deal with this moment!

or desperate enough to try to snatch away your firearm anyway. Then your ability to move decisively and without hesitation—and *know what you are doing*—will be critical. Retention procedures require practice, and they may be difficult to execute effectively against a stronger opponent or when you are facing multiple suspects. But they may be the only option you have at that particular moment.

If a suspect lunges for your sidearm while it's in your holster, your best defense is to induce some distracting, involuntary reaction in him. Go for his eyes. One or two fingers jabbed at his eyes will at the very least cause him to close them momentarily. So will a blow to the forehead between his eyes. If his build makes it feasible, a sudden punch to the solar plexus or a hard shove to his chest with your non-gun hand, palm open, may knock him backwards and off balance while you draw your gun with your strong hand. Or pivot your gun hip to the rear to protect your firearm. As you turn, deliver a hard elbow to the jaw or with your hand stiff and flat, a sharp jab that strikes his throat between your thumb and first finger. Either movement will leave you in a good position to draw and to continue hitting and shoving with your non-gun hand. It may surprise him even more if you grab his clothing with your weak hand and yank him forward. At the same time, deliver a knee kick to his groin as you push him away from your gun.

One effective alternative when the suspect tries to disarm you when your sidearm is holstered.

When a suspect manages actually to get his hand on your gun butt, you want immediately to pin his hand where it is. Clamp down *hard* with your gun hand on top of his hand as though you were going to draw your firearm. This will keep him from pulling your gun from the holster and also give you control over his hand. At the same time, use your weak hand to further hold your gun. Now, with your gun hand, curl your fingers into the suspect's palm and press your thumb into the back of his hand. Your next move involves three simultaneous actions: 1) keep your weak hand firmly on your gun; 2) pivot your gun side around to the rear so you end up facing your attacker after a 180-degree turn; 3) as you turn, twist his palm out. This will bend his wrist, forcing him to release his hold on your gun. When you complete your turn, you can force his hand and arm higher into the air, which will drop him to his knees from the pain. You want to take him down instantly; if he stays on his feet, he may be able to twist out of your hold. With him down, you're now in a position to switch hands: bring your weak hand up to continue thumb pressure to the back of his hand and use your strong hand to draw your gun.

Sometimes an assailant may jump you with the intention of grabbing your gun from its holster during a brawl. As you try to subdue him, your principal concern is the hand that is nearest your

gun. So long as you can control that, there's hope of controlling him.

In a situation where you're standing with your gun drawn, a suspect may consider grabbing your wrist or the barrel of your gun in an effort to control where you're pointing it or force you to drop it. In standard training courses, officers often are taught complicated maneuvers for retaining their firearms in the event the suspect moves with such intent. These procedures are rarely demonstrated or practiced under realistic conditions or mastered to the point they can be remembered in crisis.

A simpler, move effective approach is to *avoid* taking a stance that opens you to this kind of attack in the first place. When you are close enough to a suspect that he might reach you or your drawn gun, your gun should be in the "close quarters" position. That is, your gun hand is pulled back so that the wrist is against your side just above your hip. Your gun is *not* thrust out at arm's length toward the suspect, where it or your wrist can be grabbed. Some officers imagine that pointing a gun out at a nearby suspect like an accusing finger makes it appear more threatening. Actually, they merely make themselves more vulnerable. By keeping your gun back in the close quarters position and standing oblique to the suspect with your gun side turned slightly away from him, you can easily sidestep, move back while deflecting his hand or knock him away if he does lunge toward you. Also, you're in a good position to block him with your weak-side leg if he tries to kick you in the groin.

The close quarters position with the sidearm resting just above the hip. If the suspect now makes a sudden move, you can easily move back while pushing the suspect forward with your weak hand.

If he should somehow reach your gun or wrist, don't get into a wrestling match for the weapon. You want to get his mind *off* your gun as quickly as possible. Hang onto it firmly—while kicking him in the testicles or poking his eyes to distract him. You will maintain control. By remaining alert you often can anticipate a suspect's threatening move before it's made. If his eyes go to your gun while you're questioning him, for example, he's telegraphing to you that he's at least considering the possibility of taking it away.

Disarming

Physically disarming a suspect who has a gun pointed at you is probably the *most desperate* maneuver you can attempt. If he has taken your only gun or for some other reason you see no chance of successfully drawing and shooting, you may have no choice but to try to wrest the weapon from him. The alternative of complying with his orders, if he does not shoot you promptly, does not guarantee you will be spared. Not atypically, a Florida sheriff's deputy who was surprised at gunpoint during a five-man grocery store holdup obeyed without resistance when he was ordered face-down onto the floor—only to have one of the robbers then shoot him in the back of the head at point-blank range.

Nonetheless, *disarming should be recognized as a last resort.* Most disarming techniques are extremely difficult to pull off. Even in non-stress situations, one outstanding tactical instructor concedes that he may miss two out of ten times. Consequently, you should attempt disarming *only* in a ninth-inning situation, *when you honestly feel your assailant will kill you* otherwise.

About the only advantage you have is in knowing *what* you are going to and *when* you're going to do it—in other words, your ability to *surprise* your adversary. Obviously, a disarming attempt is realistic only when the suspect is actually touching you with the gun or if it's within your arm's length. Otherwise he'll be able to shoot before you can reach him. Your best hope is to commit yourself to a disarming tactic *immediately*, and then to follow through without stopping and with total force. If your action is delayed or telegraphed, it may only worsen your risk of being shot.

Left to their own instincts, most officers make disarming moves that are ineffective. Experiments in one midwestern police department have revealed that four out of five officers, including seasoned veterans, either pull on the suspect's gun or twist it from side to side in an effort to remove it from his hand. While doing so, many also ignore the first imperative of disarming: *to direct the muzzle so you are out of the line of fire* as you try to take control of the firearm. A few officers, unfortunately, still believe old wives' tales such as the claim that jamming the meaty part of your palm against the muzzle of a .45 semi-automatic will prevent the gun from firing because it will interfere with the slide moving. All that's really necessary to foil that move is for the suspect to pull the gun back slightly and squeeze the trigger.

Such moves will more probably get you shot than get the suspect disarmed. What's likelier to be unexpected and disabling to him is one of the following options. With each, you'll maximize surprise if you maintain eye contact with the suspect (assuming he's facing you) and use your peripheral vision to watch his hands, until you've made your initial move. Usually, you can move most effectively if you first try to distract him with talk. If you start to tell him something, he's likely to shift his concentration slightly to process what you're saying. While he's thinking about that, he can't be thinking about shooting you at the same time. In that split-second of diversion, you act.

OPTION 1: If the suspect is standing in front of you with a gun and you still have your sidearm in your holster, swing your weak hand hard, palm open, directly against the side of his weapon. Follow through so your arm sweeps across the front of your body to give your hit the most powerful impact. You probably won't knock the gun out of his hand, but the blow may push the muzzle off you for an instant. Simultaneous with this move, draw your own gun. You may be able to shoot him before he can get back on target. One limitation: you can't fully control the suspect's gun.

Option 1

OPTION 2: If you're confronted with a *revolver* that is *uncocked*, grab the revolver with your hand clamped down *hard* around the cylinder, your fingers under the trigger guard. If you clutch tightly enough, you can keep the cylinder from turning and this will prevent a live cartridge from moving under the firing pin when the suspect pulls the trigger. By simultaneously twisting the revolver so his fingers are bent backwards, you move the muzzle away from you and also inflict unexpected pain. If he keeps his finger inside the trigger guard, this move will break it. In New York City, an officer used this technique to keep an ex-convict who had already killed two policemen in a sidewalk gunfight from shooting a third whom he had disarmed and was holding at gunpoint. *If the revolver is cocked, grabbing the cylinder will not keep the gun from being fired.* Then you'll need to try to hit the revolver with your hand in the manner of Option 1. If you move fast, the bullet will likely go by you should it fire. Note: With semi-automatics, grabbing hold will not prevent the weapon from firing. But if you are able to deflect the semi-automatic and keep your grip, you can prevent the fired round from ejecting or the next round from chambering and thus jam the firearm.

OPTION 3: Clamp both hands over the suspect's gun hand. Press your thumbs hard into the back of his hands as you raise his arm and turn the gun toward him. Use your fingers to pull his fingers open as you push the barrel into him. He controls the trigger until you release his index finger, but if the gun does go off, the muzzle is now pointed at a desirable target.

OPTION 4: Where a suspect is *behind* you, say with a shotgun or rifle pointed at your back, you may be able to turn and grab the barrel. First, try to look over your shoulder slightly to see which of your arms he's closest to. That will determine the direction of your turn. If he's closest to your right side, for example, twist or pivot back quickly so your right elbow and upper arm sharply knock the gun to his left. As soon as you hit the gun off target, grab the barrel with your right hand and hold the muzzle away from you. Then use your left hand to help twist the gun away from him as you bring your knee up to his groin. Of course, reverse if he's closest to your left side. If the gun does discharge while you're struggling, it is likely to shoot into the air. Still, the blast may incapacitate you temporarily if it's near your head. If you don't

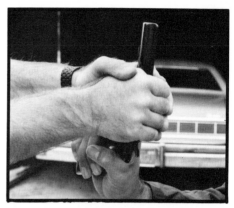

Option 2

have easy access to his groin as you turn, hold the gun away with one hand. With your other arm, reach over his shoulder and around the back of his head and hook your fingers over the length of his nose from the other side. Exerting as much strength as you can, you pull his nose to the side as if you were "peeling" his face. The force and pain will quickly twist him to the ground.

Option 3

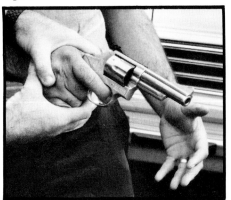

1

2

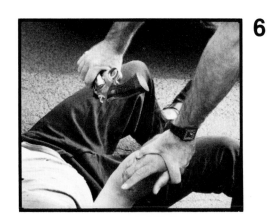

3

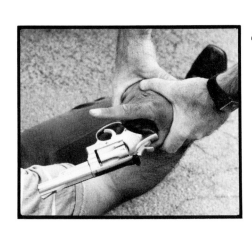

4

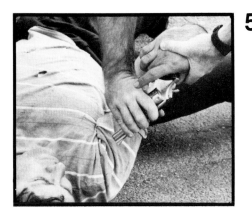

5

6

Option 4

1

2

3

4

5

6

OPTION 5: A pivoting technique can also work when your assailant is behind you with a handgun. Say he has it in his right hand, against your head. You simultaneously duck and pivot around toward your left. Your left arm goes up and hits his gun arm, knocking the gun off target and away from you as you slide your arm down toward his wrist. Grab the gun with your left hand as you complete your pivot. At the same time, slam the inside edge of your stiffened right hand into his throat (this blow can crush his larynx) and bring your knee up to his groin.

Remember, whatever disarming tactic you try—and you may know of others besides these that are effective—*don't let go once you have a grip on the gun or the suspect's gun hand.* Strike him with your knees and elbows...rake his shin with your shoe...punch or jab his windpipe, eyes and nose, and continue trying to wrench the weapon away from him, but DON'T LET GO.

Also, try to use your powers of observation before making your move. For instance, if your assailant is holding a semi-automatic, is it a double-action model or single-action? Double-action semi-automatics have the trigger in the middle of the trigger guard; with a single-action, the trigger is to

This double-action semi-automatic is ready to shoot and the safety [S] is in the "off" position. Notice the trigger [T] is in the middle of the trigger guard.

This single-action semi-automatic is cocked, but the safety is in the "on" position. Notice the trigger is to the rear.

the rear. If the gun is a single-action and the hammer is down, it means that the suspect will have to cock the gun before he can fire. This may give you an extra fraction of a second, a slight edge, to use to your advantage. If the hammer is down on a double-action semi-automatic, however, the gun is ready to shoot. Unless he's too surprised to act, the suspect can respond by firing immediately. Another factor to observe is whether the safety on a semi-automatic or long gun is on or off.

In disarming, as in so many other components of street survival, it's important that you recognize and understand firearms and their states of readiness. Having more than just a passing knowledge of firearms will significantly heighten your survival quotient.

Practice

It's not enough that you know how the tactics of surprise should be done. For survival, you need to be able to perform them, without lag time, and that takes *a great amount of regular practice* and personal commitment. Probably no tactics require more practice than disarming techniques.

In a sense, what's required is that you condition yourself as you would for a high-speed sport, so your reflexes are sharp...your coordination smooth... your movements instinctual and anticipatory. You should practice with a partner, using deactivated weapons or toy guns, but wearing or carrying all the equipment you ordinarily do on the job (except, of course, your firearms), including the accessories on your leather gear. Under the pressure of time limits, take turns springing on each other with the widest variety of attacks you can imagine. The proficiency you attain will doubtless be directly related to the amount of time you practice and the total number of times you perform each technique.

Try to involve some participants in your practice who do not know the techniques you'll be trying. There's less chance then of being able to merely waltz through the exercises with a cooperative partner. At the very least, you'll learn how very hard it can be to gain control over a suspect who has the drop on you.

Ideally, you want to condition yourself to move by *instinct* as soon as you see a gun come up against you. Move without hesitation—the same as you would if you saw a baseball flying toward your head.

153

7 COVER AWARENESS

The way some officers react when shooting threatens, you'd think they'd gotten their survival training from watching *High Noon* on the Late Show. Like the old-time western marshal, they advance on the suspect or stand their ground in the open, no matter what. Seeking protective cover is something too many think of too late.

When a small town police chief in North Carolina answered a "man-with-a-gun" call at a local residence, for example, he spotted the suspect sitting on the front porch, a .12 ga. shotgun cradled on his lap. The chief promptly climbed out of his vehicle and started across the open yard toward him...At a highway rest stop in California, a sheriff's deputy located a truck camper that belonged to a man sought for firing gunshots in a residential neighborhood. The deputy had walked directly to the side of the camper when the driver suddenly thrust a .30 cal. rifle through the window...In Cincinnati, two patrolmen were investigating vice law violations when they saw a man they had been warned was armed near a tavern. As they approached him on foot, the suspect suddenly pulled a .38 cal. revolver and fired a shot into the air. The officers stood stationary on the sidewalk a few feet from him, identified themselves and told him to stop. He turned toward them and pointed his revolver at the stomach of one, as his finger tightened on the trigger again....

Unfortunately, but not surprisingly, the officer in each of these cases was shot dead. Yet in these and numerous other instances where officers are killed, solid objects were in the immediate vicinity that could have provided a protective shield from the gunmen, had the value of cover and the ways to recognize and use it only been part of the victims' orientation.

An officer positioned on the roof of a liquor store adjacent to a robbery-in-progress. This is the suspect's visual as he exited the store.

In developing survival-mindedness, there are two points of observation that demand your constant, conscious attention. First, as you cruise your beat or speed to the scene of a crime, you should always know the last intersection you passed; you may need to relay your location without faltering in a call for help. Second, and of even greater importance, you want always to be aware of your nearest cover. As you approach any situation, you want to be in the habit of looking for cover, so you can react automatically to reach it should trouble erupt. It's difficult to go seeking it after the lead is flying. Cover awareness applies whether you are in your car or on foot—approaching a scene, searching an area, questioning a suspect, making an arrest, even eating your lunch.

This captain, standing out in the open, motions for other officers to stay back as the man on the left continues to point a loaded gun to his head. Cover was only three steps away.

155

Although cover is probably the most important single tactic for surviving a dangerous situation, about two-thirds of the officers who become involved in shootings make *no* use of it. Sometimes the action happens too fast or in an area where cover is too far away. But often, even after shots have *already* been fired, there's still the opportunity to get behind protection, if you can overcome the tendency to stand and fire from wherever you happen to be.

In many encounters, officers have stood 2 feet from a tree and shot it out with a suspect, when a quick move behind it would have given them excellent protection—and still allowed them to shoot. It's a rare situation in which *some* type of cover is not available: OUTDOORS—a wooden or metal utility pole, automobile, trash can, call or signal box, fire hydrant, mailbox, embankment, concrete or steel steps or the corner of a building; INDOORS—a store counter, walls, heavy furniture, etc. Even if the situation is so urgent that you need to fire at the suspect immediately and *then* move to cover, that's usually better than staying indefinitely in what amounts to a "free fire" zone. Remember: *No exposed firing position offers you as much insurance as firing from cover.*

Of course, when you know in advance that you are confronting a potentially dangerous firearms situation, as did the officers in the three incidents cited above, you want to know not only where your nearest cover is, you want to utilize it in making your approach. By staying behind cover in such circumstances and issuing verbal challenges to the suspect, you can:

1. buy additional time in which to positively identify your adversary (especially important in dim-light situations);

2. better evaluate the situation you are facing before making risky or decisive moves, and

3. gain the advantage of a protected position, which will allow you to return fire with less likelihood of being hit if a gunfight does develop.

To get the maximum benefit from cover, you must understand: the relationship between yourself, your cover, your gun and the suspect's location... how to select the best cover from various options you may have available...how to position yourself behind it in order to get off accurate shots without exposing your own body to gunfire...ways to overcome cover your assailant may be using...and the importance of maintaining good cover, regardless of provocation, when "blowing" it might subject you to an adversary's killing shots.

For these and other aspects of cover awareness, here are some things to keep in mind and actively apply.

Cover and Concealment

Many officers use these terms synonymously, though they are significantly different. Learning to distinguish between them is the first step to survival and effective cover use.

Tall grass and bushes offer concealment only. Because of body position, the officer on the right is less concealed than the one on the left.

An officer attempting to use a trunk lid as cover. This approach probably offered limited concealment as well because of the officer's exposed feet and the fact that the trunk was up in the first place.

157

Concealment pertains to protection from being *seen* by a suspect. It may be provided by natural or man-made objects—bushes, brush, small trees, tall grass, heavy shadows, smoke, crowds, lines of moving vehicles—anything that will *hide* your presence or movements from your adversary. Concealment may keep you from getting shot even if the suspect does detect your presence. However, concealment alone will *not stop bullets*.

Cover will—or at least deflect them or slow them down. Usually cover incorporates concealment, but its salient feature is its capacity for protecting you from hostile fire.

To illustrate: A pasteboard packing carton might provide you excellent concealment, but a suspect could shoot through it and into you as easily as he could through any other paper product. On the other hand, a six- to eight-inch concrete street curb in front of a house might provide life-saving cover against a suspect standing some distance away in the yard. If you kept your head down, shots

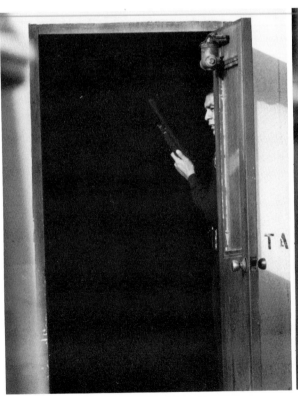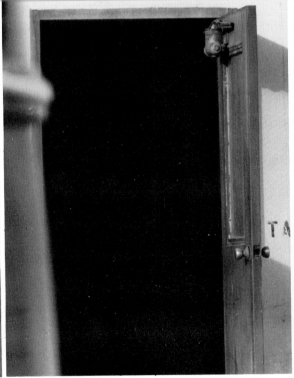

In this incident, the officer first took a "standard position" inside a doorway. Then after other officers radioed that he could be seen by the suspect, he stepped back 6 feet and was still able to maintain a visual.

he fired at your location would most likely hit the flat top of the curb and ricochet right over you.

What's tragic is that some officers have been shot to death behind what they thought was suitable cover. They crouched behind wooden fences, plywood doors, small shrubs, thin walls—without distinguishing that these objects may be somewhat concealing, but by no means impenetrable.

Neither is darkness. Because it can hide you so well, it's tempting to think of darkness as a shield. Standing back in shadows 3 to 6 feet can give you good concealment. But nighttime shadows sometimes can be turned into traps by an unexpected swing of automobile headlights. And a street-wise suspect may deliberately shoot into heavy shadows to "clear" them, whether or not he thinks you're there. Finding genuine cover and keeping it between you and your adversary is as important in the dark as it is in daylight.

Nor is distance any reason to abandon cover consciousness. With a good, solid bench rest and the right gun, if you're within the range where a suspect can see you, he can shoot—and hit. In other words, if you can be seen, you can be hit, and if you can be hit, you can be killed.

Evaluating Choices

Any cover is better than none, but certain cover is better than others. And where you have the choice, the secret is to know the difference. Often in shooting situations, officers tend to look only to size—choosing the largest object as cover, regardless of its power to stop bullets. In range training, they've probably received more emphasis on how to stand and hold a sidearm behind a plywood barricade than any real appreciation of the possibilities and limitations of cover available on the street.

Much of what distinguishes good cover from bad actually has to do with form, thickness and density. Bricks and ceramic substances tend to be good cover, concrete blocks poor; many bullets will blast right through a block wall no matter how big it might be. The wood in most modern doors, especially hollow-core doors, offers you little protection. In a scenario that is replayed repeatedly each year, a suspect inside his apartment in Wisconsin heard officers knock on his door to question him about a dispute over a hospital bill. He grabbed a .12 ga. shotgun and fired twice through the door, killing a patrolman as readily as if there had been nothing between them. In Chicago, a sniper inside

*In this shoot-out, you see two wounded
civilians plus four cover alternatives:
A patrol car, fireplug, utility pole and
metal standard. The officer being fired
at took cover behind the fourth option. Why?*

160

a high school shot through a plywood door. The bullet traveled down a corridor more than 300 feet before hitting its victim, and even then still had momentum enough to pass through both his thighs. On the other hand, a door jamb will stop a lot of bullets. And the wood of a good-sized tree is excellent cover—"almost like a sponge in taking slugs," as one survival expert puts it. "Always have a tree with you" is a good rule, where you can follow it. A telephone pole is good, too, against most ammunition you'll encounter—yet a ten-inch pole can be penetrated by a .30 cal. rifle firing metal jacketed bullets.

A concrete utility pole can provide excellent cover because you can blend in with its shape. Here the officer assumed a low position to blend in with the widest part of the pole.

Where metal is concerned, steel utility poles, fire hydrants or postal service mailboxes generally are superior to trash cans, car bodies and the like. In shooting tests, for instance, mail boxes have been known to stop a 125 grain, semi-jacketed hollow point and a 158 grain full-jacketed round fired from a .38 Special, as well as .00 Buck from 20-inch barrel shotguns—the equivalent, in other words, of most of what you'll encounter on the street. Fire hydrants are tougher. They'll break up on impact ammunition such as .30-06 full metal jacket, .308 cal. jacketed soft point and .223 cal. military rifle rounds. The damage to a fire hydrant from these powerful bullets, which could tear through a car body like butter, could be corrected with a dab of paint.

In a cover sweepstakes, solid bricks, large trees, fire hydrants and the engine blocks of cars would probably come in tops. Inch for inch, pound for pound, these objects will stop more bullets than any other cover you're likely to have available in a shooting situation.

Changing Cover

Because you have some cover in an armed confrontation shouldn't stop you from seeking better cover, provided, of course, you can change locations without getting shot in the process. As usual, you want to plan ahead; *select your next position before you move.*

If possible, you should change from place to place *behind* cover. You might be able to move around a room, for instance, by pushing or pulling an overstuffed chair across the floor while you stay low behind it. Outdoors, you may be able to take advantage of furrows, culverts, trenches or natural indentations in the ground, as well as upright objects.

Where you must cross open space with no cover, your first choice is running, as low and as fast as you can. You're safest if you can run *across* your assailant's line of fire; it's hardest to draw a bead on a target moving fast in a lateral direction. If you have to run in a path that's parallel to his gun, zigzag or move at an uneven pace.

Don't move just for the sake of moving. And in evaluating the cover you're heading toward, be sure it won't place you in an unmaneuverable position. Flexibility is important in a gunfight. If your cover boxes you in where it's impossible or difficult to move rapidly, you may end up "boxed in," permanently.

Where you must cross open space without cover, your first choice is running, as low and as fast as you can. Here an officer applies that tactic in rushing a child to safety during a sniper attack in which 2 were killed and 44 injured, including 6 policemen.

Position and Grips

Getting safe is the goal of seeking cover. Your ability to return fire from behind it and to be comfortable there are secondary considerations. Therefore, the posture you assume behind cover should be geared first and foremost to achieving maximum concealment from the suspect and protection from his bullets.

This means you want to *blend in with the shape of your cover.*

If your cover's a mailbox, crouch and spread your legs so each is behind one of the box's supports. If you're behind a utility pole or tree, your inclination may be to go to a low position if you're being shot at. But if you go low, you'll spread out, exposing your kneecaps and legs. You're usually safer to stand upright, turned sideways to the pole with your weak-side leg forward, taking most of your weight. Similarly, if you've scrambled behind a fireplug or trash can, you may be inclined to squat there. But a low kneeling position will likely give you more protection. Go down on your strong-side knee and sit back on that leg, with your body hunched and tucked in tight to keep as much of it as you can within the outline of your cover. On one knee, you can still move quickly if necessary. When you are behind large cover, like a wall, then you may reasonably have a choice between getting low or staying erect.

Two positions you almost always want to *avoid* behind cover are: 1) sitting and 2) proning out. These are probably acceptable for military uses, but for law enforcement purposes they generally allow you *too little maneuverability* in case you need to move fast to a new location. The prone

A low kneeling position is best when shooting behind a fireplug. Here you have the proper combination of cover, concealment and mobility if you need to change locations.

position, particularly, is a difficult one to shoot from if the suspect is anyplace but ground level. Over a long period of time, this position can induce considerable fatigue in your head, neck and arms. In addition, if you are on concrete or some other hard surface, these positions increase your risk of being hit by ricochet bullets. Instead of a glancing round catching you in the leg, as it might if you're standing or kneeling, you take the chance of being struck in the stomach if you're sitting or in the head if you're prone. Also, falling to get into these positions may needlessly expose you to injury from rocks, rusty cans, cactus, broken glass and other natural or man-made hazards.

There are exceptions, of course. If a low curb is your *only* cover, then it's your best, and proning out in the gutter is your only practical choice. (Generally the curb is highest—and thus most protective—near intersections and storm sewer drains.) Also if you are on or just beyond the slope of an embankment—say along railroad tracks—the prone position may work well. Here any ricochet bullets would likely bounce off the tracks and over your head.

If rolling into a curb becomes the only cover option, remember that curbs are usually highest near corners where the drains are located.

This is the view an officer saw while attempting to conceal himself from a sniper who positioned himself at the top of a 230 ft. tower some distance away.

....But from the high ground position
of the sniper [Charles Whitman], here
is what he saw. The officer was killed
with one shot from a scoped rifle.

In choosing cover and positioning yourself, remember the ostrich effect: the suspect's perspective may be drastically different from yours. If you are crouched behind cover and he is located at an upper elevation, the barrier may block him from your view—yet he may be able to see *over* it to spot you perfectly. This was the case in New Orleans where officers confronted a suspect shooting from a high-rise motel. They felt they were safe hiding behind a high brick fence, not realizing that from their assailant's high angle the wall was no hindrance at all to picking them off.

From behind cover, you want to keep a good visual on your suspect's location, if you can't see him personally. So long as you know roughly where he is, you have him contained. Unobserved, he may try to escape or move to circumvent your cover, causing you to lose control of the situation. If you can't watch him directly from where you're positioned, you may be able to utilize the reflections in windows to see his area. Or use the quick peek technique, glancing out at different levels from behind your barricade. Remember, try to peek out from low, unexpected levels and not from the same level consistently.

As you move to cover, avoid getting so close to the suspect's location that your position threatens your safety. Here an officer has positioned himself about 6 feet from occupants of a house who are shooting at police.

*If a direct assault is not imminent,
positioning yourself with your head
over the top will give you a broader
field of view.*

*....However, shooting from the side of
the mailbox will offer better cover and
concealment. What is sacrificed is
your total area of observation.*

When you're forced to stay behind cover for a long period of time, try to shift your position slightly every so often if you can do so safely. Otherwise, the fatigue and restricted blood circulation that come from rigidly holding one posture for an extended time may blur your vision and make it difficult for you to see the suspect. Ultimately, you will adopt a position that is comfortable and works best for you.

As far as firing at your adversary is concerned, you want to shoot *around* your cover when possible, rather than *over* the top of it. Visualize these two positions from a mailbox as cover and you'll see that shooting from the side will expose a much smaller portion of your vital anatomy to a suspect's hostile shots.

The exact posture you adopt will depend on the shape of your cover and the suspect's location, the idea of being to get on target while risking as little of your hide as you can. When bullets are flying and you're under stress, you want to be able to call automatically on survival skills that are simple, effective and easily applied. So, as a key to shooting, you need a basic grip that will hold your gun steady and that can be adapted to a variety of behind-cover postures. Select a grip you're comfortable with... practice it regularly...then stick with it when you get in trouble. If you can learn to shoot one way and learn to shoot one way effectively, that's a strong plus for your staying alive.

The old method involved pressing your support hand flat against the barricade with the thumb jutting out to form an "L." The wrist of your gun hand then rested in this crotch, and you braced yourself with your opposite foot forward against the wall. Even when the cover was conveniently flat, as it usually was on the ranges where this form was taught, the grip tended to be shaky. But it was even less suitable behind curved or irregular shields, like poles and fireplugs, which you are far more likely to encounter on the street.

For shooting from behind cover in an armed confrontation, you'll probably find one of these more stable grips *easier* to use and more *effective* in delivering accurate fire:

1. *the two-handed combat hold.* This is the same grip used in the basic instinct shooting stance. Basically, one hand holds your gun, and the other hand wraps around it to provide additional support. The fingers of the two hands may be firmly intertwined or locked together, or the support hand may simply wrap around your shooting hand. As you fire, the back of your support hand between wrist and knuckles presses against the side of your cover. This grip allows for a slight gun-hand push and support-hand pull which will give you a steady, solid grip on the gun.

2. *the wrist clench.* Here you hold your non-shooting arm bent and parallel to the ground and place the back edge of it against your cover. In an over-handed grip, your non-shooting hand then clutches your gun hand at the wrist. This hold allows you to brace yourself against your cover and provides some steadying of your shooting hand as you fire.

If you're comfortable using it, *the two-hand combat hold is the superior grip for shooting from cover.* You should practice it until it becomes instinctive. With it, you can shoot around anything, whether it's a square corner, a round corner, a fire hydrant, a mailbox, the hood of a car or what-have-you. The grip works whether you are standing, crouching, kneeling, even sitting or proned out. In the kneeling position, you can bolster the support it gives your gun by placing the elbow of your non-shooting arm on your raised knee to form roughly a "V" between your shoulder and gun. To keep this brace steadiest, avoid direct contact between your elbow and knee bone and instead place the fleshy part of your arm just above the elbow against the knee area.

Depending on the suspect's location, you may need to "pop out" some of your upper body from behind your cover in order to fire at him. But by moving fast and using the principles of instinct shooting, you can keep your exposure time to a minimum.

Your best position around most barricade cover will involve the two-hand hold. Notice the relationship of hands to this right-sided barricade. Also notice that at no point does the revolver actually touch the cover surface.

The proper position next to this pole is appropriate to almost every barricade cover situation.

Moreover, the amount of your body exposed during that time can also be minimized, if you train yourself to be an ambidextrous shooter, able to fire proficiently with the gun in either your left or right hand, as your cover and the suspect's location dictate. Most training on the range emphasizes only strong-hand shooting, but in some street situations, you may find yourself behind a "left-handed barricade," one that requires you to "pop out" to the left to shoot around. If you are normally a right-handed shooter, you should be able in this circumstance to shoot accurately with your gun in your left hand. There is no doubt that doing so can give you extra protection. If you don't use your left hand behind a left-handed barricade, but lean out far enough instead to shoot with your right hand, you are exposing approximately *three times* the amount of your body that would be necessary for a weak-hand shot. This additional exposure involves mostly your head and chest areas. That creates a significant increase in your survival risk, even if the exposure time involved is measured in seconds or less. In addition, weak-hand shooting can be important if your strong hand is shot or otherwise injured. If you're ambidextrous, you can still defend yourself.

Although most officers have a strong psychological urge to use their strong hand in shooting from behind both right- and left-sided barricades, weak-hand shooting can be developed to the level that you *will* use it under stress. It is learned behavior, and you can learn it well. The tactic is well worth the effort, but learning it does require *extensive practice.* In addition to training your hands, you have to condition yourself so you don't stick your head all the way out to shoot with both eyes or with your stronger eye. If you haven't practiced to the point that you can use weak-hand shooting comfortably and confidently, you *will* revert under pressure to shooting with your stronger hand, which, in certain circumstances, can be lethal.

For weak-hand shooting, of course, you use the same grip. Just transfer your gun to your weak hand and employ your strong hand for support. (If you're using a semi-automatic, you'll find a definite awkwardness in operating the safety and slide release, which is normally done with the thumb of your shooting hand. These levers will have to be moved with the index finger of your weak hand.)

The proper body and shotgun position behind a right-sided barricade. Notice that the shotgun does not touch the barricade.

Reverting to the strong-hand position [left photos] around a left-sided barricade will expose your head and torso every time. The same is true when holding a shotgun.

In applying barricade cover, both feet are placed firmly on the ground, with your gun-side foot placed back a comfortable distance.

In shooting with either hand, a proper foot placement is important for balance and control. If you're in a standing position behind a barricade, the foot on the same side as your gun hand should be placed about one step back. Again, you'll probably need to experiment to find the position that offers you the best combination of comfort, balance and accuracy. Remember to shift your weight on the balls of your feet from time to time during periods of inactivity to relieve fatigue.

Be sure when shooting that *no part of your gun touches your barricade.* Be conscious of where the barrel is (cylinder, too, if you're using a revolver), and keep it slightly away from any surface. You may have shot on a range by resting your gun on a little sandbag, but this is not comparable to a hard surface that has no "give." If your gun is touching such a surface, it will bounce when you fire. This change in the recoil action will make your shots inaccurate and lengthen your recovery time for getting back on target for your next shot.

Be careful also to keep your muzzle completely clear of your cover. In Illinois, an officer suffered a painful ear injury while shooting from behind a railroad embankment. He unwittingly let the barrel of his shotgun drop down so part of the muzzle was pointing into the train track he was trying to shoot over. This can cause not only an unusually intense sound reverberation which can injure your eardrums, as happened in this case, but also can cause your ammunition to deflect dangerously, bringing injury to yourself or fellow officers.

Even without mishap, *shooting from behind cover is different from shooting in the open.* Your accuracy rate is likely to be lower. The only way to correct that is by adhering to the one unchanging survival principle: *practice builds proficiency.*

Patrol Car as Cover

A lot of shootings go down near patrol cars. Often your closest source of cover is your car itself. If you're inside it, you may be able to move quickly to a protected position just by shifting a few inches in your seat. Outside the car, there are several places where the vehicle's construction offers you excellent shielding. If nothing else, you may be able to *drive* your unit to a position where good cover is available.

There are, however, some popular misconceptions about patrol car cover.

MYTH: You have good cover by crouching behind a wide-open vehicle door and shooting through the open window. Actually, this position leaves you vulnerable in several ways. Your legs are exposed below the door; they can be knocked out from under you by ricochet fire from the suspect's position. Your head and upper torso are exposed as you rise up in the window to shoot. And if the suspect is smart and has enough firepower, he can likely shoot right through the door and hit you. Indeed, there's enough firepower for that in a .22 cal. rifle hot load. (If you *must* use a car door for cover, try to angle the door in relation to the suspect's fire. Then there's a greater chance of his bullets ricocheting off.)

If you've ever considered a cover tactic like this, consider yourself lucky you've never tested it during a shooting confrontation.

Patrol car doors make for poor cover and much blood.

MYTH: Flopping over the hood, over the rear fender or over the car top is a good way to return fire. Some of the same lethal problems apply. You're exposing a sizeable portion of your body to hostile fire once you get above cover. If you're shooting over the top, for example, at least your head and shoulders are exposed on the roof and your mid-section is vulnerable through the windows. And your assailant still may be able to take out your legs by skipping bullets. Indeed, positions like these may invite shots. They certainly have in the past.

Avoid any barricade cover position with a vehicle in which this much of your vital organs are exposed.

MYTH: While seated in your car, you can shoot through the windshield and hit your adversary. This may work in Clint Eastwood movies, but *don't* try it in real life. The bullet actually may travel down the glass, rather than through it, and deflect into your car. Or it may just lodge in the glass. At the very least, your eardrums will experience pain from the shot fired within the confines of the car.

One way to remain inside your patrol car and shoot effectively, at least when your assailant is in front of you, as might be the case in a traffic stop that goes sour, is to use the back brace position. With your door at least partially open, you slide over in your seat so your back is resting against the door post. One leg stays inside, you keep the other up off the pavement by bracing your foot against the open door. *Scoot down low* and position your sidearm in the crotch formed by the front edge of the door and the windshield post. The metal can serve as a bench rest for your hands, enabling you to get off more accurate rounds with either your sidearm or shotgun. In this position, your face and chest are partially protected behind the heavy metal of the windshield post, and, depending on the exact location of the suspect, you may achieve additional shielding from the car's engine block. Of course, you keep your engine running so you can back up or pull out of there fast if necessary or desirable.

One tactic for using your vehicle as cover is to position yourself like this. Brace your foot to keep the door open. This position also keeps your legs clear of low rounds.

If the suspect is positioned where you're better off or have time to exit your patrol car, you want to exit on the side away from hostile weapons fire. If you're the driver and it's safe to exit through your door, hit your seat belt release and at the same time tuck your left arm under the shoulder harness. You shed the harness with a pushing motion and open the door latch with your left hand. Then push the door open with your left knee, leaving both hands free as you start out. (If you're the passenger officer, use your right hand and knee for this maneuver.) You want to roll out of the car, landing on your hands and knees and keeping low until you reach cover, say behind a wheel.

If you need to exit from the side of the car opposite where you're sitting, duck down, stretch out across the seat and open that door. Grab the edge of the seat and pull yourself across on your belly and side, and continue to slide on out. You can use your feet against the opposite door for an extra push forward. This keeps your head and chest, your most vulnerable areas, as low as possible and allows you to present the lowest profile while exiting—and that's your top priority. *Do not* try to draw your gun while going through these maneuvers. You may end up accidentally shooting yourself. Draw after you're *outside*, when you're capable of returning fire safely.

Vehicle exits are usually given little attention in basic training. But one of the things you'll learn quickly in trying an opposite-door exit is to keep the equipment that you store on the front seat to an absolute minimum. Consoles, radar and other necessary equipment that may be in the way will slow you down enough. If a suspect's bullets are turning your unit into a sieve, you don't want extra debris to further hamper your getting out!

Outside the patrol car, move immediately to where you have maximum protection. Crouching or kneeling behind one of the wheels is likeliest to fully conceal you and protect you from ricochet rounds and also puts a barrier of rubber and metal—possibly two of them—between you and a suspect's direct fire. Behind a front wheel, you may also be protected by the engine block, the least penetrable component of any vehicle. *Beware of standing or kneeling between wheel bases.* True, you've got the whole length or width of the car as cover, but your legs are exposed underneath. In the infamous Texas Tower incident in 1966, an ambulance driver took such a position outside his vehicle, thinking he was safe from the sniper shots crackling around him. Charles Whitman struck him at least once by using ricochet shooting under the ambulance.

The proper cover exit from the passenger side of a one-officer patrol car. The success of this move is based on using your feet to catapult your body across and out.

Outside your patrol car, seek cover behind the wheel base. [The officer on the right uses the "quick peek" technique].

The front of your patrol car can also become effective barricade cover. Here you shoot from a kneeling position. Your legs should be as close to the wheel as you can comfortably position them.

Again, depending on the suspect's location, you may be able to most safely sight him by quick peeking under the car. If you're up front and he's situated appropriately, one way for you to shoot that maintains good cover is to rock forward and fire around the front of the car, just above the bumper. This tends to be a better position than the traditional one, taken by two officers in Maryland who tried to apprehend a teenage bank robbery suspect. When he fired at them with a .20 ga. shotgun, they shot back *over* their patrol car. He killed them both with blasts to the head.

If your assailant changes location and you need to move from one side of the patrol car to the other, under fire, stay low as you circle the end of the car. Keep a visual on the suspect through the car glass, so he's under constant surveillance. As soon as you round the vehicle, again take cover behind a wheel.

Most suspects will expect you to remain by your vehicle. Moments after this picture was taken, the officer with the shotgun was killed by sniper fire from a hotel across the street.

182

Under stress, we all tend to revert to sources of strength. In a crisis, with officers, a principal source tends to be the patrol car. It's familiar...it's mobile...its radio may symbolize a lifeline. But in some situations, to save your life, you'll have to abandon it. Your position there, even if you make the best possible use of the car as cover, may be too vulnerable. This was tragically illustrated in a midwestern incident where two officers were fired upon in their patrol car by two suspects in another car. The officer who was driving was killed in the first volley. One of the suspects then climbed out of the suspect vehicle and approached the patrol car on foot. The passenger officer saw him emerging but instead of exiting the patrol car for cover, he stayed inside to radio for help. He was then shot like a sitting duck by the suspect firing through the windshield.

As you maneuver in and around your patrol car, *keep in mind your other cover options*. Remember, your car has definite limitations. There should be no umbilical cord tying you to it if you can safely reach something better somewhere else. This may mean sacrificing your communications contact unless you have a portable radio. But protecting your life is, after all, your top priority. A solid shield will probably do that better than a microphone in an imminent shoot-out.

Penetration Power

Many officers think that what they can't see they can't shoot. A vivid test of this that rarely fails is performed regularly by one instructor in survival tactics. One at a time, he arms his students with a deactivated revolver and tells them to "shoot" him as he sits facing them, about 2 feet away. The trick is that he holds a sheet of typing paper in front of him. Almost invariably, a curious choreography promptly develops: the student moves the gun to try to shoot *around* the paper, the instructor jerks the paper in front of the muzzle, the student shifts the gun, the instructor blocks it with the paper and so on, ad infinitum. Hardly anyone ever "shoots" *through* the paper, though a bullet obviously would punch right through to the instructor. On the street, the same sort of thing sometimes happens. One officer saved his life by holding up his open palm in front of a suspect's gun and continuing to move it as the suspect tried to shoot around the officer's hand.

Sometimes it's the suspect who capitalizes on the failure to acknowledge penetration power. In

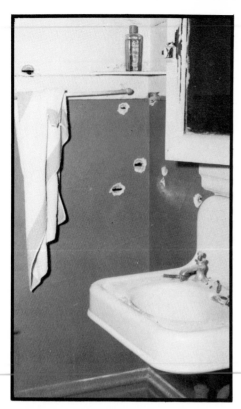

Bullets do penetrate walls. A suspect being hunted on a felony charge heard an officer walk into his bathroom during the search. Once the officer's presence was revealed the suspect shot through the wall from another room and killed a target he didn't need to see.

more than one armed encounter, the offender has ducked behind a hedge—and the officer has stopped shooting at him, even though his location is known and the officer's ammunition is clearly capable of penetrating to it. The officer waits to shoot until the suspect's head pops up.

With a firearm and ammunition that are powerful enough, you can penetrate virtually *any* cover. With a high-velocity .30 cal. rifle—like a .308 or .30-06—you can punch through about anything. Even with your service handgun—and especially with a shotgun loaded with rifled slugs rather than .00 Buck—you can shoot through many objects a suspect might commonly hide behind, including doors, exterior and interior walls of many buildings and certain parts of cars.

If a suspect pulls a gun on you as you approach his door in a traffic stop, for instance, you may be able to shoot him by firing through the door as you drop into a protected position below the window level. Years ago, when cars were made differently, this might not have been possible. But today, despite some claims to the contrary, car bodies often *can* be penetrated by standard police ammunition, especially if you are a few feet back from the car so the bullet has a chance to gain some stability before it impacts. In one California incident, an officer fired 9mm rounds from a semi-automatic at a suspect sitting in a Ford Pinto. Eight bullets went through the trunk lid, the back seat, the front seat, into the suspect and out again. (Where car doors are concerned, the chances of penetration are greatest if you shoot straight on. Even a shallowly angled shot is likelier to ricochet off the metal. If the window is down, that's another factor hampering penetration. Cold weather may be, too; ice on the metal would tend to heighten the ricochet effect.)

Sometimes firing through cover is the surest way of incapacitating your assailant. If he's shooting at you from a window, for example, you may have a tough time catching him in the opening. But with a wood or stucco building you could possibly fire through the wall to either side of the window or below it and hit him while he's standing or crouching there between shots.

In a situation like this, incidentally, your first shot should probably be to the right-hand wall as you face the window. If the suspect is right-handed, as 90 per cent of the population is, that's where he's likeliest to stand.

ONE CAUTION: shooting through cover is risky. Many departments discourage it. It should be attempted *only* when you are 100 per cent *certain* of the suspect's identity...certain of his exact location...and certain there is *no one else* with him

In some cases, penetrating the suspect's cover [here a car door] can be combined with rapid movement outside of the kill zone.

185

behind his barricade who might be struck by your bullets. You should also consider what might happen if your rounds should deflect from the cover and ricochet to other locations. If you ignore these provisos and shoot just because you *can*, you may end up with a tragedy—and facing an indictment— instead of a dead assailant.

The potential for miscalculation is memorably illustrated by a case in the midwest where officers arrived outside an apartment in response to a disturbance call. Through the door they could hear loud sounds like a woman being tortured. They ordered the door opened. No response. Then they tried to kick it in, but it felt as if someone on the other side was holding it shut. The sounds grew louder and more anguished. In frustration and concern for the victim, one officer shot through the door. Later, they discovered the noises were being

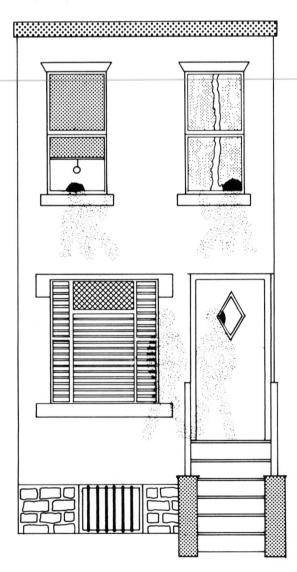

If it's completely safe to penetrate the armed suspect's cover, shoot at the surface most likely to contain the largest part of the suspect's body.

186

made by people in the apartment "trying to imitate disco sounds." There *was* no crime-in-progress. Fortunately, the penetrating bullet failed to hit anything but the floor on the other side of the door.

Penetration power, incidentally, is one of those two-way streets that an astute suspect will try to make use of, as well as you. Making sure he can't, of course, is your prime consideration in selecting your cover.

"Blowing" Cover

Once you have good cover, *maintain it*. Don't "blow it" and sacrifice your safety because you:

- want to reach your radio. Some officers have been killed because they left good cover under fire and tried to run to their patrol cars. They would have been better off running away from the car and using someone's telephone to call for help.
- want to help a fellow officer who has been injured. If you are shot in the process of trying to get him to safety, you only complicate the situation. It's a natural impulse to want to help, but there's a good possibility that since he's down, he will not be fired on again. Wait.
- want to get the action over with. A sobering example of how impatience defeats survival procedures is found in a case where two heavily armed ex-convicts, recently paroled as "rehabilitated," were surprised by police while robbing a neighborhood supermarket. Realizing the market was surrounded by officers, the bandits took cover by running upstairs to the manager's office. For the next 20 minutes, the sergeant in command called on the two to surrender, but they did not respond. Suddenly, a patrolman left the protected position where he had been waiting and started up the stairs, revolver in hand. The sergeant ordered him back behind cover, but he muttered, "Those bastards don't scare me any. Let's get this over with." He was six steps from the top when simultaneous blasts from two sawed-off shotguns reverberated from the manager's office. His fellow officers below watched in horror and disbelief as his body tumbled backward down the stairs, his head blown almost entirely away.

8 | SHOOTING TECHNIQUES

A patrolman had just gotten off duty and was walking to his car parked on a shadowy Chicago side street, when a man driving by suddenly slammed to a stop. The stranger got out of his car and for no known reason fired at the officer with a nickel-plated revolver. Good cover was too distant to reach...the assailant was only 10 feet away; the officer had little choice but to shoot back in the most effective way he could. He drew his revolver and fired four shots at the suspect, killing him on the spot.

The method he used is what we've referred to previously as "instinct shooting." This technique allows you to get on target fast and to conclude the confrontation as rapidly and effectively as possible. Without doubt, it's the most efficient means today of firing at most assailants in most law enforcement situations.

Instinct shooting is an adaptation of a tactic developed by American soldiers in Vietnam to deal with an enemy who frequently surprised them at close quarters in areas with little available cover. Because suspects commonly confront officers under just those circumstances, it's ideal for use in law enforcement. Basically, it involves taking aim at your target by *pointing your gun as you would point your index finger*, at the spot you want to hit. It allows an ideal balance of speed and accuracy and power—the triple header that wins gunfights—without using the conventional sight picture procedure. It can help you get the edge when everything seems to be against you: poor lighting, irregular terrain, an obstructed view, the cover and move-ment of your adversary—not to mention the tremen-dous physical and emotional stress that sledge hammers you from the moment you perceive danger. Instinct shooting is simple...easy to learn...can be used behind cover as well as in the open...and is versatile enough to serve you in a variety of positions, including, as we've mentioned pre-viously, kneeling and falling down.

Ironically, the principle behind this technique is unconsciously employed by most suspects. They rarely have illusions of being trained marksmen; they just point their guns and pull the trigger. John Wilkes Booth did that against Lincoln...Jack Ruby against Oswald...countless nameless, faceless as-sailants over the years have done it against count-less officers...and the bad guy who takes *you* on will probably do it against *you*.

His version of instinct shooting, however, is likely to be a relatively crude, one-handed form that depends mostly on suddenness and surprise for success. What you can perfect is a polished pro-cedure that is equally fast but also is designed with specific survival needs in mind.

Sept. 29, 1978. Female suspect shoots into unoccupied patrol car in the start of a siege which involved an exchange of 15 shots. Note the one-hand hold and close distance factor similar to Booth's.

April 14, 1865. Booth's shooting tech-nique conformed amazingly with today's patterns of encounter.

Knowing how to shoot, of course, is only part of the prescription for successfully resolving an armed encounter and probably the last component. Among other things, you must also be proficient at: properly identifying your target...dealing with more than one assailant in a single episode...and coping with unpredictable reactions by yourself and by the suspect if hit. In addition, you need to understand clearly when the risk of shooting is greater than the probable benefit and be able to avoid firing in those situations.

That's a lot to coordinate in a matter of a few seconds, when you're ducking bullets some suspect has decided have your name on them. It demands a keen level of mental and physical conditioning. What follows will help you achieve it.

Bear in mind that any shooting we discuss here is assumed to be legally justified. We're not concerned with evaluating *whether* you should shoot, only with *the methods* you can best employ if shooting is demanded.

Instinct Shooting Position

In a typical shooting, your assailant will fire first. He'll be standing still or moving toward you. And he'll be so close you'll have little choice but to shoot back immediately, in an effort to put *him* on the defensive and perhaps allow you a chance to move to cover. So long as you subject him to effective fire, his shots are likely to be ineffective. In military parlance, this is called establishing and maintaining fire superiority.

Under pressure, you will revert to whatever position you have practiced.

You don't have to be an "expert" shooter, in the usual target practice sense. But you do have to have good eye-and-hand coordination and be able to position yourself correctly and bring your gun into action quickly and properly, without conscious attention to the mechanisms of firing.

If you've trained correctly, the necessary mechanisms will come instinctively when you're faced with a crisis situation. On the other hand, crack target shooters who have no trouble hitting a stationary target 20 yards away but who have not trained for instinct shooting may not hit a moving, firing suspect only 6 feet away. A case in point occurred in an eastern city when a suspect grabbed a cleaning woman in the federal courthouse, put a gun to her head and demanded to see a bankruptcy referee. During the negotiations that subsequently developed, a plainclothes policeman posing as a lawyer was able to get close to the gunman. The officer was armed with a snub-nose revolver in a concealed ankle holster and was rated as an excellent target shooter. At the right moment, the officer drew his revolver and started shooting. The suspect was less than 5 feet away—little more than an arm's reach. Yet when the officer fired, he *missed* the suspect four times out of five.

From analyzing reports of officer-involved shootings, it's obvious that many officers in high-stress situations tend to hold their guns with one hand and shoot one round. This is because *under stress* they fall back on what they know best—basic academy range training, which usually emphasizes a one-hand grip for firing one shot at a time.

Draw your sidearm before your approach to danger. Upon contact with your sidearm, your hand and fingers should be positioned for the proper shooting grip.

Occasionally, one-handed shooting may be necessary; you may be wounded in the other hand, or you may be holding your gun in one hand while crawling through a window or up a fire escape, for example. Usually, however, your preferred option is the better-controlled two-handed shooting, firing multiple shots in rapid succession. This gives you the best chance of effectively stopping a suspect who is threatening your life or someone else's.

DRAW: If you've anticipated danger, you'll already have your gun unholstered and in the firing position (not at your side) when you need to shoot. If not, you begin moving into the instinct shooting position as you draw.

Most officers' draw consists of a series of jerks: the hand comes up, the hand comes down, the gun goes up, the gun goes out. This back and forth sequence is inefficient. For good instinct shooting, your draw should be one continuous motion, with *smoothness more important than an attempt at speed alone.* You want to bring your gun out to the same place with the same fluid maneuver every time you withdraw it from your holster. As you draw, your hand should be positioned for the proper shooting grip so that you do not have to readjust it once the gun clears leather. This helps enhance your accuracy. With the draw, as with other instinct shooting components, speed is fine; accuracy is final. Your adversary must be *hit* to be incapacitated; the mere noise of your firearm going off won't do it.

To draw, grasp the stock of your gun firmly, with your shooting hand high on the grip panels. Your thumb and fingers should be in position for shooting—except for your trigger finger. Keep this finger extended outside the holster at first, parallel to the barrel, and allow it to fall alongside the frame above the trigger as you withdraw the gun. This will prevent an accidental discharge. Draw from your wrist and arm. Bring the muzzle up so the barrel becomes parallel to the ground as you extend your shooting arm toward the suspect. Simultaneously, you swing your other arm up so your hands come together in a supported grip, just as your gun enters your peripheral vision.

These movements should be *fast* and *forceful,* taking about 1 to 1.5 seconds with practice and culminating in your hands and arms *punching* the gun out at your target, much as you'd throw a low punch to his body. *You don't look down at the gun as you draw* any more than you'd look at your hand if you intended to jab him or shine your flashlight on him. *Concentrate on the suspect.* For safety, even if you intend to fire immediately, your finger should stay outside the trigger guard until your gun has cleared the holster and the muzzle is pointing forward, clear of your body.

GRIP: In a shoot-out, you'll be so scared you can taste it. Your heart and lungs will kick into high gear...your brain will race furiously...adrenalin surge into your bloodstream...your muscles possibly tremor. Unless your grip steadies and strengthens your shooting hand, your accuracy may be seriously affected.

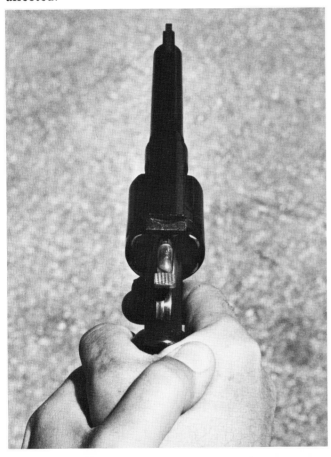

High angle view of one of the accepted grip positions for instinct shooting.

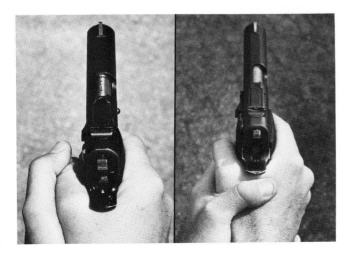

The recommended grip for a semi-automatic is with the thumb of the weak hand alongside the thumb of the strong hand (left photo). Otherwise, with the traditional placement of the weak-hand thumb (right photo) the slide may scrape your skin as it moves back in firing.

For the recommended, two-hand combat hold, your support hand comes up under or alongside your shooting hand as you move your gun on target. There are several options for how your hands are ultimately positioned. You may: 1) solidly lock the little finger of your shooting hand between the first two fingers of your support hand; 2) wrap your support hand around the middle, ring and small fingers of your gun hand, or 3) cup the palm of your support hand under the butt of your sidearm and cross the fingers of your support hand over those of your gun hand. In each case, the thumb of your support hand either overlaps that of your shooting hand, or both thumbs lie along the left side of your sidearm (assuming you are right-handed). Your shooting hand should be high on the back-strap of your gun, and your support hand should encompass and reinforce as much of your shooting hand as possible. By the time your hands are locked together in final position, you should be ready to shoot. This grip works both as a brace and a bench for your gun and allows you to move it in any direction. Moreover, with practice, it is no slower—and much more stable—than one-handed shooting.

You want to keep a firm hold on your gun, but *don't clutch* it. Clutching can make your hands shake, destroying the purpose of this "layered" grip. Also, if you are using a semi-automatic, be sure your hands are positioned so that the slide can come back when you shoot without eating up the skin on your thumb(s) or knuckles.

If for some reason you must shoot one-handed—say you've been wounded in the other—you can still make your non-shooting arm useful by positioning it to provide support, even if you can't use that hand for gripping. You hold the arm taut and place it under your shooting arm at the wrist. This provides something of a bench rest for your shooting hand while firing.

STANCE: Your grip should be part of a solid, firm stance that lets your whole body work at keeping your gun steady so you can concentrate fully on making your shots count. Two basic positions are suitable for instinct shooting. By experimenting in your practice sessions you can learn which is more comfortable and effective for you. Rather than just planting your feet and facing downrange, try these positions extensively on surprise targets at different angles and distances to get the feel for how they'll work in a real confrontation.

For our purposes here, we'll describe each stance as it's assumed if you are caught in the open in a gunfight. With appropriate modification, each can be adapted for use behind cover, where you need to conform to the shape of your barricade.

The proper tactic for shooting one-handed when your gun-hand has been disabled.

196

The more commonly taught stance is the isosceles or combat stance position, so called because your arms are extended away from your chest like two equal sides of a triangle. As your gun comes out and up, you face the suspect squarely, and if you're right-handed, you move your left foot straight out to the left so your legs are in a solid, braced position and you have maximum mobility in any direction, should you want to move to cover, engage a second opponent, etc. Bend your torso slightly forward from the hips and flex your knees to assume a crouch similar to that of a baseball infielder.

As your arms move up for the supported grip, you thrust your hands out at the midline of your body, straight out from your chest. Neither arm dominates; in the final on-target position, both are pointed straight toward your assailant. Your wrists, elbows and shoulders are firmly locked, with the muzzle of your gun at or just slightly below eye level. In effect, your gun becomes an extension of your arms and fingers. Remember, *straight arms help to shoot straight.* Also, they carry the recoil back into your shoulders to help reduce the shock to your hands and keep you from "bouncing" off target when you fire.

The proper isosceles stance for instinct shooting involves locking your wrists and elbows with your torso bent slightly forward. Your arms will absorb the recoil and prevent you from pulling off target.

Some theorists claim that crouching, except behind a low barricade, lessens accuracy and slows you down. But knowledgeable shooting veterans understand that this movement lets you get your gun up and "on" quicker. Both your sidearm and your eyes are at about the chest level of the suspect, which should help your aim. Also, the crouch provides better balance. Real-life shoot-outs often unfold in icy alleyways or on tenement staircases, and on these uneven surfaces you'll need all the balance benefits you can get. By getting low, the crouch makes you a smaller target and capitalizes on the fact that many suspects tend to shoot high with a handgun, especially when the shoot-out takes place in dim light.

Forming the isosceles stance can be thought of as a logical extention of the one-hand hold. The one-hand hold offers limited control for most officers in a shooting.

The other basic instinct shooting position is the Weaver stance, named for its California inventor. Here you stand essentially erect with your feet shoulder-width apart, your weak foot forward so that your body is turned at a slight angle to the suspect. Your shooting arm is held straight out at shoulder level or flexed just a bit. Your weak arm provides a supporting grip but is flexed sharply at the elbow, 30 to 45 degrees, depending on your bone structure. In effect, it is positioned similar to a weight lifter's when curling a dumbbell. By pulling back at the grip with your support hand and simultaneously pushing forward from the shoulder on your strong side, you produce a certain isometric tension that helps steady your gun and reduce the recoil.

The Weaver stance involves positioning your weak-hand at a different angle than your gun-hand.

Its proponents argue that the Weaver stance "turns a handgun into a rifle—shot from the strong shoulder and braced from below by the weak arm and hand." Unfortunately, a handgun, being a tool for close combat, never really approximates a rifle. But the Weaver stance is especially suitable for accurate, fast shooting when you're using heavy loads or a hard-kicking sidearm, because of the shock-absorber effect created by the bent elbow and push-pull pressure. This pressure tends to hold the firearm down and in place as it discharges. Using this stance properly, some shooters can control even a .44 Magnum under very rapid fire.

However, the Weaver requires considerable practice to master. The exact alignment of bent arms is something many officers have to fumble for. In a few words, it's not as natural for most people as the straight-out, locked-in isosceles stance, especially if you have been taught to crouch.

A shotgun, as well as your handgun, can also be quickly positioned for instinct shooting. Again, you have several options.

In the traditional stance, you stand erect with feet apart, weak foot slightly forward and knees bent, somewhat like a boxer, and swing the gun up to your strong shoulder so your cheek is against the stock. Your strong hand grasps the stock just behind the trigger guard; your weak hand holds the shotgun's fore-grip or slide with your weak arm bent at the elbow. The weapon is held just slightly below your eye level. The barrel is therefore positioned in your peripheral vision as you keep your primary vision fixed on the suspect. This position has a "business" look about it that's psychologically intimidating, especially if you rack in a round. In the vast majority of cases in which a shotgun is used, this psychological impact suffices; a round is never fired. Yet in the event you do need to shoot, firing from the shoulder position is likely to give you the most effective target acquisition.

In cases where you don't have time to bring the shotgun to shoulder level, there are several alternative instinct-shooting positions, all of them keeping the gun lower.

The lowest position is with the side of the stock pressed firmly against your hip on your shooting side. (Just press the stock against your sidearm if it's in the way.) Here you bend slightly foward to make a smaller target, grasping the fore-grip with your weak hand, and locking the elbow of that arm straight; if it is bent, the recoil will cause the barrel to jump up and throw off your accuracy. Although this position may lessen the psychological impact of a suspect looking directly down the barrel of your shotgun, it's still a good one to use for quick response and when you are advancing on a suspect. You can shoot a new round with every step you take with a reasonably effective range.

Other low-level positions involve pressing the shotgun stock firmly against your rib cage, about half way between your hip and your armpit on your shooting side. Or bring the stock up into your armpit, so your strong arm clamps it tightly into your side.

After you rack a shotgun, consider extending the index finger of your support hand along the outside of the slide, at the suspect. This will help guide your shots. Take care not to touch the barrel, though, because the metal heats up from shooting and can burn you.

The proper stance for instinct shooting with the shotgun positioned against your rib cage. This stance will prevent any contact between the shotgun stock and your holstered firearm.

AIM: With instinct shooting, you don't waste time trying to line up a sight picture of the suspect. With the top of your gun at or slightly below eye level, your eyes function as your sights, whether you are shooting a handgun or a long gun.

You aim the gun by pointing it, as you would your finger or your flashlight. You keep your eyes focused straight ahead, looking over the top of your gun. Your eyes concentrate on the suspect, not on your sights. If you are ready to shoot, rather than trying to concentrate on his whole body, look at the center of his chest.

The top of your gun barrel will be in your peripheral vision and as you look along it at the area or body mass you want to hit, the muzzle will tend to line up accordingly, just as the tip of a pointing finger would. In other words, *your hands—and gun—will instinctively follow your eyes.* Bullets are very dependable; they tend to go where they are pointed. When you squeeze the trigger, the bullet should go where you are looking.

Historically, getting a target in precise sight alignment has been emphasized for long-range shooting where there's a desire for pinpoint accuracy. But for the close-range firing of most street

In most cases, your adversary won't give you the time to leisurely close one eye and line up a sight picture. Your primary vision must be on your suspect, not your sights.

confrontations, careful alignment is not needed. Indeed, it may be a hazard to your survival because it will delay you in getting off the fastest possible shots.

You can hit just as well—and much faster—with the aiming procedure described above at distances of 7 yards or less. With extensive practice you may be able to develop proficiency at 12 yards or more.

At night or in low light level conditions, you can still aim accurately with this procedure. An officer depending on traditional sight alignment, on the other hand, would be lost because with insufficient illumination he wouldn't be able even to see his sights. Painting the front sight white may help, but instinct aiming is likely to be more reliable. *If you can see or point at your adversary, you can hit him*, whether your sights are visible or not.

The secret, regardless of light quality, is to keep your eyes "out there" to guide your gun. *Don't look down*, don't bring the barrel of your gun up too high. If you do, you'll get hooked into trying to form a sight picture and lose your edge. Remember, *drawing and sighting to shoot takes over 2½ times as long as drawing and shooting with the instinct technique*.

FIRING: Your shots should always be fired double-action because that's faster and a natural component of the instinct procedure. Don't pump or jerk the trigger, but squeeze it smoothly and quickly. If you're firing a revolver, your trigger finger should be placed so the trigger falls between the first and second finger joints, to allow adequate leverage for the cocking/firing mechanics of a double-action pull. The same finger placement works best for most officers on a shotgun trigger. With a semi-automatic, you want the fleshy portion of your first finger joint directly on the trigger. So you can anticipate the time to reload, try to count your shots or your trigger pulls. If possible, you want to avoid shooting your gun dry.

If you're shooting with a handgun and your shots are hitting high, low or wide, it's most likely because you are allowing your wrist to flex when firing...because you are holding the gun with a weak grip...or because you are erratically snapping the trigger. Sometimes, in addition to being dangerous, a very wide trigger or a grooved trigger will also adversely affect accuracy.

With a shotgun, you may tend to shoot high from the hip position because your hand comes off the stock or your arms bend when you pull the trigger, and this allows the muzzle to elevate. You can compensate for this by aiming for the suspect's abdominal area, if he is at some distance. Buckshot

Double-action shooting requires a smooth trigger squeeze with any firearm.

tends to rise and thus should hit his chest area when it impacts. If you aim for his chest, as you would with a handgun, your shots may go over his head. Again, practice squeezing, not jerking, the trigger.

Perhaps the greatest impediment to your shooting, unless you've properly conditioned yourself for survival, will be your own mental attitude. Shooting at people is different from shooting at paper targets. You may balk at doing it. But remember: a humanistic attitude on your part at the wrong time can get you, your partner or some innocent civilian killed. If you are legally justified in shooting (an obvious prerequisite), then shoot. If you must take a life to save innocent lives, that is simply part of your job.

Multiple Adversaries

When you're confronted with more than one assailant—as happens to officers in at least 40 per cent of all armed encounters— you'll need to combine instinct shooting with the utmost expression of mental discipline. Extraordinary demands for your physical and emotional attention may come simultaneously from several suspects, placed perhaps at widely different angles, different ranges and/or different elevations. They're hard to deal with because your depth perception may be adversely affected by your excitement and stress. Yet you must force yourself to concentrate on one adversary at a time, no matter how briefly, and deliver the most destructive rounds you can to him before confronting the next. Multiple assailants are extremely dangerous not only because of the obvious tacical problems handling them presents, but because they tend to energize each other. Where one man alone might surrender, two or more together may give one another the "balls" to take you on, and to keep shooting even after you shoot back.

If conditions permit, you want to fire first at the suspect who presents the *greatest* or *most immediate* danger to you. Usually, that means the one with the largest caliber gun; facing one assailant with a sawed-off shotgun and another with a .38 Special revolver, for example, you're probably best off to take your chances with the .38 while you try first to knock out the shotgun. Sometimes, though, proximity becomes a factor; an assailant 2 feet away from you with a hunting knife may be of more immediate danger than a second assailant 20 yards away with a handgun.

You'll have to process this information at computer speed, or the purpose for selection will be nullified. The idea is to decide fast—and shoot. Don't become encumbered with mental processes... don't get "target fixation" on the first gunman and block out his partner(s).

Besides deciding whom to shoot first, you'll have to assess the confrontation in terms of how many shots to deliver before moving on to the next assailant. To the degree practical, you'll probably want to spread your risk. Hit the first suspect with a two-round burst, then engage the next most dangerous, then turn back to the first if he's still not down.

If there is no cover available and you must remain in the open, try to move like a gun turret on a tank or battleship when you shift your firearm from one assailant to the next. You are in the instinctive shooting crouch, arms locked at the shoulder, elbow and wrist. Keep your feet planted as they are, knees flexed. Now swivel your torso, head and arms as one unit from your flexed knees. You want to point your whole body trunk at the next suspect you're going to shoot.

This method of moving maintains the eye-gun-shoulder relationship necessary for good instinct shooting. If you swing your arms freely rather than moving them locked in place with your upper body, you risk swinging past your adversary and "overshooting" him, because your arms will be hard to stop directly on target.

With the "turret traverse," you can fire controlled rounds within a 180-degree arc with speed and accuracy, without moving your feet. If you need to turn in a wider angle, pivot; keep your weight on your strong-side foot and swing the other out and around you as you turn.

As in single-suspect confrontations, you'll want to fire as many of your shots as possible from behind cover. If you're not there when you first encounter your multiple adversaries, move there at your first opportunity. Good cover offers your best insurance against injury or death, and it will allow your more time for target selection and for reloading, too, if that becomes necessary.

Don't make assumptions about the number of adversaries you are facing. Those you see may not be the only ones present, and the ones you don't see right away may be the most dangerous. An off-duty officer was walking with his girlfriend in New York City when a civilian ran from a bank, shouting that it was being robbed. The officer told his girl to call for help. He then ran into the bank, where he saw two men with guns. He identified himself and ordered them to drop their weapons. Unknown to him, a third robber was standing behind the bank's entrance. As the officer concentrated on the suspects he saw, the third one killed him with one shot.

Center Mass

However many adversaries you face, you don't shoot to scare...you don't shoot to wound...you don't shoot to disarm. You shoot to *stop the action* of a threat being made to your life or someone else's. You want to get the suspect to cease his illegal attack as quickly and efficiently as possible. Whether he survives or dies from your rounds is not the consideration. Getting him stopped is.

Shooting at certain parts of his body will likely accomplish this goal more readily than shooting at other areas.

The area in which impacting bullets prove most devastating and immediately incapacitating is shaped like the letter T. The crossbar, 2 to 3 inches wide, extends across the forehead just above the eyes. The vertical portion, about the same width, runs down the center of the body to the lower stomach. In this zone lie the brain...the major blood vessels...the spine...and most of the vital organs—in short, the body's life-support structure.

A hit to a suspect's head is highly effective. A bullet of any caliber to the brain will undoubtedly produce the greatest and most instantaneous incapacitation. But the head constitutes a relatively small target. Also, the suspect can easily and instinctively move it out of your line of fire by bobbing, ducking or weaving if he sees your muzzle pointing at it. Even at ranges as close as 3 feet, you'll likely miss if you aim for the head.

Some theorists argue that the best spot to shoot is the suspect's abdominal cavity, because slugs punching into him there will cause him to "relax" and pitch forward. Practical experience indicates that that concept definitely is more theoretical than realistic. Shooting to this area does threaten the bladder, the lower intestine, some important arteries and veins and may also shatter the pelvis. But the shocking and incapacitating effect is likely to be slower than you can afford.

If you are using *large* caliber bullets, say in the .45 semi-automatic range, a wound in a nonvital area *may* be fatal through a phenomenon called "hydrostatic shock." Because the body is composed largely of water and because liquids are noncompressible, the shock of a high-velocity entry by a large bullet can be transmitted throughout the body, in a wave of pressure. This may cause widespread organ damage, disruption of the nervous system and even death.

Still, *the best place to shoot for maximum stopping power is "center mass,"* the portion of the T that crosses your assailant's chest area.

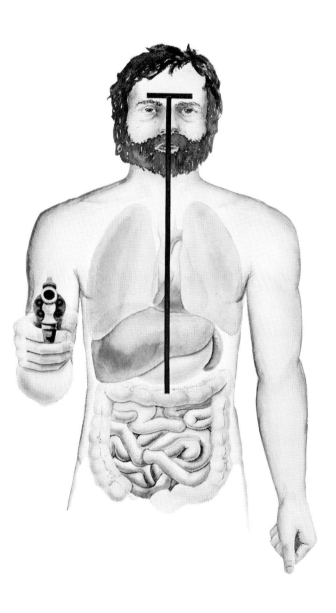

The "T" zone, 2 to 3 inches wide, spans above the eye brows and intersects in the middle with an imaginary line which extends to the navel.

Usually, hits to the center mass area are the most devastating because they penetrate vital organs and shatter bone.

The sooner you are able to cause major interference with a suspect's life-support structure—by directly puncturing vital organs, shattering bones or by inducing profuse bleeding—the quicker he is likely to collapse. This will probably require more than one shot and may take many, depending in part on the efficiency of your weapon and ammunition.

Some officers make the mistake of shooting once and then waiting to see what the round is going to do. It may miss entirely. Statistically, most bullets fired in gunfights do just that. Or your shot may have freak consequences. A New York officer recalls firing on a suspect who tried to rob him after duty early one morning. They were no more than 2 feet apart, and the officer assumed his bullet hit the suspect's abdomen and relaxed after shooting. Actually, it struck the cylinder of the robber's revolver, leaving him able to flee before the bewildered officer could get off effective fire. And even if your first shot hits, it may do little more than just get the suspect's physical defense system reacting, especially if he's high on drugs or in some other altered mental state. Of course, you try to make the first round count, but you should *not* be trying for the single, perfect shot. Instead, you should be reacting, subconsciously, to this question: *"How many rounds can I get into him before he kills me?"* As a *minimum*, it's wisest to fire two shots in rapid sequence; two bursts of two shots each will deliver even more incapacitation.

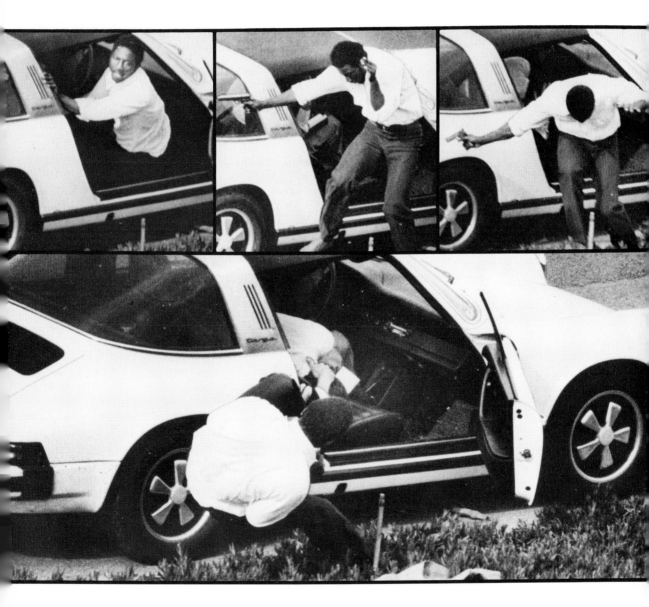

Unique series of photographs of a kid-
napper who barricaded himself in his
car with a hostage, then leaped out to
open fire on the police. Notice the
body's tendency to go back slightly,
then the upper torso moves forward as
the body falls to the ground. As these
moments were captured on film, the
offender was shot with multiple rounds
to the head and chest.

The upper torso is likely to be his biggest body region and take longest for him to move, so aiming there offers you the best chance of hitting as well as incapacitating him. You want to look directly at the center of his body, at about armpit level, halfway between his breast nipples, where you want the bullets to hit. As they slam home, he may move backwards in reaction to the pain, throwing him off balance for delivering effective return fire. Perhaps most important, shots to his center mass are likely to prove doubly devastating to his vital organs. Going in, there's a good chance your bullets will shatter one or more bones. Sharp fragments of bones will fly out inside his body at the same velocity with which your bullets hit. This internal "shrapnel" will contribute to the impact and to the severity of his wounds and his rapid incapacitation.

However many shots are necessary, you should keep shooting—fast and accurately—until the suspect ceases being a threat. If he's armed and determined to shoot, every second he's on his feet and able to respond brings you closer to death. Try to count your shots so you can anticipate the need to reload, and move behind cover if your are not already there.

Note: If center mass shots have no effect on the suspect, he may be wearing body armor. Many officers believe that bulletproof vests can be sold only to law enforcement personnel, but in fact no federal or state law prohibits the sale to anyone with the money. Use of body armor by criminals dates back to the days of John Dillinger and Baby-Face Nelson. Some suspects today fashion their own chestplates out of fiberglass boat repair kits; others buy vests through military surplus stores. Where a suspect appears armored, superior firepower may still bring him down. In Detroit, a gunman wearing body armor shot it out with police, wounding one officer. The suspect was finally killed by a volley of .30 cal. carbine fire which pierced his handgun-rated vest. With conventional weapons, consider shooting at the suspect's head or, more practically, shooting low. Shots at or below the waist can be fatal, as witnessed by the fact that nearly ten per cent of the officers killed in an average year are shot there. If nothing more, you may break the suspect's hips or pelvis or knock his legs out from under him. In California, an assailant who killed two detectives with a .45 cal. semi-automatic carbine while he was shielded by a bulletproof vest was finally cut down by a sheriff's deputy who got into position where he could fire at the suspect's back. From that angle, one blast from a shotgun did the job.

Ricochet Shooting

In some cases, you may not have to fire directly at an assailant to hit him, because of the ricochet or "bouncing bullet" phenomenon. As we've seen in discussing cover, slugs can glance off hard surfaces and cause serious injury. While you want to protect yourself from being wounded by such fire, it's something you may be able to use to your advantage against a suspect. For example, ricocheting your shots off a wall if he's shooting from a doorway farther down...or off the pavement under a car if he's behind it...or off a sidewalk if you've already dropped him but he's still firing at you from a prone position may be the surest way to deliver bullets that will finally stop the action.

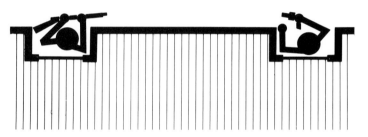

Ricochet shooting works against any hard surface. [You are positioned on the left.]

As you adjust your position while maintaining cover, shoot to impact the surface at less than a 45° angle.

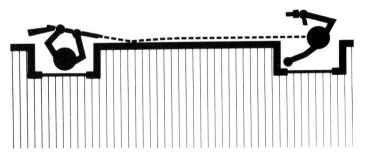

The bullet will then flatten out and travel between 1 and 8 inches off the surface until impact with the armed suspect.

In each of these circumstances, the suspect is a difficult target. You may be able to see only a small portion of him, like his head and shooting arm sticking out of the doorway or his legs under the vehicle. Or, if he's close to the ground or proned out, his position may effectively make his body smaller. With so little to aim for, direct hits are tough. Ricochet shooting, for practical purposes, expands the target. Hit the wall, the pavement or the sidewalk at any point in front of and in line with his body and the bouncing slugs will travel the rest of the way to him.

That's because lead deflects off a hard surface differently than does a rubber ball. A ball bounces off at the same angle at which it impacts. But slugs or buckshot tend to flatten out from the force of hitting and then fly in a slightly erratic manner at a very low angle above the surface.

You can see evidence of this at most indoor firing ranges. Usually as a backstop to targets a range uses heavy steel armor plate, tilted at about a 30- to 60-degree angle. Bullets strike the plate and ricochet down into sand or a bullet trap. If you look at the bottom of the backstop where the deflected rounds end up, you'll notice that they land close to the steel plate. In other words, their angle of deflection has been very slight.

The same holds true off hard surfaces like you'll encounter on the street. Occasionally, a freak "flyer" behaves differently, but most handgun bullets and buckshot will skim along from the point of initial impact to where they finally connect with your target with a deflection of no more than 1 to 8 inches off the surface (assuming there's not some defect in the surface that interferes with the flight). The harder the surface, the less the deflection. Because the slug flattens out, it tends to make a more devastating entry when it does hit the suspect, although it will have lost some velocity after impacting with the hard surface.

To deliver ricochet rounds, you use the same instinct shooting grip and aim that you do for direct shots. Some officers think they get the best results by aiming for a spot on the wall or ground about two-thirds of the way between them and the assailant. However, the ideal angle will depend on the surface and the type and velocity of the rounds you're using. Consequently, you'll want to practice using your gun(s) and ammunition off a variety of surfaces to develop an approach that's best for you. For your practice sessions, you can use balloons or cardboard silhouettes to simulate armed suspects.

Normally, we think of ricochet shooting working off concrete, asphalt, bricks or other rock-hard,

To deliver ricochet rounds, you use the same instinct shooting grip. Notice the officer's position relative to cover.

nonporous surfaces. But it may also work off turf, flat packed sand, even still water or ice under certain conditions. The effective range usually is up to 25 yards or a bit more. If you try and bounce bullets into a suspect much beyond that, results become erratic and the ricochet effect is of little reliable value.

Some rangemasters think ricochet shooting is only a gimmick. But applied properly, it has a reputable place among your survival options. Occasionally, when there's an obstacle between you and the suspect, bouncing bullets may allow you your only shot at him...or innocent people in the vicinity may make direct shots unsafe. Of course, you should *not* consider ricochet shooting a proper substitute for well-aimed, direct fire in all or even most armed encounters.

And you want to remember that assailants, as well as officers, sometimes know this tactic. That's one reason proper cover is so important. In a small midwestern town, for example, a uniformed officer approaching a liquor store where a burglar alarm was ringing was confronted by two suspects who bolted out of the front door. The officer dove to the pavement and assumed a prone position, from which he yelled, "Police! Halt!" One of the burglars fired at the concrete 6 feet in front of the officer. The slug ricocheted and slammed into the officer's skull, just below the bill of his hat.

Ricocheted bullets can bounce off walls as well as pavement. Consequently, you want to avoid positioning yourself near any wall in such a way that the surface can be used for ricochet fire by a suspect against you.

Sometimes suspects' guns achieve this effect strictly by accident. In a western city, a detective fired at a fugitive who had drawn a semi-automatic after being cornered in a modern steel-and-concrete building. The officer's shot hit the suspect, and he stumbled backward. Reflexively, he fired at the tilted concrete floor several feet in front of the detective. The bullet ricocheted up and severed an artery in the officer's thigh, causing his death. Again, proper cover in all probability would have deflected the bouncing bullet and assured the officer's survival.

Muzzle Flash

When you fire a shot, an incandescent burst of light flares out of the space between the cylinder and the barrel and also from the muzzle. This so-called

Muzzle flash during even daylight hours can be seen at a distance.

"muzzle flash" is caused by the sudden release of high energy gaseous powder particles as the bullet blasts out of the chamber and exits the end of the barrel. Under adequate lighting conditions, you'll hardly notice it. But in the dark or in dim light, its sudden, accentuated vividness may seriously affect your proficiency, both by startling you and by briefly destroying your night vision.

By anticipating muzzle flash and getting yourself accustomed to it through night-firing practice, it will come as less of a disconcerting surprise. Then you'll be in a good position to use this phenomenon to your advantage.

If, for example, you're up against an armed burglar inside a warehouse where the light is so bad you can't see him, try throwing something away from where you're standing to draw his fire. Then watch for the muzzle flash from his gun to position him. For an instant, the flash will partially silhouette him. Afterwards, even if you can no longer see him, you still may be able to hit him. You will only shoot, of course, if you are positive of your identification of the suspect.

Shoot on both sides of where you saw the flash, firing first just slightly to the right. Because most people are right-handed, that's where his center mass is likeliest to be, if he hasn't moved since firing. In the dark, with only muzzle flash as a guide, most people tend to shoot high, so consciously keep your shot slightly down. A high shot is worthless, but a low shot might at least produce an effective ricochet.

Remember, a smart suspect may try to use your muzzle flash to his advantage. If you're not in a good protected position, try to move to one as soon as you shoot. If no cover is available, at least try to shift location after each series of shots to thwart his hitting you by firing at your flash. An untrained or poorly trained shooter or one who doesn't practice much has a tendency to jerk the trigger, and this, in turn, sends his shots to his left. That may well be the case with a suspect. So on the good chance he'll shoot to your right (his left as he faces you) you're probably safest to move to your left after you fire. As you move to cover, keep low to increase the odds of his shooting over you.

Unpredictable Reactions

Among the least predictable aspects of a gunfight are what the reactions of yourself or the suspect will be if hit. In either case, your survival may be directly affected. Where the suspect is concerned, rounds that should drop him may not; he may keep going—firing back—with a stamina that defies credibility. By contrast, you may succumb to a relatively minor wound that should be "survivable," unless you are prepared psychologically for the physical and emotional impact of being shot.

Medical researchers have established that nearly *20 per cent of the time, suspects who are shot will not be incapacitated by just one round,* even though they are fatally wounded. They're dead...they just don't know it! Some 13 per cent will keep going up to five minutes; nearly 7 per cent, even longer. In Philadelphia, an assailant was shot square in the heart—yet he managed to walk down a flight of stairs and open two doors before he collapsed. In New York, a suspect hit in the stomach, bladder and gallbladder ran three blocks before collapsing. Even multiple shots will not bring down some suspects. In Los Angeles, another suspect kept firing through *20 hits*, before the 21st finally dropped him. In another case, a suspect was shot 33 times with 9mm rounds before ceasing his threatening movement. Even hits from multiple shotgun rounds have failed to immediately stop some assailants.

Liquor store robber who was shot 33 times with 9mm rounds before becoming incapacitated.

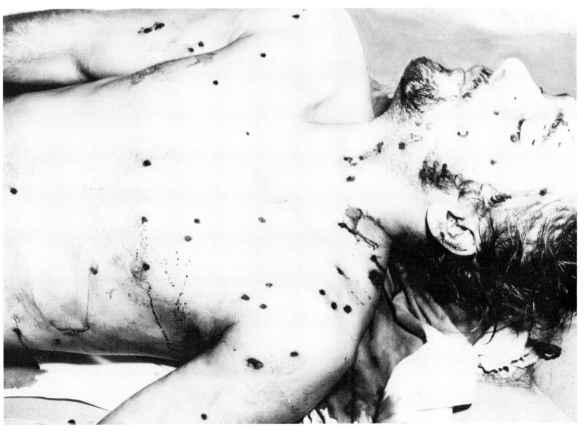

The damage a suspect can inflict during this so-called "ambulation after death" is substantial. In an attempt to thwart the robbery of a tavern, an officer shot one suspect in the chest and stomach and watched him fall to the floor. After lying motionless for a few seconds, the robber, to the officer's astonishment, scrambled back to his feet, grabbed the shotgun that had fallen from his hands and began shooting again. He killed the officer immediately and wounded several patrons of the bar before he finally died. During another tavern holdup in California, an off-duty sheriff's deputy who was a patron in the place shot a suspect in the chest, a wound that proved fatal eventually. But in the meantime, the robber engaged the officer in a struggle and managed to beat him to death with a sawed-off rifle.

In still another case, an officer emptied his .38 revolver at contact distance into the chest of a suspect who was trying to shoot him after having wounded his partner. The bullets broke several ribs, penetrated both lungs and punctured enough blood vessels to produce massive internal bleeding. Yet the suspect fell only temporarily and came back off the ground still clutching his 9mm semi-automatic. He pointed it directly at the officer to resume the gun battle. This officer saved his life because he was alert enough to use surprise. He dropped his own empty gun and lunged for the revolver on the belt of his wounded partner. With this weapon, he shot the suspect through the head, dropping him instantly.

Some officers blame their ammunition for shot suspects not falling when they should. It's true that in experimental testing the kinds of rounds used by many law enforcement agencies do not always display as much "stopping power" as some other commercially available ammunition; because they fail to "spread" or flatten out much as they travel through tissue, some traditional "police" bullets tend to penetrate too extensively, while not expanding in flesh and incapacitating. On the other hand, single shots of standard .38 Special handgun ammunition, like that carried by innumerable officers, have killed 350-pound bears, whose weight and body mass far exceed those of most suspects.

There's probably less hard information available about bullet effectiveness and potential on the human body than about any other facet of ballistics. Experts can measure velocity, range, trajectory and answer some other questions about bullet performance with a high degree of accuracy and professionalism. But when it comes to how a man or woman will react when shot, too many variables are involved for pat answers. The idea that a "heavy" round like a .45 cal. bullet, will spin a suspect around and knock him down even if it strikes him on the thumb is pure myth. No handgun bullet will do that. In addition, you have to remember that while a larger, heavier bullet may perform its intended task more efficiently, it will also give you a harder recoil, louder muzzle blast and brighter muzzle flash—all of which may adversely affect your accuracy, the most important factor in whether a bullet does its job.

Multiple shots to the suspect's center mass are your best hope of producing instant collapse, whatever factory ammunition your department specifies. However, *no* pattern of injury is *guaranteed*. Suspects with identical damage to the same vital organs have responded radically differently. Factors other than bullets' impact may temporarily dominate—and the problem seems to be getting worse.

For instance, you're more likely today than say ten years ago to confront an assailant who's jacked up on drugs, including powerful hallucinogens and PCP. These people, along with the steadily proliferating number of drunks and psychos, very often fail to react to bullets like they "should". Frequently, their sensitivity to pain is dulled, allowing them to absorb an unbelievable amount of it. At the same time their altered consciousness may imbue them with enormous strength to keep going. Even normal suspects may draw great staying power just from the adrenalin and steroids that rush into their bloodstream automatically during an alarmed state.

One argument for officers making greater use of the shotgun in armed confrontations is that its superior destructiveness will instantly bring down the assailant in a greater percentage of cases. Yet some suspects have managed temporarily to withstand being hit even with a rifled slug fired from a 12 ga. shotgun, considered the ultimate in power in police weaponry.

The lesson here is clear: any firearm you're using may not do what you think it will. *Don't bet your life on a suspect reacting the way he's supposed to when you shoot him.* AND NEVER ASSUME HE'LL REACT LIKE SUSPECTS DO ON TELEVISION. Be prepared to *keep on firing* until he ceases to be a threat, even if you've already hit him with "fatal" rounds.

Just as you prepare for the suspect's reaction to being shot, you want to prepare for your own so you don't overreact. Some officers seem to be conditioned to believe that if they are hit during a gunfight that automatically means they must die. Police surgeons tell of those who simply abandon the fight and succumb to wounds that are superficial and should not have been fatal, like the Illinois officer who fell down and died after being shot in the arm with one .22 cal. bullet. What doctors call "psychosomatic death"—that is, sudden death in which emotional states like hopelessness, helplessness and feelings of abandonment are primary contributing factors—is being increasingly recognized as a significant factor in officer killings.

The effects of traumatic shock, stress and fear when you are shot can be profound and can, of course, do strange things to your body. Not all are within your ability to control. Nonetheless, *a positive mental attitude* can have a remarkable influence on your survival. *Because you are shot, even in a critical area, does not necessarily mean you will die.*

If you are hit, try to keep on fighting back. A sense of purpose and a strong will to survive will help you stay alive. When the smoke clears and you can assess the damage, your wound may not be as bad as you thought—particularly if, by sticking with the encounter and marshalling the survival tactics you've trained to use, you are able to incapacitate the suspect and prevent him from hitting you again.

Don't fall into the trap of assuming that because you are hit, the suspect will stop shooting. Trying to play possum or hoping that you'll be left for dead or given mercy if you go down are risky games. In fact, once you fall and stop shooting, the suspect is more likely to try to finish you off. Two New York City incidents illustrate this point vividly. In one, two patrolmen were shot from behind by two members of a black revolutionary group. As one officer lay on his back, wounded, he raised his arms and pleaded, "Don't kill me!" The suspects shot him 13 times. In the second case, two other officers fell wounded in an ambush. The suspects then approached and deliberately shot the eyes out of one fallen officer and shot the other twice in the genitals.

If you don't already have your firearm in hand when you are wounded, you want to draw it immediately. You should practice so that you can draw your sidearm with either hand, from any position, including lying on your face or back.

Never give up! Instead, *act* to survive.

RELOADING
UNDER FIRE

Based on statistics, it would seem that reloading is not an important part of gunfights. The *average* confrontation is over before either side fires even as many as three rounds, and only about four per cent of officers in shoot-outs ever find it necessary to reload under fire; the closer the encounter, the less the chance that reloading will become a factor. For gamblers, these odds might be reassuring. But part of conditioning yourself for survival is learning to cope with the exceptional as well as the common-place.

All the statistics belittling reloading won't help you a bit if, like an unfortunate minority of officers, you have to expend more than the "average" number of rounds during a long foot chase or all-out firefight or against one or more well-protected assailants—and still face an adversary who's unhit and firing back when there's nothing left in your own gun to shoot. Whether it's "supposed to happen" or not, when it does *you're better off with a sack full of rocks than standing there with an empty gun.*

The faster your recovery rate—the speed with which you can replenish your ammunition and get back on target—the stronger your chances of emerging from the confrontation alive. For the action doesn't come to a halt while you reload; indeed, it may escalate to a new and more dangerous level.

While you're out of commission:

- the suspect may change locations. If you're distracted with reloading, you may not be able to find him immediately when you're ready to start shooting again. And he may have moved to a vantage point where he can kill you with his next round;

- he may rush you. In a street battle with a burglar, an Ohio officer crouched behind his patrol car to reload. The suspect, who had been near the front of the car, ran around the side and attacked the officer from the rear, shooting him in the head;

- he may get a good "free" shot even without moving. A Georgia patrolman approaching the scene of a domestic disturbance got into a gunfight with a suspect who was armed with a .22 cal. rifle. The officer was away from his patrol car when the shooting started and was pinned down by the suspect's fire so he couldn't get back. But with his .38 cal. revolver he managed to keep the assailant so off balance that he missed consistently, even with his superior weapon...until the officer had to reload. In that momentary pause, the suspect got the one good shot he needed. He killed the patrolman with a bullet to the chest.

Efficient Recovery

There are ways to reload that minimize such risks while maximizing recovery efficiency. Some of the mechanical procedures vary, depending on the type of firearm you're using. But regardless of the gun, there are certain survival principles regarding reloading you will want to follow whenever possible:

1. As a general rule, *try to reload during a "tactical pause"* or break in shooting and especially before you advance your position. Even if the ammunition in your gun is not all expended, consider using any lapse to get your gun full again; there may not be another opportunity, and it's better to choose your reloading time than to be forced into it. Say, for example, you shoot two or three rounds at a suspect, who then runs into a residence or store and seizes hostages. After you position yourself to wait for back-up, you want to reload so when the action resumes your gun is full. During a pause in the shooting, you can slip in a new magazine with a semi-automatic. With a revolver, eject

all the cartridges in your gun—live and empty—on the ground and load in all fresh rounds. If there is no tactical pause, shoot until you are out of ammunition, then reload immediately, whether your adversary is still standing or not. Whatever the circumstances, dump your spent shell cases directly on the ground; that's fastest.

2. *Communicate with your partner*, if you have one. Ideally, you want to avoid running out of ammunition and being "down" at the same time. Through prearranged signals, you may be able to swap off on reloading, provided, of course, that you each count your shots and know where you stand in terms of remaining rounds. With preplanning, you may even be able to con the suspect. If, by practiced arrangement, you both yell, "I'm out!" at the same time, when it isn't true, the suspect may think he has a free shot. He may then come out in the open to attack, allowing the hit you need to end the confrontation.

3. *Reload behind cover*, or at least in a concealed position, especially if your gun is a revolver. A "wheel gun" requires a longer recovery rate, which means a longer period in which your assailant can shoot at you with impunity. You need a good barricade to shield you.

4. *Reload by feel* so that all the time you're filling up you can *keep your eyes on the suspect* or the suspect's location, not on your firearm. Any move he is able to make without your surveillance can only work to your disadvantage. If you keep your eyes focused on where you want to hit him, you'll be ready to shoot as soon as you have live rounds. Also, if you keep the elbow of your gun hand touching your side, it will help you sense exactly where your gun is.

Swift, effective reloading requires that you combine shrewd tactics with manual dexterity. Here are some of the things you need to know to pull it off, tailored to the type of firearm on which your life depends.

Revolver

Getting fresh ammunition into a revolver is more complicated and difficult than with either a semi-automatic or a shotgun. To fire your last shot from a revolver...dump your cases...fully reload and fire again may take you 10 seconds or more, depending on the type of cartridge carrier you use. While

Unloading a revolver efficiently will make you feel confident about maintaining your gaze in the direction of the armed suspect.

you're reloading, your gun is inoperable. With the cylinder swung open, it's extremely vulnerable to dirt, mud, slush and other foreign objects...and you are literally defenseless. You don't want to panic when faced with a reloading situation...but you do want to hurry.

To unload, open the cylinder as soon as you decide to reload, whether or not you have fired your last round. Hold the gun in your weak hand with your palm under the trigger guard and curve your two middle fingers around through the frame so they rest on the cylinder. This will keep the cylinder from closing. Now invert the gun so the barrel is straight up. Place your thumb on the tip of the ejector rod...trigger finger around the barrel...and your little finger over the hammer or behind the hammer spur. This gives you a firm grip on the gun; even if you trip or fall, you can retain it. While stabilizing the cylinder with the tips of your middle fingers, rapidly eject the spent cases with a single downward stroke of the rod. If you keep the gun vertical, the cases will eject cleanly without hanging up or catching on the gun grip on their way out. *Let all the brass fall directly onto the ground.* Some officers have been killed because they took extra time to catch the ejected cases and put them in their pockets, as they'd done when shooting targets on the range. As you're moving your revolver into position for ejecting the spent rounds, your strong hand should be reaching for fresh ammunition.

For reloading, you'll be getting your fresh ammunition from one of three primary types of cartridge carrier: belt loops...dump pouches...or speed loaders. Each has unique advantages and disadvantages that will influence your reloading capability. The type you use will depend on the functional trade-offs you are willing to accept (or that your department is willing to accept for you).

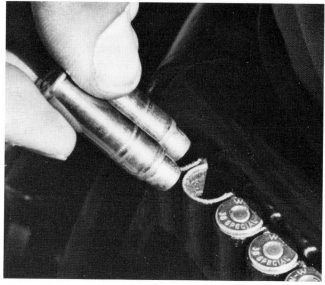

For speed, two cartridges at a time should be activated from the cartridge carrier by pushing them up from below. Then grasp the cartridges by the primer end.

If you use a vinyl speed strip, make sure it is grasped properly for easy removal. The speed strip will load two cartridges at a time.

Reloading either with belt loops or the dump pouch requires nimble fingers. Leather loops provide dependable access to additional ammunition, and they allow you a choice of how many rounds to remove from your ammunition carrier for reloading. Loops may be hard to draw from, though, when your fingers are sweaty, cold or trembling. You can make the job easier by pushing the cartridges up in the loops from below as your first reloading step. Push up every other cartridge, or all six. Either way, with practice, you can learn to grasp two rounds at a time, rock them up and out of the loops together and chamber them simultaneously. Still, there's a lot of repetitive back-and-forth motion to get the cylinder full. Also belt loops allow your ammunition to be exposed to the weather and elements. Unless your cartridges are changed frequently, a green corrosion may build up on the metal, making them difficult to draw from the loops.

When unsnapping a dump pouch, cup your fingers so cartridges won't fall out prematurely.

As the dump pouch is lowered, all the cartridges should fall easily into your hand.

With the dump pouch, you get six bullets in your hand at once, often facing diverse directions. You have to position them properly before you can load. Moreover, a dump pouch is hard to activate properly should you be in a prone position. Leather loops may provide a more dependable access to additional ammunition. They allow you a choice of how many rounds to remove. Also, with a dump pouch, you'll probably need 12 to 14 seconds to reload. Taking two at a time from belt loops, you can fill up in about 10 seconds. Because every second you take means more exposure to risk, it's essential to shave time where you can.

To reload once you have one or more loose rounds, either from loops or a pouch, ready in your fingers, retain the grip you had on your revolver for unloading and tilt the muzzle toward the ground at about a 45-degree angle. The palm of your weak hand should be cupped under the cylinder to catch any cartridges that drop. With the thumb and middle finger of that hand, grasp the cylinder. You want your thumb and finger in adjacent grooves; that will help you judge where the cartridge goes, since each cylinder opening lies between grooves. As you rotate the cylinder with thumb and finger, you load the ammunition with your strong hand. When you're finished, close the cylinder and resume your firing position.

Some gunfight veterans insist that the fastest carrier for fully reloading a revolver is the round speed-loader, which holds six cartridges in position for simultaneous insertion into a cylinder. With practice, a speed-loader can cut your recovery rate to three seconds or less—almost as fast as changing magazines in a semi-automatic. Also, the advocates of speed-loaders say, these devices will allow you to reload smoothly, with minimum hand movement, in the dark...when you are running or crawling...with gloves on...when the weather's so cold you can't feel your fingers, much less your ammunition. Critics argue that it's difficult to reload with a speed-loader without closely watching what you are doing in order to line up six cartridges simultaneously, especially in the fear and tension of a gunfight situation. With extensive practice, however, you can master this technique so your eyes won't have to be diverted from watching the suspect in order to watch your gun. It's no more difficult than learning to type without looking at the keys. Like other methods of reloading, speed-loaders are gravity dependent. If you're on your back, they won't work well. You have to get into a position where you can point the muzzle of your gun down perpendicular, so the rounds will feed straight in when you push or twist the cartridge release. Be careful not to drop the loader as you reach for it with your strong hand. Some types will spill their cartridges if dropped, forcing you then to draw your spare revolver or to reload from the ground. Again, know your equipment thoroughly before you get into a situation where your life depends on your operating it at top speed. Also, take care not to activate the cartridge release *before* you've fitted the bullet noses into the chambers. This has happened to officers under stress or by accident when they stumbled or fell in pursuit of a suspect. The cartridges then are lost, instantly. Once the cartridges are in your gun, toss the speed-loader aside. You can recover it later, after the action is over; don't take time under fire to put it in your pocket or back in its carrying case.

Whatever type of ammunition carrier you use, you'll need to reload strictly *by feel*, not by looking down. Partly that's to make you proficient in the dark, when you may have trouble seeing your gun,

If you carry speed-loaders, use a double leather case and practice opening the snap for efficient removal.

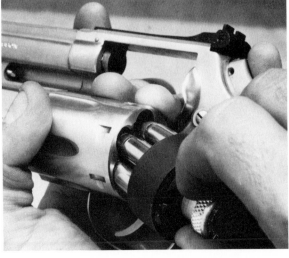

Many officers assure themselves that the six rounds will load properly by touching one of the bullets against its cylinder hole at a slight angle. This contact then becomes a guide for all the cartridges to enter the cylinder directly.

hands and ammunition and when use of a flash-light for reloading would only silhouette you as a target. More important, working by touch alone lets you keep your eyes on your assailant or his location at all times. To facilitate this continuous surveillance, you should face toward him through-out your recovery period.

You may want to consider bringing your revolver up to eye level with your elbows touching your side, while you reload. This allows you to see what you're doing while still watching the suspect in your peripheral vision. However, this position increases the time it takes to get new ammunition from its carrier to the cylinder and also increases the risk that you'll drop some enroute. If you're practiced enough, you're better off with the gun at belt level, as close to the ammunition source as you can get it. What your fingers are doing should be automatic; your mind and eyes should be free to concentrate on the suspect(s) and the action you're facing.

When cartridges are loaded, always make sure that the cylinder closes properly.

Where you are using some method other than speed-loading, *you may not want to reload a full cylinder* under certain circumstances. If you're out of ammunition but under fire...behind poor cover... or your assailant is coming at you, your survival savvy may dictate that you quickly dump your empties...load only one to three fresh cartridges...and get back in action. *Don't get cut down loading a sixth round in your gun.* That's exactly what happened to a western highway patrolman; just as he finished loading the last round, his assailant, who had been watching, shot him in the head. If he'd loaded only two, chances are *he* could have been the one to surprise the suspect.

Proper technique for reloading a revolver one-handed.

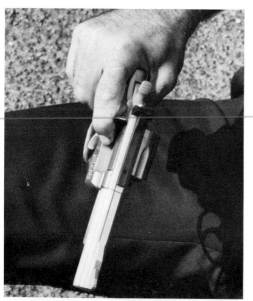

1

2

3

4

With partial reloading, the position of the cylinder holes you fill will be important. Ideally, when you close the cylinder, you want your ammunition positioned so that a *live round comes under the hammer the first time* you pull the trigger. That means you have to know the direction in which your cylinder rotates; otherwise you may have to stroke the trigger several times to move a round into detonating position, and this can cost you time. Smith & Wesson cylinders rotate *counterclockwise*; you want to load these high on the *right* side. Colt cylinders turn *clockwise*; load them high on your *left*. If you're using a revolver from another manufacturer, know how your cylinder rotates.

You can reload a revolver one-handed. This is convenient if one hand, arm or shoulder has been disabled by hostile fire or some other injury and also if you need to reload while driving. You activate the cylinder lock and force the cylinder open with your good hand. Stick your thumb through the frame to keep the cylinder from closing and use your trigger finger to plunge the ejector down and dump your expended rounds. Stick the barrel of the empty gun into your waistband, with the cylinder open and away from your body. The ejector rod should be outside your belt to help hold your gun. Load with your free or good hand, close the cylinder and you're set.

Here, too, there may be circumstances in which one-handed reloading will surprise your adversary. One officer, for instance, entered a warehouse during a nighttime prowler call and was immediately fired upon by an assailant perched somewhere up high. Zigzagging between crates and piles of merchandise, he finally located the shooter, far up in the rafters. Directly beneath him was a steel ladder leading to his location. In the gloom the officer managed to reach it without being seen, but in the process he shot his revolver dry. On the way up the ladder, he stuck the gun in his waistband, loaded in three cartridges and waited, hanging on a rung. Momentarily he heard his assailant starting down the ladder to look for him. The officer fired three rounds with deadly accuracy at the startled suspect from a distance of about 8 feet.

When you're able to choose your location for reloading, try to load over an area that will provide some cushion for your cartridges should you drop any. There have been instances where bullets have exploded from the primer falling on hard or rough surfaces, like concrete or pebbles.

Also, for safety reasons, *keep your finger outside the trigger guard* at all times while unloading and reloading.

Never reholster an empty gun. When the shooting is over and you reload your gun to return to duty, be sure you *load the cylinder fully.* On the range, you may load only five rounds to make scoring easier. On duty, too, some officers use a five-round load so they can carry the gun with an empty chamber under the hammer. Actually, there's no safety benefit to this if your gun's in good working order, plus it reduces the number of rounds you have available in a shoot-out. One midwestern detective who habitually loaded only five rounds in a six-shot revolver was making an entry in his notebook in his unmarked car one night when a suspect suddenly appeared from between two buildings and ordered him out of the car at the point of a .38 cal. snub-nose. The officer complied and was forced to lie on the ground while the offender went through his pockets, taking his money and his badge. Before he could grab the detective's gun, a witness in one of the buildings knocked on the window, the robber became startled and ran. The officer chased him down the street and fired four shots along the way, then ran into an alley after him and fired his last remaining round. With the next trigger pull, the firing pin clicked into the sixth—empty—cylinder hole. With a "free" shot, the assailant killed the officer and fled in a waiting car.

Semi-Automatic

Probably the fastest firearm to reload fully is a semi-automatic.

For maximum streamlining, you want to anticipate reloading before you run dry and draw a spare magazine from your leather gear with your weak hand. You can hold this magazine alongside your weapon while your weak hand is in the support position for firing. This will somewhat lessen the support you're able to give your grip, but you'll be ready with fresh ammunition the instant you dump the old; you don't have to spend valuable seconds reaching for the replacement.

To change magazines, depress the magazine release button on your semi-automatic with your gun hand, while keeping the gun in shooting position and your eyes on the suspect. As the empty magazine falls out, bring the new one under the gun with your weak hand without looking down. Your forefinger should lie along the magazine's front edge, with your thumb at the back to guide it into the magazine well. Seat the new magazine firmly by tapping it into place with the heel of your weak hand. You don't need to slam it hard to get it to lock; in fact, doing so may damage the magazine and lead to malfunctions. If you've changed magazines before shooting dry, you are ready to resume firing immediately upon the new magazine being in place. On the other hand, if you shoot all your original rounds before changing, the slide will have locked to the rear after you fired your last cartridge, signaling that your gun is empty. With the new magazine in place, you'll need to release the slide with the thumb of your gun hand and let it fly foward into firing position before you shoot again.

The proper weak-hand placement of a fresh magazine prior to speedloading a semi-automatic.

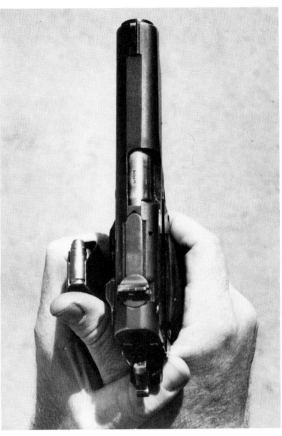

An advantage of *some* semi-automatics is that you can still fire even while reloading. So long as the slide remains forward on a semi-automatic, a round is chambered, even though you remove the magazine. With a Colt .45 semi-automatic, for example, you can shoot that one round without any magazine being in the well. If you do, though, you'll have to manually chamber a new round when the new magazine is inserted. Not all semi-automatics have this firing feature, however; Smith & Wesson models 39 and 59 and the Browning Hi-Power 9mm, for example, do not. Unless the magazine safety disconnect on these guns has been altered, they will not fire without a magazine in place even though there is a live round in the chamber. So *know your equipment*.

It takes longer to load a semi-automatic one-handed, but it can be done, if, for example, one of your hands is useless because it has been wounded. After you drop the old magazine, place the gun tightly between your knees, angled so that the muzzle is pointed down and away from you and the

Proper technique for reloading a semi-automatic one-handed.

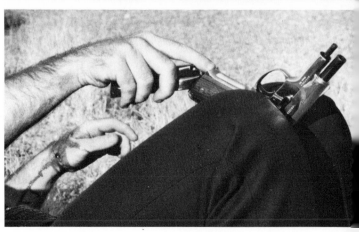

butt is up and out in front of you. Insert the new magazine and tap in into place with your good hand, then grip the gun with that same hand and return it to shooting position. With a quick press of the slide release, you're ready to go, having reloaded in about five seconds or less.

Note: If, to maximize the speed of reloading, you simply release the old magazine and let it fall to the ground, do *not* later replenish it with new ammunition and return it to your gun or magazine carrier without careful inspection. You want to be certain that the drop did not dent or crack the magazine or bend its lips. Such damage could result in feeding problems, if undetected.

Shotgun

When you take a shotgun into action you want to have at least ten rounds along, counting those already loaded in the gun plus extras. You can carry your spare ammunition in your weak-side pocket because under fire you'll reload with your weak hand. Or you can carry an "ammo sling" on the stock of the shotgun so you'll always have extras whenever you have the gun.

Count your shots. That will help you anticipate the need to reload. If possible, you want to avoid shooting the shotgun dry. In moments of tactical pause, you can load fresh shells into the magazine loading port underneath the gun. You can do this on the move...with the shotgun in the firing position, rather than straight up on your hip or cradled in your weak hand as in the conventional loading mode. That way, you don't have to move the muzzle off the suspect's position.

Working by touch with your eyes concentrating on the suspect, withdraw live cartridges from your weak-side pocket or sling one at a time. As you pull

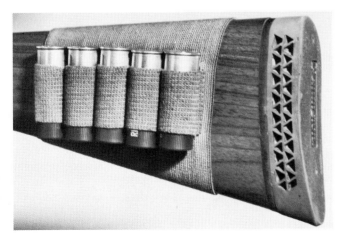

An accessory like this ammunition sling can be effective for speedloading the shotgun but only if it's positioned on the side nearest your body with the shells stored primer-end up.

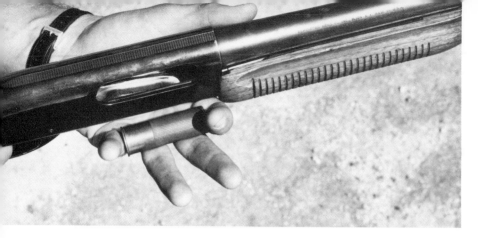

In speedloading a shotgun with a side ejection port, eject the last spent shell. Now cup the first shell in the curls of your fingers.

Now reach under the receiver to the open ejection port and insert the first shell.

Then pull the slide forward while you prepare to insert additional rounds. Your gaze remains in the direction of the suspect's location.

Additional shells are also loaded by feel, from underneath into the bottom loading port.

a round out, feel for the brass. You want the shell lying across the folds of your fingers, with the primer end resting against the inside of your little finger. If necessary, this allows you to grasp the foregrip of the shotgun and fire without dropping the shell.

Bring each shell under the gun, up against the forward end of the trigger guard, then slide it forward into the tube. Use your thumb to push every shell in until it is firmly seated.

If you should fire your last round before reloading, here's an option for getting back into action fast that will work on police shotguns featuring a side ejection port, such as Remington, Winchester, Hi-Standard, Mossberg and Smith & Wesson. After you shoot your last round, pull the slide back to eject the spent shell—but *do not* run the slide forward. This leaves the side ejection port open. Keeping the gun in the firing position and working by feel, bring your weak hand with the first live cartridge up under the stock receiver and press the shell into the open ejection port on the side. This way you are loading directly into the chamber. Then move the slide forward to rack the round in place, and you can fire immediately. If you're under attack, you can repeat this cycle: advance...shoot...eject... reload one shell, so long as you have spare ammunition. By loading four additional rounds into the magazine loading port underneath the gun, you can fill your shotgun with five live rounds, so in effect, you've gained an extra shot. (With the bottom-loading Ithaca brand, which some departments use, you can't load directly into the side ejection port because it doesn't have one. But you can still get live shells back into your gun without taking it out of a combat position by loading directly into the magazine loading port, as we've described, as soon as you shoot dry. Then rack the action. The last spent shell will eject and as you move the slide forward, a fresh round will chamber.)

Remember, though, if you lose count of your shots and unwittingly kick out the last shell and then run the slide forward on an empty chamber before reloading any shotgun, you'll have to pull the trigger and dry fire once or hit the slide release button on some models to be able to rack a live round in place.

Back-Up Gun

The fastest reload is a second gun. While you're not required to carry an alternate weapon, about 50 per cent of all officers do. It's good insurance—

provided you have practiced with your back-up gun to the point that you have the same proficiency with it as with your service firearm. Some officers simply carry a duplicate of their primary gun. The fact that both weapons mechanically operate the same aids proficiency; there's no need to switch tactics or thought processes as you switch weapons. Also, the same type of ammunition will fit both weapons. Most officers carry four-inch barrel revolvers as their primary weapon and choose the two-inch snub-nose as a back-up gun.

Typically, a back-up gun is used when you're out of ammunition or disarmed. It can also help you recover from a mechanical malfunction. Two Chicago officers responded to a call of "shots being fired on the street," and when they arrived they were fired on by the suspect. They took cover and returned fire. But on one officer's second shot, his .357 Magnum jammed. Later he learned that the firing pin was defective, but at the moment the malfunction caused him little concern. He holstered the revolver...immediately drew a .45 cal. semi-automatic from his second holster...and helped his partner quickly resolve the confrontation. In another instance, an officer approaching a grocery store where a robbery was in progress reached for his service revolver—and discovered his holster was empty. A defect in the holster had allowed the gun to slip out unnoticed while the officer was still in his patrol car, and it now lay yards beyond his reach between the seat and the door of the vehicle. Because he carried a second gun, a snub-nose .38, he was able to draw it from its holster and proceed with his approach, where his life otherwise might have been in considerable jeopardy.

Not to be overlooked is the possibility that a back-up gun can give you one more edge in using surprise against a suspect. More than once a suspect who *thought* an officer was reloading has decided to jump him. But instead of rushing a defenseless man, the suspect has rushed toward a back-up gun, which dropped him then and there.

FINAL APPROACH

The shooting's over...the smoke has cleared...
your assailant is down or seems ready to surrender.
Don't relax! You're entering one of the most dangerous phases of an armed encounter.

Even in incidents where there has been no
shooting—or even any evidence of firearms up to
now—your final approach for an arrest is fraught
with hazard. Year after year, the greatest number of
officers are killed during the period when they are
moving in and trying to take a suspect into custody,
regardless of what has gone before.

A small sampling shows just a few of the many
ways in which things can go wrong:

After a gun battle with a suspect who'd shot a
woman, officers kicked open the door of the bedroom from which he'd been firing and found him
lying on the floor, apparently dead. They relaxed
and holstered their guns as they walked toward him.
Suddenly he rolled over and came up with a revolver
in his hand. He shot two officers before the others
got back on target...At an emotion-packed shooting
scene, where an officer had just shot an assailant, a
back-up officer ran up to the body and grabbed the
suspect's .45 cal. semi-automatic, which was lying
by his side. "I've got the gun! It's all right now!"
he yelled—then, in his stress and excitement, he
inexplicably turned in the direction of other officers
and let loose two shots...In North Carolina, a small
town police chief arrested a man whom he'd found
in a suspicious car with a sawed-off shotgun.
Having recovered one weapon, the chief didn't

bother to look for others. The suspect had a second gun concealed in his clothing. He drew it and fatally wounded the chief in the shoulder...A state trooper successfully apprehended three jailbreakers single-handed in Arkansas and handcuffed them as they lay docilely face-down on the ground. His technique for handcuffing multiple suspects was improper though, and as he was getting the prisoners to their feet, one managed to draw a .357 Magnum and shoot the trooper dead...In Washington state, a young patrolman was placing a man under arrest in connection with a disturbance complaint when the suspect unexpectedly started to struggle. He grabbed the officer's service revolver and fired five fatal shots into him at close range...Undercover officers in Atlanta ordered three teenagers up against a van after spotting them breaking into autos. They appeared to be unarmed, but as the officers approached, one of the suspects whipped out a hidden handgun and sent a fatal shot blasting into one officer's head...In Texas, a sheriff's deputy arrested a teenager for burglarizing a service station, but failed to search him thoroughly before placing him in a patrol car. Enroute to the sheriff's office, the suspect drew a .22 cal. handgun, shot the deputy in the head and chest, then fled in his patrol car... Elsewhere in the southwest, a patrolman was trying to arrest a man on an outstanding traffic warrant. As he concentrated on this suspect, a second subject whom he hadn't seen rushed him from behind, knocked him to the ground and shot him fatally in the chest.

Sometimes a final approach snafu escalates on a giant scale. In a west coast university town, a middle-aged sergeant was trying to handcuff a prowler he'd arrested when the suspect started to scuffle. Before the incident finally ended, the suspect: grabbed the sergeant's .38 cal. service revolver...killed him with a shot to the head... was attacked with a hand axe by a civilian witness... shot and wounded the citizen...ran into a nearby residence, where he took two persons hostage...shot and killed one of the hostages, a four-year-old girl... and was eventually killed himself hours after the episode started, by one of the officers who surrounded the residence.

Much of the hazard of a final approach, of course, is built in. If you haven't been close to the suspect before, the final approach forces you there. The closer you come, the greater your chance of being injured or killed. Once you move within arm's length, you're in the zone where the most trouble occurs—and the most officers die. You're under pressure, too, to get the incident concluded; if you've been shot at by the suspect already, you naturally want to bring him fully under control before he can attack again, and if he hasn't yet presented threats of violence, you want to restrain him before he gets the idea to. There's much to do—disarm, handcuff, search, transport, perhaps deactivate dangerous weapons, deal with hostile crowds, preserve evidence. It's easy to get distracted. And if you have more than one suspect to deal with, your responsibilities, stress—and risks—are multiplied.

As with your initial approach to the scene, the first rule for surviving your final approach is: *do not rush*...don't be in a hurry to put your gun away...take your time. The action may not be over yet, and your gun will only serve you best if it's in your hand. Speed breeds carelessness and the inadvertent overlooking of lifesaving details.

In this photograph stands an unhandcuffed suspect who surrendered to police after he abducted his wife at gunpoint and assaulted a hospital therapist during the abduction. A search later revealed one .12 ga. shotgun and two semi-automatic pistols in his house. Which one is the offender?

If a suspect appears to be submitting, don't assume that he is. Appearances can be fatally deceptive. An officer sent to stop a bar brawl in Philadelphia positioned himself outside and ordered the participants to come out and surrender. One man, wearing a white apron, emerged with his hands behind his head. He looked compliant, but what the officer couldn't see when looking at the man head-on was that in one of his hands the suspect held a .45 cal. semi-automatic. A noise distracted the officer momentarily. The suspect whipped his hand down from behind his head, fired and hit the officer squarely.

A suspect's hands, as always, should be the focus of your attention, especially those you can't see. Some officers as they get close tend to look into a suspect's eyes. *His eyes can't kill you, but his hands might.* Keep track of what they're doing.

Remember, any arrest, even for the most insignificant offense, should be regarded as a potentially dangerous situation. An offender you're approaching because of a minor crime may be wanted for a serious offense elsewhere, or he may be mentally unstable and unpredictable.

There are a variety of tactical considerations you should be conscious of as you move in. If you've gotten this far without getting shot, the right procedures now can successfully carry you over this last tricky and perilous hump. For the remainder of this chapter, we'll assume there has been an armed confrontation or that you've seen a weapon, so you *know* the suspect you're approaching is dangerous. However, many of the same principles will apply in situations that seem nonviolent, also.

Disarming

Before you move out from behind cover, you want your assailant disarmed of any visible weapons. If you've shot him, he may have dropped his gun already. Otherwise, he may respond to verbal commands. As a first step, you want him to put his trigger finger outside the trigger guard. Then you want him to release his hold on the gun.

Often suspects are reluctant to drop a gun on a hard surface, especially if they've paid for it rather than stolen it. This will certainly be true where the "suspect" really is an off-duty or plainclothes officer. Also, some firearms, notably shotguns and certain semi-automatics, may discharge if dropped, exposing you to the risk of an unintentional hit. So you may do best if you order your assailant to lay down his gun *very slowly*. In Phoenix, police tried, unsuccessfully, to get a barricaded mental patient to drop his rifle out of a window. He'd just bought it and was concerned about getting it scuffed up. He finally did agree to wrap the gun in a towel and put it outside his door.

Once the suspect relinquishes his gun, have him (and any other suspects) take at least three steps away from it so it is out of reach. (This applies, incidentally, even where the suspect's weapon is not a firearm. Two Illinois officers spotted a man walking down a ghetto street with a seven-inch butcher knife in his hand. Four times they ordered him to drop it. Finally, he stuck it in a wall behind him. The officers, however, neglected to have him move away, and when they got close he grabbed the knife and tried to attack them. In this case, the suspect was shot; had his weapon been a gun, the outcome might have been much different.)

On issuing commands to the suspect, speak slowly and in short phrases so there will be no doubt that he understands your intentions. *Under no circumstances should you leave cover to accept a gun directly from a suspect.*

Incapacitation

A suspect is safest for you to approach if he's in a position that makes it difficult for him to struggle...try to grab your firearm...or to reach a hidden gun. If he's lucid enough to understand and follow orders and able to move, you can get him situated *before* you start toward him. If you're working with a partner or back-up, only one of you should give the orders. Tell the suspect first, *in summary*, what you are going to want him to do, but make clear he is not to move until you give the command and then do *specifically* what you say and *no more*. Let him know that if he disobeys, you'll be forced to take "appropriate action."

There are several positions in which a suspect's capacity to move will be limited. The traditional tactic is to use a wall or other vertical surface, like the side of a van. If you use this approach, choose a spot away from windows. The suspect may try to escape by plunging through a window or the glass may reflect your movements behind him. With the suspect facing the wall, order him to spread his fingers and place his hands against the surface about 3 to 4 feet apart. Then have him spread his legs and move his feet back 4 to 5 feet from the wall.

Searches should focus on controlling the hands. Yet with this position, consider the possibilities for the suspect to kick your groin, grab your hand or tell the suspect next to him to assault you or disarm you.

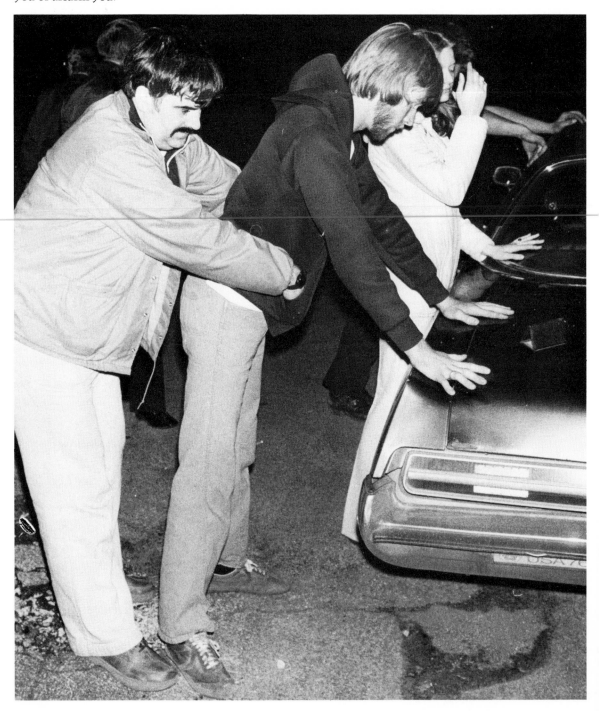

This slants his body at about a 45-degree angle from the wall, hampering quick movement on his part.

If you're out in the open, you can have the suspect kneel, facing away from you, with his fingers intertwined behind his neck or head. His right ankle should be crossed over his left. Again, this hampers any abrupt, major movement, and, as we'll see, gets him in a position where you can control him during your handcuffing and search. If you notice a gun stuck in the suspect's waistband while maneuvering him into this position, it's imperative that he not be allowed to move his hands from behind his neck. If he's a three-time loser, looking at a long prison term or the death penalty, he may try to go for the gun and take you out even with the odds heavily against him. From the kneeling position, tell him to fall forward without taking his hands down. Even if it knocks his teeth out, this may be the safest position for you.

Probably the all-around best position for temporarily incapacitating a suspect is to have him prone out. If he's against a wall, he may try to spin off, or if he's kneeling, he can still reach for a hidden gun. Prone, he has the least opportunity for movement. Order him face down on the ground, arms outstretched straight from his body, with his palms turned up. You want his head away from your intended route of approach. Try to get his head turned so his vision is fully blocked—like looking into a tire, rather than out at the perimeter of action. To the extent possible, you don't want him to know what you are doing...you don't give him any slack he might use against you.

Approach Position

As you move in close, you want to shift your gun out of the two-hand, instinct shooting hold. For close proximity, a gun out at your arm's length is an open invitation for a suspect to try to grab or kick it and disarm you.

As you get within 10 or 6 feet of the suspect, you should pull the gun back in your shooting hand and ''lock'' it in just above your hip. Your elbow will be bent and the heel of your hand touching your side between your lower rib and the top of your hip bone or gun belt. Only the gun's muzzle should extend out beyond your stomach. In this position, you can still fire ahead at close range or pivot to engage several suspects and be reasonably certain of hitting them in an effective spot. Also, this position leaves you a hand free to contact the suspect or shove him back if he lunges for you. You can advance with this hand up and ready, holding your handcuffs, which you take from their carrier on your weak hand side. Note: This hip or "close combat" position for your gun should be used *only* during the final approach period and *not* as a substitute for the instinct shooting positions more appropriate for other distances.

Try to approach so the suspect cannot observe your movements without turning and looking to find you. Order him to turn his face away from you. If he tries to look, instruct him firmly not to do so. If he's down, approach from his feet; it'll be harder for him to see you, and you'll have slightly longer to react if he tries to attack. Be extremely cautious if he has fallen with his gun still in his hand or within reach. *He may be faking death or serious injury.*

If possible, approach from an angle that lets you take advantage of available cover and that will give you a clear field of fire, without endangering innocent civilians or fellow officers. If you have to shoot, you want to concern yourself only with hitting the suspect and protecting yourself.

A suspect wanted in three homicides is approached by an officer making body contact with a shotgun. Maintaining a safe distance from any suspect avoids the possibility of your being assaulted or disarmed by a suspect who knows you're within range to receive a kick or grab the barrel of your firearm.

Always make it a rule to approach any suspect so he can't see your approach. How would you approach this armed suspect?

A suspect may try to talk to you, to explain his actions...heap on abuse...plead for a break...or ask questions. Tell him to *shut up*; refuse any request he makes. Chatter will tend to relax or distract you. You want *no unnecessary conversation* until after he has been secured and searched.

Above all, STAY ALERT. The suspect may have a hidden gun you haven't seen. *Do not take a verbal surrender at face value*, no matter how sincere it sounds or how badly wounded your assailant may seem to be.

Handcuffing

When you have a partner or work an approach with a back-up officer, he covers you as you move in, using an instinct shooting hold on his gun and making sure neither of you is in a cross-fire position. You give the orders and your partner remains quiet, except to warn you of danger. Even though he is covering, you keep your gun out, in the close quarters position, until you make physical contact with the suspect and bring his hand under control for handcuffing. In numerous cases, officers have been shot during a final approach, despite the presence of a partner. They think that with him providing cover, he'll do what needs to be done and drop their own guard.

If you're alone, you'll also want your gun drawn until time to cuff. You want it ready to fire, double-action...not cocked. You've possibly seen officers—at least the television actors who don't know too much about guns—place the muzzle of a cocked gun against the head of a suspect while they bring him under control. This is a highly dangerous tactic. A gun close to a suspect's body may encourage him to try to grab it. Moreover, a cocked firearm requires only a fraction of normal trigger pull to shoot; if the suspect moves or you slip, you could easily fire and kill him unintentionally. In one midwestern community, a narcotics investigator who allegedly used this tactic shot reflexively when a suspect butted backwards and hit him in the groin. The round fatally wounded the suspect. At this writing, the officer and his partner are facing a lawsuit of nearly $1 million, brought by the victim's family, charging excessive use of force and wrongful death. Sometimes it's the officer who ends up shot. In the stress of the moment, you may unwittingly return your gun to its holster cocked, where a hard blow or careless draw can cause it to fire.

When it is time to reholster your sidearm, do so without looking down at your gun, so you can

Putting a cocked revolver to the head of an arrestee like this purse snatch suspect increases your risk. You also want to avoid placing your firearm in reach of the suspect.

keep your eyes and attention fully on the suspect. Refasten the restraining strap and *remain aware of your gun*, even though it's no longer in your hand. ALWAYS keep your gun side turned away from the suspect to safeguard your firearm.

When you're alone and have your shotgun that you've taken into the confrontation, you'll be able to sling it over your shoulder if it has a strap, thus keeping it on your back and out of your way. Where this is not possible, your safest option is to unload the shotgun...move the slide to the open position... put the safety on...and lay the gun down where it can't be disturbed, while you handle your adversary. If bystanders or other factors make that impractical, your best bet probably is just to keep your assailant covered and under control until back-up help arrives.

The suspect who's down, either dead or injured, should be approached with the assumption he's still alive and dangerous. You and your partner should consider approaching him simultaneously, guns drawn, because with a suspect in this position, it's hard with only one of the officers approaching

When you and your back-up assume an "L" or right-angle position to a suspect, you minimize the possibility of a cross-fire situation. You're also making it difficult for the suspect to shoot both of you.

While a back-up officer provides cover, you approach the incapacitated suspect from a safe angle.

You step on his wrist to prevent any arm or hand movement which could result in a discharge.

to avoid a cross-fire situation. You want to come at him in an "L" position—one of you approaching from his feet, one from his side. With this deployment, each of you can shoot without hitting the other. If your assailant has his gun still in his hand, one of you should walk up on the side where the gun is, but never approach or stand so the muzzle is pointing at you. When you reach his side, step on his wrist hard to prevent any arm or hand movement that would enable him to shoot. Use your foot nearest his body for best balance. Holster your gun without dropping your eyes from the suspect. Make certain his gun is uncocked. Then use both your hands to twist it out of his fingers. Clamp your strong hand over the cylinder or slide to control the gun while simultaneously pulling his finger away from it with your weak hand. Once he's safely disarmed, handcuff him behind his back, search him thoroughly for other guns, unload the suspect's weapon(s) and then check for vital signs.

With a suspect who's kneeling or against a wall, you can approach alone with your partner covering in the "L" position. You want to use your feet in

After securing the suspect's firearm, you now step backward while maintaining a visual on the suspect's hands.

making physical contact. If he's spread against a wall, first place your non-gun hand between his shoulder blades and press down slightly. This puts additional pressure on the suspect and allows you to feel any attempt he might make to push off the wall and turn on you. Once your hand is in place, the traditional approach is to hook your right foot to the inside of his right one while you take control of his right hand. Should he try to push back from the wall, you can shove down hard between his shoulder blades, forcing his head into the wall, then quickly slide your hand down to his waistband and pull back hard, while simultaneously kicking his leg out from under him.

In a wall search you want to keep the suspect off balance with his feet spread wide apart with his body angled sharply to the wall.

Keep your sidearm in the close quarters position. Some departments also recommend the suspect's head be turned away from the side being searched, with his palms turned out.

After handcuffing, the suspect's head position against the wall plus his body angle give you control in moving him away at your command.

1

One kneeling arrest position begins with the suspect's gun placed on the ground with the suspect having taken three steps away from the gun. The suspect's fingers are interlaced against the back of his head as you maintain cover at the rear of the vehicle.

2

As you maintain your aim at the suspect's center mass, you continue to use precise commands to maintain suspect control by his assuming the kneeling position.

3

Commanding the suspect to spread his legs as far apart as possible will keep him off balance. The fingers are still kept interlaced at the back of the suspect's head.

4

You now grasp the suspect's interlaced fingers with your weak hand while simultaneously using your gun hand to push him forward. This has the effect of bowing his back and keeping him off balance.

5

Have the suspect cross his ankles then stride your foot forward in front of his left knee and apply pressure against his hip with your knee.

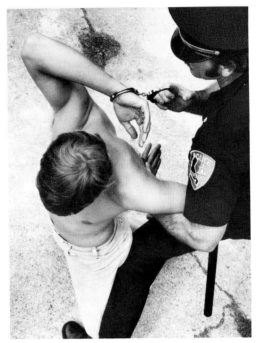

6

Handcuff the suspect's right hand first. Place three fingers inside the handcuff ring and hold it as the suspect's left wrist is brought behind his back.

7

The right arm is now brought down and around as you maintain pressure against the suspect's hip.

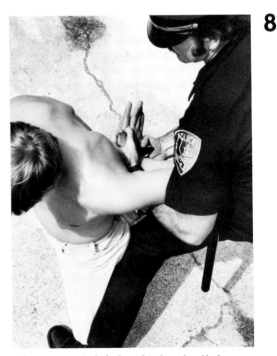

8

The suspect's left hand is handcuffed while you hold his left hand at the wrist.

9

The suspect is now put at a further disadvantage by moving his head to the ground while kneeling. A search can now be safely continued for weapons.

10

The suspect's legs are also searched for weapons as you maintain control of the suspect's hands.

11

While keeping your leading foot against his knee, use your weak hand to grasp his left arm. Your strong hand now holds onto his left hand as you begin to bring him to a standing position.

12

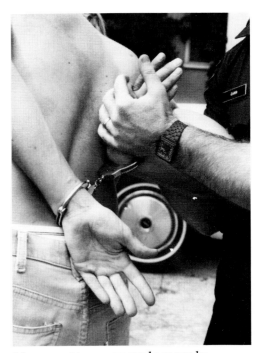

Movement to your patrol car can be achieved by using the wrist-lock on the suspect's right hand. He is now ready to transport safely.

1

In starting a prone arrest position, issue commands from behind cover. Command him to interlace his fingers behind his head.

2

The suspect is then commanded to his knees and told to spread his legs far apart.

3

With his arms out, palms up, order him to cross his legs and face away from your approach.

4

Raise his wrist as you push in on the back of his hand with your thumb and pull up with your fingers.

254

5

Once you know you have a good wrist-lock on the suspect, you slide your right arm down the forearm of the suspect while you maintain pressure on the wrist.

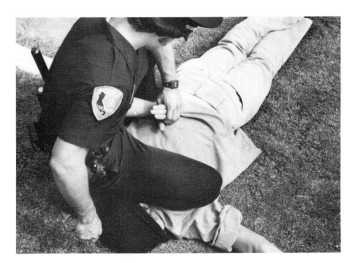

6

As you maintain pressure, drop your right knee across his shoulder blade and neck, while taking out your hand-cuffs.

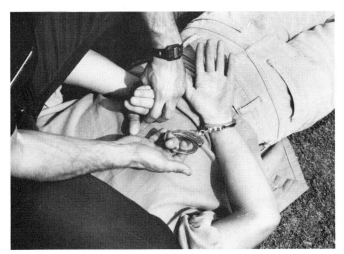

7

By maintaining pressure on the suspect's right wrist, you start handcuffing his left wrist first. You maintain security by holding onto the other cuff with three fingers.

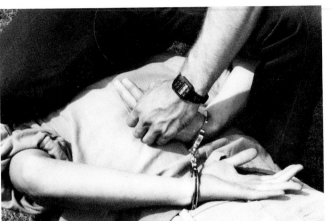

8

At this point you can easily cuff the other hand by raising it first, then cuffing. You now resecure the wrist by reapplying the wrist-lock.

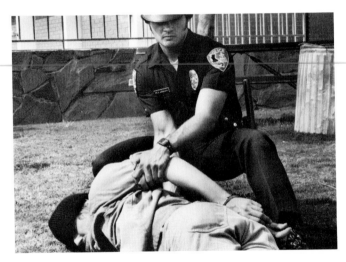

9

You now assist the suspect in safely rising to his feet. You do so by placing your left hand on his left arm and your right hand on his right arm. As you pull up, you twist him into a sitting position.

10

You now instruct the suspect to tuck his right leg under his left thigh for balance as he rises.

As the suspect is raised, apply a wrist-lock to his right hand. The thumb of your right hand also maintains pressure on the suspect's right elbow.

If he's kneeling, one approach is to come from behind and place your left foot between his crossed ankles as you simultaneously grasp the top three fingers of one of his interlocked hands. Pull him backwards with the small of his back resting against your knee so he is off balance. Then, with your shin pressing against his top ankle, slide the ankle forward until it's in the hollow behind his left knee. This position, which has been tested against black belt karate experts, allows you to keep both feet on the ground and changes his center of gravity so he is thoroughly off balance for moving. (You can put him more off balance by pulling back slightly as you grip his fingers.)

There are two variations of this tactic: 1) stand with your left foot on top of his crossed ankles. If he resists, you can jam your foot down hard and either break his ankle(s) or at least inflict considerable pain. This position, however, tends to put you off balance and susceptible to falling; 2) stick the front of your foot under his ankles as they are crossed behind him. If he moves, lift your foot sharply, and he'll pitch forward onto his face.

As you slide your foot into whatever position you decide is appropriate, quickly handcuff the suspect's right wrist. Unless you know him to be left-handed, his right is cuffed first because the chance is 90 per cent that it's his strong hand. Bring it around behind his back. You want to have his arm and wrist under control so you can inflict pain, if necessary, should he struggle or resist. Then instruct him to bring his other hand behind him. You can steady him if he's kneeling; if he's against a wall, he can support his weight with the top of his head. *You want to cuff a suspect's hands behind him only.* If they're in front, it's too easy for him to grab for your gun or to swing his manacled fists as a powerful weapon in and of themselves. If possible, slip the free end of the cuffs through his belt before cuffing his left hand. This will further restrict his movements and prevent him from stepping through his arms to bring his hands to the front of his body. Cuff him so both his palms are facing out, the fronts of his wrists against each other. And be sure to double-lock the cuffs.

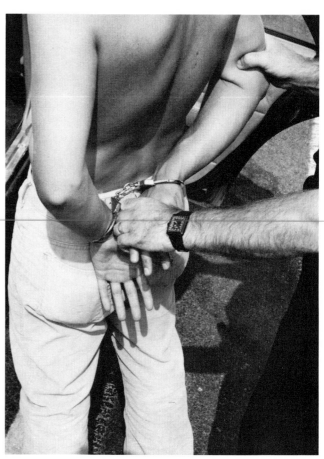

This is the correct handcuff position wherein both palms of the suspect are facing out. By holding the suspect in this manner, you can apply pressure to the fingers of his right hand and his right arm should he resist.

Your opportunity to maintain suspect control is diminished when handcuffing right hand to left hand or left hand to left hand with an officer sandwiched in the middle.

On rare occasions, you may need to handcuff a deformed or injured individual who can't bring his hands behind his back. Here you can reduce the risks of front cuffing somewhat by turning his belt so the buckle is in the rear. Then pass the cuffs through the front of the belt and cuff him with his palms out. This keeps his arms close to his body and lessens his ability to attack.

When you have several suspects to handle, your options may include:

Handcuffing two prisoners with one pair of cuffs. With the suspects side by side, order the one on the right to bring his right hand behind his back. Turn his palm out and attach the cuff, then pass the free end of the handcuffs through his belt. Now have the second suspect bring his right arm to the rear. Attach the cuff to his right wrist. This leaves both prisoners in a somewhat awkward position, lessening the chance of their running or coordinating arm movement. Although it violates the general rule about front cuffing, an acceptable alternative where only one set of cuffs is available is to cuff both prisoners' right wrists together in front of their bodies. This, too, is awkward enough to hamper extreme movement. *Never* handcuff two suspects right hand to left hand. This affords them too much freedom of movement. (Some officers carry two sets of cuffs, which makes handcuffing two prisoners less of a problem.)

Handcuffing two prisoners with two pairs of cuffs. Cuff the first suspect with his hands behind his back, palms out. Then have the second suspect interlock his right arm through the other's left arm before you handcuff him in the usual palms-out manner.

Handcuffing three prisoners with two pairs of cuffs. The first suspect is cuffed to the rear, palms out. The right arm of the second suspect is then interlocked through his left arm. Now use your second set of cuffs to handcuff the wrist of this interlocked arm to the wrist of the third suspect's right arm. When they're locked together, all the suspects should be facing in the same direction.

Handcuffing four prisoners with two pairs of cuffs. This procedure is an *extremely risky* one because of your necessary close proximity to all four suspects. You should not attempt it unless you have a partner who can cover you. You should be unarmed, and the suspects, in this case, should be searched before you start the cuffing. Position the first two suspects so they are facing each other, and handcuff their right wrists together with the first set of cuffs. Think of these two suspects as the lateral points of a four-pointed star. The other two suspects will be positioned as if they are the other two points. With your second set of cuffs, first cuff the right wrist of suspect number three. Now place the remaining cuff around the links of the first set of cuffs and lock these links inside the cuff, along with the right wrist of suspect number four. Because of the difficulty they'll have in moving, it's hard to transport suspects who are handcuffed in this fashion. This manner of cuffing is usually practical only as a holding procedure.

Remember that your survival from this point on may depend heavily on your getting your assailant handcuffed firmly. With female prisoners, especially, officers often leave cuffs too loose so as not to cause pain or discomfort, thereby enabling the suspects to slip out of the cuffs entirely or to more easily step through their arms and bring the cuffs out front. Some officers, foolishly, are reluctant to handcuff female suspects at all. In each case, cuffs not only should be squeezed snug but should also be double-locked. Once the cuffs are on, squeeze the suspect's fingers together to make sure his hand is not small enough to allow him to slip through the handcuffs.

Regardless of how cooperative he or she may seem to be, *never handcuff a prisoner to yourself.* Besides the obvious risk of his trying to overpower you, he may decide to leap in front of a car or off a roof, making you an involuntary victim of his suicide attempt.

Searching for Firearms

Most often, a suspect can—and should—be searched at the location where you arrest him, after he is cuffed and incapacitated as much as possible. Sometimes, however, especially in concentrated urban areas, hostile crowds may try to release or threaten your prisoner and it seems desirable to get away from the scene as quickly as possible. In those circumstances, officers may place the handcuffed suspect in the patrol car and search him thoroughly while driving away. Even then, however, you should perform a cursory search before placing him in the car. You can pat down his belt area, for example, while walking him toward the car. To continue the search in the car, have the suspect sit in the back seat on the passenger side, with one officer seated next to him directly behind the driver-officer.

This technique has some obvious hazards and limitations. Where possible, a better alternative is to call for sufficient back-up to contain and control the crowd while search procedures are conducted at the scene.

When you search the suspect, you'll of course want to confiscate anything he might be able to use to pick the lock of your handcuffs. A bobby pin or a small strip of brass from a wooden ruler can be used to disengage the teeth in the ratchet, and the ink cartridges from some ballpoint pens are almost identical to handcuff keys. Some suspects keep an actual key hidden on their persons, under a bandaid, in the waistband of their pants or inside a belt, for example.

Your primary concern, however, is finding weapons. Because your assailant has displayed one gun or you've recovered one early in your search does *not* mean that's *all* he has. During a final approach at a drug store where police had interrupted a robbery, a patrolman in Indiana successfully used a verbal challenge to disarm a suspect who was holding a revolver in his hand. But the officer neglected to search for an additional weapon. Moments later, the suspect whipped a .357 Magnum out of his waistband and shot the officer in the head. Sometimes a suspect's most dangerous weapon is his second one. During a domestic disturbance in Texas, a detective took a large Bowie knife from a man who later, as the incident appeared to be winding down, produced a .45 cal. semi-automatic and shot the detective in the back. If you see or find one weapon, *don't omit or cut short your search*. Your suspect may have two—or three. Often assailants carry multiple weapons on the assumption that an officer won't find them all.

Your search should be systematic, so you cover his entire body from his head to his toes. A good place to look first is around the suspect's midriff. Many people who carry guns illegally mimic what they see on television or in the movies. They don't wear a holster belted to the side or carry the gun in the small of the back, but stuck in their waistband close to the front of their body. Often they have it in the cross-draw position, believing (erroneously) that this is quicker and more impressive. As one observer has noted, "Most of these people are in the ranks of the losers." But if your search is slipshod, they can quickly make you a loser, too.

After checking the waist area, go to the top of his head and check all areas down to his toes. Work from top to bottom, right to left—and maintain the same search system on *each* suspect. That way you won't forget any area.

No area of the body or item of clothing should be immune from searching. Adversaries have been known to carry guns in the crotch of their pants... inside their hats...up their sleeves...on cords around their necks...under coats and vests...or fastened to their arms or legs by rubber bands or tape. Sometimes, they hide them in slings and bandages. One female subject in California was found to have a Colt Python hidden in her vagina! Others have carried guns taped in their arm pits or under their breasts.

A favorite spot for concealing weapons, often overlooked, is inside boots. Some survival conscious officers will not place any suspect in their patrol cars until after he has removed his boots, using only his feet to do so. In circumstances that are duplicated often in the annals of lost lives, a county policeman in Virginia handcuffed a shoplifting suspect and placed him in his patrol car, without searching his footwear. Enroute to the station, the suspect managed to pull a handgun he had concealed in his boot and shot the patrolman at point-blank range. In Tennessee, the assailant in a similar case was a young drunk whom a deputy sheriff was driving to jail. This suspect had a .38 cal. derringer hidden in his cowboy boots. When he pulled it and started shooting, the deputy tried to defend himself. He shot the suspect three times...but it was the deputy who died, shot once in the head.

Male officers (and female officers, too, for that matter) are often reluctant to search a male suspect's crotch area. Because of this hesitation, two New York officers were about to place an arrested suspect in their patrol car without a thorough search, until one's sixth sense became alarmed and he decided to check out the suspect further. While the officer was searching the suspect's crotch, he was ridiculed by the suspect with remarks like, ''Are you queer, man?'' and ''You must be a faggot, a closet queen!'' Even the officer's partner laughed a little—until he found a .25 cal. semi-automatic hidden in the suspect's pants.

Similarly, male officers may be hesitant about searching female prisoners on the street, and seasoned suspects may try to capitalize on this fact. But a suspect is a suspect, regardless of sex; women kill law enforcement officers the same as men do. In searching a female, first pull out her blouse tail if it's tucked in; sometimes guns or other weapons will fall out. Also consider unsnapping her bra and shaking it by its straps; that's another common hiding place. Most areas of her body can be searched the same as you would a man's. In checking between and under her breasts, on the insides of her thighs and around her crotch, use the edge of your hand. This can protect you against accusations of improper advances.

Even a suspect who appears to be defenseless should be searched and handcuffed before he's transported from the scene. After a shoot-out in which the assailant was badly wounded in Ohio, the police recovered the .25 cal. semi-automatic he had used in the fight, but they didn't search him further before loading him into an ambulance. The suspect still had another gun secreted on his body. In this case, the prisoner died enroute to the hospital, but with lesser injuries he might have used it to shoot his way to freedom.

Remaining Alert

During your search, as in other phases of the final approach, you'll need to exercise a difficult form of mental discipline. You'll have to concentrate on what you're doing, of course, but a survival orientation demands that you not succumb to the natural tendency under stress to concentrate *only* on that. A shooting encounter is *not* a "linear" situation, a progression of single, isolated events from the beginning through the end. Rather, at each stage of the encounter, many important things are going on simultaneously. When you are searching a suspect, you may at the same time have to be alert to a crowd of bystanders collecting around you, to back-up officers arriving and deploying, to evidence that needs to be preserved, to the possibility that the suspect, even though handcuffed, can still use his legs to kick or run or his head to butt you, and so on. The temptation is to block out everything but the most powerful, immediate stimulus so you can concentrate better. But you can't afford that kind of tunnel vision. You'll need to keep part of your awareness focused on everything else that's taking place in the scene around you.

For example, additional assailants often appear in this period. If you're not alert to the possibility of their presence, their use of surprise may overwhelm you and put you at such a disadvantage that you can't recover. Yet, just as many officers are not attuned to the possibility of a second weapon, many fail to consider extra adversaries; they get one under control, and they relax. In law enforcement, we've used back-up men as a patrol tactic for years. It's time we acknowledged that offenders are using them, too, with increasing frequency, just as they use back-up guns.

A very high percentage of armed robberies, for example, are committed by two or more people. Bank surveillance photos at a series of bank robberies in New York City show how one team worked. While one suspect presented himself to a teller and announced the robbery, his partner remained farther back in the teller line, appearing to be an ordinary, uninvolved citizen. If the robbery went well, this man simply waited until the robber was headed out of the lobby, then ducked out of the line and exited behind him. If something went wrong, the back-up man was there with unexpected fire power. At one bank, for instance, a security guard gave chase to the robber. The back-up man came up behind him, drew a gun and shot him.

If your response to a call is fast enough or if you happen to be at the scene when a crime goes down—as often happens with off-duty officers at tavern or grocery store robberies—the extra assailants may not have yet made their presence known when you intervene. They may blend in with the environment, yet be located in tactically advantageous positions. If it's a tavern, one or more back-up men may be seated at the bar or in a booth, watching the action like the other patrons. At a truck hijacking, another assailant may be standing nearby as if waiting for a bus or be "fixing" a flat on a car down the block. On traffic stops, a passenger may attack you as you're taking the driver into custody. Or the extra suspect may be hidden altogether; perhaps you've flushed one adversary out of a closet with a verbal challenge, but another, unbeknown to you, remains secreted inside.

In any case, the back-up man may wait until you are involved with the complex and easily distracting problems of a final approach to strike. In Virginia, for example, two officers who'd staked out the parking lot of a motel where numerous thefts from vehicles had occurred spotted two teenagers suspiciously looking into certain cars. They ordered the youths to halt and were approaching them when a third suspect, whom they hadn't seen, emerged from inside a nearby vehicle where he'd been hiding. He fired one shot from a .25 cal. semi-automatic, fatally wounding one of the officers in the chest.

Sometimes an additional assailant has no connection with the suspect(s) you're handling. One gunfight started in Detroit as officers were handcuffing a traffic violator when an uninvolved motorist pulled abreast, pointed a gun at one of the patrolmen and yelled, "Hey, you black motherfucker, I'm gonna kill you!" In a somewhat similar case, three Colorado officers had quieted a disturbance at a trailer court and were returning to their cars when a man uninvolved with the incident suddenly emerged from his trailer nearby. Shouting a string of obscenities, he hoisted a .12 ga. shotgun and shot one of the patrolmen fatally in the back.

264

Often, a new assailant is part of the crowd that forms to watch, and something about your presence or the action sparks a violent response in him. Several officers were in the final stages of investigating a hit-and-run traffic accident in Kansas, when a man who'd been watching the proceedings from a crowd across the street suddenly darted over to them, knocked a reserve policeman to the ground and grabbed his service revolver. A deputy sheriff standing nearby shot the assailant in the throat, but before he fell, several more shots were exchanged. The deputy was wounded, and the reserve officer was killed. In Wisconsin, a motorist who'd been stopped for driving an improperly registered car started to struggle when the officers took him into custody. As they focused on getting him under control, a bystander walked up and shot both officers in the head with a 7.65mm semi-automatic. As the Dallas Police Department learned when Jack Ruby assassinated Lee Harvey Oswald, *on-lookers or crowds of any kind in any location bear careful watching.*

Probably the person you least expect trouble from during a final approach is the victim of the crime. Yet in some circumstances it's not uncommon for a victim to transform suddenly into an additional assailant. This is particularly true at the scenes of domestic disturbances. More than one officer who has managed to rescue a wife from being kicked, beaten or killed by her husband has been startled to have the ''grateful'' victim then turn on him when he moved to arrest the husband and transport him to jail. The rules here are: don't automatically rule out anyone as a potential assailant...remain aware of where your gun is in relation to the victim, as well as the suspect...and be conscious, too, of any other weapons that the victim may have access to. For example, try to avoid arresting suspects in kitchens; there are usually too many knives around.

One possibility to stay alert for is an extra assailant who isn't human. Trained attack dogs are being used increasingly by criminals. Certain narcotics dealers in one city are known to keep German shepherds penned in closets that can be opened with the trip of a latch, sending the dogs charging at policemen who attempt arrests.

The most difficult area to watch during a final approach is to your rear. If possible, try to get a wall or other solid barrier behind you while you're approaching, handcuffing and/or searching a suspect to lessen the risk of attack from that direction.

To help all your senses (particularly your hearing and your peripheral vision) remain alert to what's happening around you, you want to minimize your exposure to distraction. In one case, a sheriff's deputy shifted his attention away from a subject he was arresting on a highway just long enough to listen to his patrol car radio. The suspect reached back into his car and got a gun, which he used to kill the deputy and the deputy's wife, who was in the patrol car. In other cases, civilians have approached to ask questions or register complaints during a handcuffing or frisking, and suspects have capitalized on the diversion to seize officers' guns and start shooting. Often the suspect himself will try to distract you, by moving unnecessarily or by asking permission for favors, like going to the toilet, taking medicine, getting his coat, etc. If he needs a coat, go with him or send an officer to get it and thoroughly search it before letting him have it.

Suspects may try to con you by attempting to make you look foolish or by playing on your sympathies. But *under no circumstances should you permit a suspect to move out of your immediate presence*, even if denying him a request seems harsh. A city marshal in Kansas had arrested and handcuffed a parole violator he recognized driving around town with his four children. As he was being put into the patrol car, the suspect asked and was granted permission to return to his own vehicle for a moment to speak to his bewildered children alone. There he obtained a .357 cal. handgun, which he managed to fire twice at the marshal's chest even though his hands were cuffed behind him. As the marshal lay dying, the assailant stole his service revolver and fled, with one of his kids driving the car.

There's not much we can learn about police work from the movie roles of Clint Eastwood, but he did have a pertinent piece of dialog in one of his films. Commenting on a fellow officer who'd been shot and killed because he relaxed his alertness toward a prisoner out of sympathy, Eastwood remarked: ''The color of pity is red—blood red.'' It's a line worth remembering when you're trying to maintain firm control over someone who may have the will and the way to take your life.

One way to protect yourself is always to treat a prisoner as if he is armed, even though a thorough search has convinced you he's not. If he needs to communicate with someone else, you carry the message for him while he remains locked in the back of your patrol car. Don't permit other people to stick their heads in your car, kiss the suspect or otherwise approach or touch him. By allowing any physical contact, you open the possibility that a confederate will transfer a small caliber firearm to the person you have in custody.

Recovering Firearms

The gun(s) you recover at a crime scene may pose a dilemma. On one hand, you may need to handle them and possibly unload or otherwise de-activate them to make them safe to transport away. On the other hand, the guns *as they're recovered*, may constitute important physical evidence against the suspect in the court hearings ahead. If, for example, the gun is cocked or has been fired at you, the position of the hammer or the empty cylinder hole(s) may bear on your assailant's intent and on your justification for having used deadly force. At the scene of a shooting death, particularly, the exact positioning of the weapon may be important and may help determine whether the incident was a homicide or suicide. Change the condition of the gun and you may change the case. Similarly, if you destroy latent fingerprints by handling the weapon, you weaken the evidence.

This man was found in a street after witnesses said he turned the rifle on himself and pulled the trigger. Unless this rifle's position presents a danger to you or others, there is no reason for patrol officers to touch this important physical evidence.

In making decisions about a recovered firearm, you'll have to weigh the immediate danger the gun presents to you and other people against its evidence value. If you are confronted with a dead body in a secure area (such as inside a room) and no one else is present, leave *everything* alone, including firearms. Secure the room and wait for specialists. Where safety is threatened, you'll have to act otherwise. *Preserving lives takes priority over preserving evidence.* Still, try in each case to handle or change the condition of a recovered firearm no more than is absolutely necessary to make it safe. By unnecessarily handling or changing the gun, you may give rise to accusations that you planted it...switched it...loaded it...cocked it...or otherwise misrepresented facts about its recovery.

When any weapon is taken from a person under arrest, all officers present should visually examine it so they are in a position to testify about the circumstances of its recovery and to recognize it when it is presented in evidence. However, unnecessary *handling* by several oficers and the related confusion increases the risk of an accidental firing. *One* officer only should be responsible for actually deactivating the firearm.

Unless you are a highly experienced gun expert, many street firearms you recover are likely to be unfamiliar to you. That alone is reason enough to handle a gun minimally, regardless of the evidence factor, or *leave it alone* (but not unattended) if at all possible until someone familiar with the gun can handle it. You can easily discharge a gun unintentionally if you're not familiar with it or if it is in poor working condition, as assailants' firearms often are. Moreover, the gun may have been "set up" to discharge unconventionally, and if you're not familiar with the weapon, you may not recognize that it is rigged. Officers have been killed and injured by handling such guns with overconfidence. If you must handle the gun and can locate and recognize the safety on an unfamiliar gun, engage it. With your finger away from the trigger, carefully lift the gun by making as little contact with it as possible. For instance, you might stick a pencil or pen through the trigger guard, behind the trigger. Or, better, you can use a shoelace. When you lift a gun with a shoelace through the trigger guard, there's no chance it will slip off and no way the trigger can be pulled. (Note: If you use a handkerchief or gloves to lift the firearm, you wipe away fingerprints. Similarly, the old movie trick of lifting a gun with a pencil in the barrel is *not* recommended because it can alter the rifling and residue, which may constitute evidence.) As you lift the gun, keep the muzzle pointed in a safe direction, remove the ammunition and do not squeeze the gun in any way. Homemade firearms and some semi-automatics have pressure-sensitive plates that can cause them to fire, without the trigger being pulled.

Some departments have armored containers you can use to transport firearms in any condition. If these are available, you can use them as a means of preserving both evidence and safety. Otherwise, you'll have to consider other options.

A shoelace placed inside the trigger guard, behind the trigger, can be used to pick up a firearm. This technique avoids the necessity for touching the firearm at all.

One technique for handling firearms is to pick up the weapon by the grip panels, the one area least likely to retain fingerprints.

To unload this M-1 carbine model, activate the manual safety. The "safe" position is straight up and down.

Depress the magazine release lever and gently withdraw the magazine.

As you move the bolt to its locked position, visually inspect the chamber to make sure no live round is present inside the barrel.

These procedures may apply either when you recover a gun from an assailant or, as sometimes happens, you locate a discarded firearm during your tour of duty that has no immediate connection with a crime scene.

If you are alone and you recover a handgun that is uncocked, you can secure it temporarily by unloading it and separating the ammunition from the firearm by placing them in your pockets. Here they're out of the suspect's view and because the gun is unloaded you are protected from an accidental discharge. *Never* put a loaded gun in your pocket, belt or waistband. As soon as you have an opportunity, lock the recovered gun in the trunk of your patrol car for transporting. When a shotgun is recovered, make it inaccessible until the suspect is handcuffed, searched and secured, then bring it to your vehicle. Before transporting it, you lessen the chance of unintentional discharge by unloading the shotgun and making it inoperable by opening the breech or moving the slide or bolt to the rear, if it has one. Be sure to remove any rounds that have been chambered and to collect any live rounds that may have fallen to the ground. Separate the firearm and the ammunition and leave the breech open when transporting.

Some other long guns are best transported unloaded, too. One is the M-1A1 carbine. To unload it, you move the safety selector switch on the right side of the trigger group to the "on" position and rotate the gun so it is resting on its sights. Grasp the upper portion of the stock with one hand, while grasping the magazine with the other...and depress the magazine release lever. Then pull the magazine up and forward until it is separated from the gun. Now turn the gun back over and pull the bolt and slide rod back firmly toward the rear sight. This will eject any chambered rounds. With the bolt as far back as it can go, engage the bolt locking pin and carefully release the bolt to travel forward. Check the chamber visually to be sure all rounds have been cleared.

When you're faced with a cocked gun that could go off accidentally, you want to reduce the threat it presents before you leave the scene, but after the suspect himself is well under control and you have holstered your own sidearm. With a revolver, one option is to point the muzzle in a safe direction and put the thumb of your weak hand across the hammer track as a block between the cocked hammer and the revolver's frame. Keep the fingers of your weak hand away from the muzzle. With your other thumb holding the hammer under control, apply just enough pressure to the trigger to release the hammer. Take your finger off the trigger...guide the hammer down slowly and with slight reverse "braking" until the firing pin touches your weak hand thumbnail...then slowly remove that thumb and lower the hammer the rest of the way. (This method of rendering the gun safer will work even if the weapon is in the hand of a dead suspect. Place your weak-hand thumb between the hammer and frame and disengage the weapon from the suspect's hand with your strong hand. Then follow the uncocking procedure we've described.) Or: if you decide to unload the revolver, consider identifying each cartridge to indicate which one was in the firing position at the time of confiscation, as a means of keeping the evidence solid. You will want, also, to note the exact position of the other rounds as they were found in the cylinder. Sometimes officers need to uncock their own revolvers after an armed confrontation. Under stress, they revert to inappropriate range training and prepare to shoot single-action. Then, when things quiet down, they're left holding a cocked weapon they don't know how to render safe.

The same procedures for deactivating a suspect's revolver will work on your own. You don't have to resort to the preposterous and dangerous options chosen by two eastern officers. One decided to uncock his service revolver by firing it into a toilet, with inevitable results. The other carried his gun around in his holster with the hammer *taped back*, so it couldn't go off under any circumstances!

To render a cocked semi-automatic safer to transport, first attempt to engage the safety and then remove the magazine. But remember—even with the magazine out of some semi-automatics, a live round may still be in the chamber and able to shoot. Assume that one is. If the gun incorporates a mechanical ejector (most do, except for some cheap .22s), you can clear the chamber by moving back the slide. Hold the gun in a shooting grip, but with your finger outside the trigger guard. With your weak hand, come over the top of the gun from the rear and pull the slide back, or hold the slide stationary and push the gun forward. (If the gun is a 9mm Luger, which you may occasionally encounter, the same effect is accomplished by using your thumb and index finger to firmly pull the two bolt hubs up and back.) The movement should cause the chambered round to be ejected, and you can inspect the chamber and look down the magazine well to be certain the gun is clear. You can stuff your handkerchief or a rag into the opening to keep the slide back and the gun inoperative.

*The proper technique for lowering
the hammer on a wounded suspect's
revolver.*

1

2

3

4

5

The proper technique for deactivating a semi-automatic held in a wounded suspect's hand.

1

2

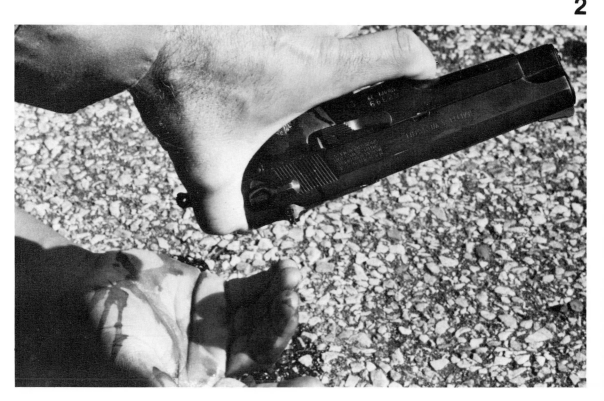

3

4

*The proper technique for deactivating
a .25 cal. Beretta.*

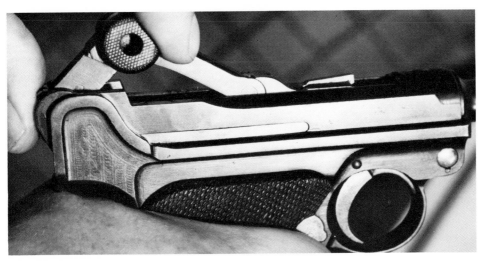

*The proper technique for deactivating
a suspect's 9mm Luger.*

If the gun lacks a mechanical ejector, as some commonly recovered semi-automatics do, like the Beretta .22 cal. and .25 cal. models, moving the slide to the rear won't eject a chambered round. Here you'll have to empty the magazine and then activate the release lever on the left side of the weapon. When you move the lever, the springloaded barrel will "pop" up, and you can take out the live round.

Whatever your method, *be sure you keep the muzzle pointed in a safe direction throughout.* An Ohio officer was trying to deactivate a .45 cal. semi-automatic he had found hidden in a fire hose in a hallway when the gun unexpectedly discharged. Because he'd pointed the muzzle carelessly, he shot his partner.

When you are working with a partner, one of you takes responsibility for securing *all* recovered firearms, while still keeping his primary attention on helping control the suspect. If it becomes necessary to pass a suspect's gun(s) between you, keep in mind your options for minimizing the possibility of an unintentional discharge—or hit—in this circumstance.

The safest way to pass a revolver is to open the cylinder and place your index and middle finger through the opening under the top strap, so the cylinder cannot swing closed. Point the muzzle down and hand the gun to your partner with the

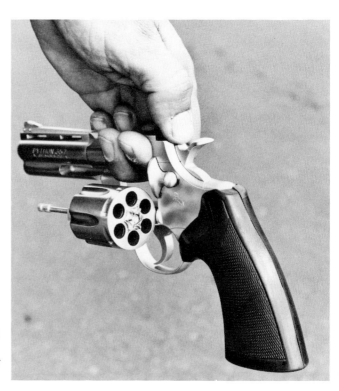

Any suspect firearm should be passed with the muzzle pointed away from anyone. If it's a revolver, the cylinder must be open.

butt toward him. The revolver can then be safely carried by the top strap, with the cylinder open. A semi-automatic is safest to pass if you first remove the magazine...pull the slide back to clear and inspect the chamber...then lock it back, even if it means using a cloth or rag to plug the ejection port to keep the slide from flying forward.

Whether you're recovering, deactivating, passing—*anytime* you're handling a firearm—two survival principles always prevail. They can't be repeated too often: 1) *keep the muzzle pointing in a safe direction*...2) *keep your finger outside the trigger guard*.

Departing the Scene

The last phase of your final approach is taking the suspect away. Again, guard against the natural tendency to relax. Many shootings occur in patrol cars enroute to the station. Others erupt at the station, while a suspect is being booked or fingerprinted.

In walking a handcuffed prisoner to your car, you can maintain control of him through pressure holds. Assuming you are right-handed, walk slightly behind the suspect on his right, so your gun side is away from him. With your weak hand, tightly grip the fingers of his right hand and pull them up and back toward the under side of his arm. With your gun hand, apply thumb pressure on the artery in the fleshy part of his inner arm just above the elbow. These grips allow you to inflict whatever pain is necessary to keep him under control and also permit your gun hand to move quickly to your sidearm if need be. To any civilians who are watching, you will not appear to be using undue force.

No suspect should be permitted to enter your patrol car without having been handcuffed and *thoroughly* searched. The incidents in which assailants have pulled concealed firearms or grabbed officers' guns once they are inside a patrol car are legion. In a case that is all too typical, two South Carolina highway patrolmen placed a husband and wife in the back seat of their unit after arresting them for public drunkenness. The officers had neglected to search the man's combat boots, however. Enroute to the county jail, he drew a five-shot revolver and shot the passenger officer four times through the front seat. A fifth shot ricocheted and hit his wife. When he put the gun to the head of the second officer and pulled the trigger, the firing pin clicked on an empty cylinder hole; he was out of

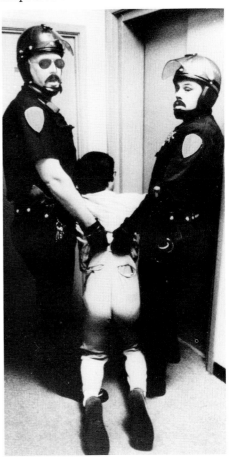

The primary benefit of the wrist-lock, unlike this tactic, is that it forces the suspect to do all the work.

ammunition. This officer then shot and killed the suspect, but by then his partner was dead from his wounds. A deputy sheriff in Oklahoma was killed while he was transporting a mentally deranged subject to a hospital. Because his passenger was entering the hospital voluntarily, the deputy decided not to handcuff him. At a stop sign, the man started a struggle in which he obtained the deputy's service revolver and shot him fatally in the head and chest. In Illinois, two prostitutes were put in the back seat of a patrol car for transportation to the lockup, but they were neither thoroughly searched nor handcuffed because their arrest seemed "routine"—this despite the fact that the arresting detectives were seasoned veterans, with 20 years of service apiece. Of course, one of the girls had a .25 cal. pistol stuffed in her bra. She drew it and started shooting. The officers killed her—but not before they each had been shot twice.

For maximum control, remember to walk prisoners to your car with your gun side away from them...not like this.

Besides having your prisoner cuffed behind his back, you want to strap him in with the seat belt— and pull it tight. Then he can't wiggle his hips and legs through his arms to bring his cuffed hands out front. If you are alone, be extremely cautious about transporting a prisoner in the back seat of a patrol car without a cage. It's hard, if not impossible, for a single officer to adequately watch a suspect in the rear. You may be better off to have him up front with you, but strapped in so he has little movement. Better yet, call for back-up. And always notify communications of your location and destination before starting out with a prisoner.

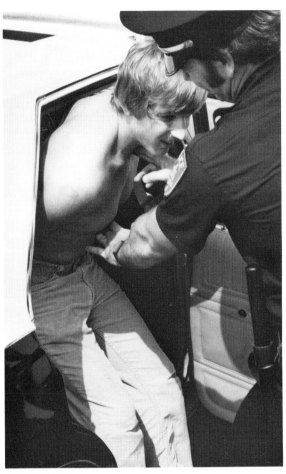

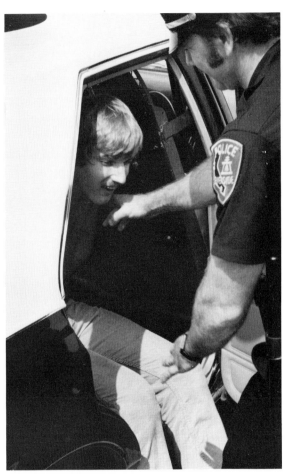

The technique to consider for safely placing your prisoner in the back seat is to place your right index and middle fingers on his throat. The index and middle finger of your left hand are gently applied to his abdomen.

Based on the degree of resistance you encounter, your application of pressure at these two points will keep him at the disadvantage until he is seated.

Some survival-conscious officers refuse even to permit apparently innocent civilians, like traffic accident victims, into their patrol cars without a frisk first. Where women are involved in such situations, you should at least insist on keeping their purses with you up front while they are in back.

At the station, constant vigilance is still required. Unless the suspect is locked in a cell, you want to keep him under direct observation at ALL TIMES.

When you are involved in fingerprinting a suspect, remove your gun as you would when entering a psychiatric ward or a jail; in numerous instances, suspects have grabbed officers' guns and killed them during the fingerprinting process. Have your partner safeguard your sidearm or place it in a locker. Search the prisoner thoroughly again before freeing his hands. For the printing, release only one of his hands at a time, keeping the other cuffed to his belt.

From start to finish during your final approach:
- *Think mean* - that's survival!
- *Be deliberate* - that's survival!
- *Never quit looking* for the "other" bad guy or the extra firearm!

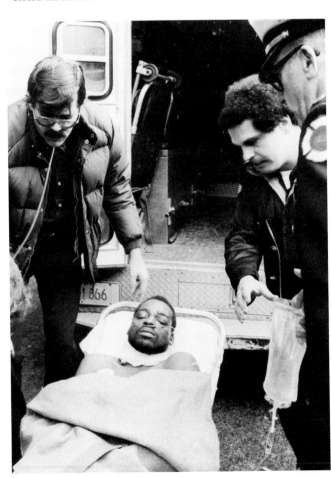

Control of a wounded suspect at the scene does not end until the ambulance exits for the hospital. This man, who had just been convicted of murder, pulled out a loaded gun in the courtroom and was shot by a sheriff's deputy. The defendant had been out on bail and was not searched prior to sentencing in his murder trial.

AFTER-BURN 11

There's a psychological violence connected with gunfights that can be a dangerous enemy, as well as the physical violence. Sometimes the effect makes itself felt almost immediately. The instant the shooting is over, you may burst into tears... throw up...wet your pants...lose control of your bowels...shake so badly you have to put your gun down.... One rookie officer in California responded to a domestic disturbance call with his partner and encountered a woman who threatened them with a shotgun. As the rookie drew his revolver, his partner grabbed their patrol car's shotgun and ordered the woman to drop her weapon. When she refused, he let fly two rounds that literally severed her head. The new officer stared at her remains in horror, then threw down his revolver. ''If this is what being a cop is all about,'' he declared, ''I don't want anything to do with it!'' He walked off and was never seen again by his fellow officers.

Suspects, too, sometimes have extreme immediate reactions. About five per cent of those who kill police officers then commit suicide, either right away or shortly afterwards.

Most often, though, the impact is not so swift for the officer. It's likelier to set in days, weeks, even months after the shooting, through a phenomenon some therapists call ''after-burn.'' This refers to the tendency of the human mind to dwell on unpleasant, emotion-charged events in the wake of

In extreme circumstances, officers who are unprepared emotionally for a shooting have committed suicide off-duty as a way to cope.

their actual occurrence. In after-burn, you relive and react to an experience, churning over and over what you and others did and what you might or should have done differently. This continual reminding and reassessing can be as vivid as the original event—and even more psychologically upsetting.

After a minor fight with your spouse, after-burn may keep you irritable and on edge for a day before you let go of your angry or guilty feelings. After a truly significant event—like shooting at someone, especially if you kill him—after-burn may permanently change your life...unless you are prepared for it and able to respond appropriately.

A classic illustration occurred several years ago in Tennessee to a 33-year-old patrolman. One bleak winter night he was on stakeout in the back room of a liquor store, hoping to apprehend a team of robbers who'd been knocking over late-night business places with aggravating regularity. As he watched, two men entered the store and announced a hold-up. When one struck the storekeeper on the head with a gun, the officer burst out of his hiding place and leveled his shotgun at the offenders.

"The guy with the pistol turned and started to aim at me," the patrolman recalled later. "That was when I cut loose on him. I had to do it. It was

Police officers cling to each other in relief after a high-speed chase and gun battle in which the man on the ground was killed. Moments before he had killed a highway patrol officer.

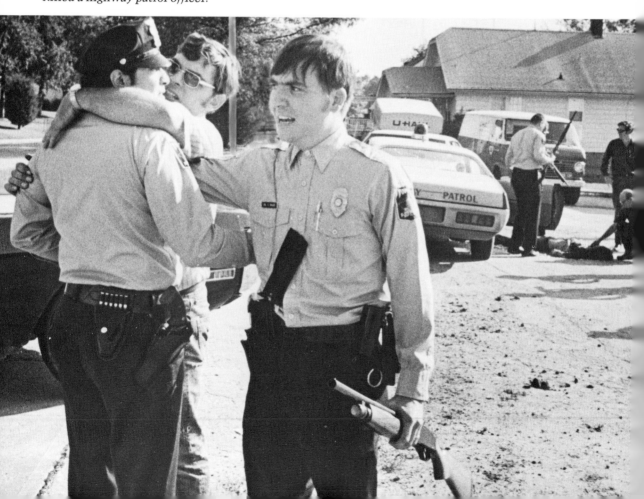

either him or me or the manager." This suspect was killed instantly. "The other robber hesitated a moment, and I begged him to give up. I said, 'Please don't run, or I'll have to kill you.' He ran, and I shot him just as he went through the door." This suspect did not die for nearly thirty minutes. As his life ebbed away, the officer could hear him gasping for breath. "If you ever have to kill a man," he told fellow officers later, "never look at his face." A few days after the shooting, the patrolman's friends gave him a fifth of whiskey in "celebration." Over the label they'd pasted a police photo of one of the dead bandits sprawled on the liquor store floor.

At the time of the shootings, a psychologist later testified, the patrolman was "a stable, hard-working, family-oriented type of fellow with a good circle of friends." His reaction to the incident, however, was "very severe anxiety and depressive neurosis, insomnia and a lack of concentration."

He relived the killings night after night in his dreams. Within six months, he had become an alcoholic. Eventually, his wife left him because she could no longer tolerate the changes in his personality. Six years after the incident, the police department fired him because his uncontrollable drinking had made him unsuitable for duty. He was unable to hold another job. In effect, his life was wrecked. Finally, eight years after the shootings, his city's pension board awarded the ex-patrolman an annual lifetime disability pension of $5,500, the first it had ever granted for psychological injuries.

Should you be shot during a confrontation, the after-burn can carry physical and financial as well as psychological ramifications. An 11-year police veteran in Wichita, for example, was shot in the right arm with a .357 Magnum when he responded to a robbery-in-progress call at a liquor store. At first, he says, "I didn't know if I was hit in the arm, the chest, the head or where. I just remember the pain, the immediate pain." Because he was able still to give chase to the gunman, he figured that his injury would not affect his work. But when his wound failed to heal properly, he found himself assigned to desk duty.

Under his department's regulations, he is prohibited from holding a part-time job outside to help make ends meet, because of this "light duty" assignment. His financial position is further strained because his physical condition keeps him from doing repairs and "other little things" around home. "If something needs doing, I have to pay someone to do it." He's limited, too, in the activities he can enjoy with his four-year-old daughter, who asks him repeatedly when his arm will be well, when he will be

Memories of a shooting are often slow to fade.

able to do this and that, who shot him and why. His wife, who ''was really shook up'' by the shooting, has pressed him to leave law enforcement. Understandably, he has lost a lot of sleep worrying about his future as an officer and a family man. ''I miss patrol work,'' he says, ''but if I have to go out and wrestle someone, I just can't do it. I'm still steadily going through pain in my arm.''

After more than 19 months of therapy, he is scheduled at this writing to undergo surgery for the fifth time. He has been informed that if his arm ''doesn't come around'' after this operation, he may have to retire.

Under the best of circumstances, we all know that the psychological strain of being in law enforcement is immense. There's no time that the strain is greater than *after* a fatal confrontation. During the gunfight, you may not be consciously aware of the recoil, the muzzle flash or other things that are happening as you fire your gun. If you are working on strict survival instinct, trying to stay alive, you may not even be aware of stress at the time. But *afterward*, regardless of how justified or imperative

your shooting a suspect may have been or how seemingly minor a wound to yourself may seem, you are almost certain to feel a psychological impact in some form. And this stress is likely to be greatest when you take a suspect's life.

When you take an assailant's life in police work, you usually do so to save your own life. But how you handle your reaction to that event will in the long run determine whether you are indeed able to "save" the kind of life you had before the incident.

Officers who've been involved in shootings know you can never predict exactly how you will react afterwards. Men and women who least expect to be sandbagged psychologically may be hit the hardest. What you *can* do is understand the nature of the subtle and not-so-subtle forces that are likely to play on your mind after an armed confrontation and learn how best to prepare for them...cope with them...and help fellow officers who may experience them. Our discussion here generally assumes circumstances in which you inflict injury or death on another individual. But many of the principles will also apply where you are the injured party.

Passages

Some psychologists and psychiatrists argue that a lot of officers are like little kids playing war; they "get off" on the neat equipment, the excitement, the crusading aspects of good guys versus bad guys. Obviously, that's not *all* there is to police work or to policemen. But if we're honest, we'll concede that many of us probably have been drawn to this profession, subconsciously anyway, for at least some childlike reasons. Though we may mask it with a macho image, a lot of what's deep inside us is still "little kid."

Many people postpone growing up as long as possible. But a law enforcement officer runs into situations where he has to confront the end of childish fantasies and the existence of awful adult realities a lot sooner or a lot more intensely than "ordinary" people. For many people, this moment comes when they experience the death of a parent or loved one or are involved in a natural disaster or some other public tragedy—some fateful development that they feel is beyond their control. For officers, the telling event is often a shooting, where their own actions have helped determine the outcome. *In a shooting situation, an officer in effect suddenly goes from being a "kid" fooling around with a gun to being an arbiter of life and death.*

If you shoot and kill someone, you're likely to feel deep in your heart that what you did is "bad." It may have been necessary and fully justified from a legal standpoint, but most officers have rather simplified standards of right and wrong, and however much you may rationalize your action, at least a part of your psyche "knows" that killing someone is morally "wrong." You're likely to experience a feeling of sadness, of loss of innocence, which, with your possibly exaggerated childlike core, may itself be exaggerated.

One thing you need at this point is empathy, an understanding from other people about how you feel. But if you're someone who's not actively in touch with his emotions, you may not even recognize or acknowledge how you're feeling yourself. Many officers fall into this category. The last time they had a feeling was back in 1963. They can't admit to themselves that they are at all upset, much less ask anyone else to listen to them or to share their emotions. For such an officer, a post-shooting conversation with his wife might go: "How was your day?" "Fine." "Anything interesting happen today?" Silence...or, "Naw." If she's astute, she may see something's up...but she can also see the wall her husband has erected around his emotion.

Even if you *want* to communicate on an honest level, you may have trouble doing so. Your work may already constitute a strain between you and your mate, and if you start talking about a gunfight, it could be just another nail in the coffin. Your fellow officers may be busy lionizing you for what you feel bad or ambivalent about. They're likely to come on with comments like: "Great job! Boy, I can't wait 'til I can get in there and blow somebody away." Or: "Well, kid, now you're a man!" Or: "Where's the notch on your gun?" Or: "You only shot him once? Why didn't you empty your gun into the asshole!" Command level personnel in your department may be unapproachable or more concerned with bureaucratic technicalities than personal crises. Friends outside the department may reflect the duality of fascination and repulsion held by society as a whole toward the use of deadly force. People you don't even know and who have no appreciation of the circumstances or of the amount of terror that can be involved in a shoot-out may add to your inner turbulence by writing blistering letters to the editor condemning what you did, as was the case in Chicago recently after a young policewoman shot and killed a man who tried to rob her at gunpoint. If you're not a religious person, the traditional avenue of appealing to the deity is shut off.

You may wind up alone with the after-burn, feeling shaky and somehow threatened. Some officers try to block out, discount or repress what happened in the strongest possible terms. Some start drinking. Some show their turmoil by doing little crazy things, like locking the keys in the patrol car or forgetting roll call or coming in for a shift they're not on or chewing people out over inconsequential annoyances like not being able to find the paper clips in the squad room.

And unless they get help, some officers go really crazy.

Reactions differ, of course, with individual personalities. But psychologists have identified certain psychological stages or "passages" that officers commonly go through after they've killed or sometimes even seriously injured suspects.

At the scene of the shooting, you may experience a sense of depersonalization ("This isn't happening to me") or puzzlement ("What's all the fuss about?"), as well as physical excitation. Time may seem to slow down or stop. Usually some pressing responsibility intervenes that forces you into real-life activity: you need to call in on your radio, or help handle a crowd, or talk to your supervisor, or fill out a report. This distraction offers a "psychological break" that delays the impact of the event.

Eventually, though, the reality of what has happened hits. If you're a sensitive, intuitive, understanding officer, this may happen fairly soon, because your defenses are rather permeable. You're likely to enter a sober period, in which you feel very disturbed, shaken or thoughtful, though for reasons we've explored, you probably don't talk about it. You may develop an urge to "make up" for what you have done, to express your regret or apologize in some demonstrative way. Often officers will attend the suspect's funeral, either in disguise or under the pretext of looking for clues or other offenders. Consciously or subconsciously, they may see this as a way of saying, "I'm sorry for what happened."

If you are less sensitive, intuitive or in touch with your emotions, you may seem unfazed by the shooting or try to belittle it ("It's no big deal"), even claim you "liked" it. While this may allow you to avoid an obvious negative reaction at the onset, your denial that anything extraordinary has occurred may, in fact, only delay the impact. As time passes, you may develop seemingly unrelated symptoms that really stem from your deeply buried psychological turmoil: headaches...backaches... stomach problems...jittery nerves...absent-mindedness...a short temper that ignites flashes of inappropriate anger. Some officers experience nightmares they can't remember or repeatedly wake in the night in inexplicable panic.

If, early out, you do not sit down and acknowledge that a serious event has occurred...frankly examine your feelings...confront what is happening...and decide what you are going to do about it—*if you continue to deny and repress honest emotions, the effects can escalate into full-blown psychiatric problems.*

A full investigation of the shooting is likely to develop, especially if you have killed a suspect. In many respects, it will resemble any other homicide investigation. Evidence will be gathered, reports will be required, command-level personnel will be involved. You will be under scrutiny, and the press may treat you as a "suspect." Some officers who are unable to keep all this, plus their own emotions about the shooting, in realistic perspective become genuinely paranoid. They believe they are *unnaturally* watched or picked on. They may experience flashbacks, where they see someone in a crowd who looks like the suspect they shot. Or they talk about feeling "cursed," of "people looking in my eyes and seeing I have killed someone." Some become obsessive. One state trooper had shot at a burglar who then ran and disappeared into a swampy woods in a rural area. The officer irrationally fantasized that the suspect was lying in agony somewhere among the trees, slowly bleeding to death. Day after day, he compulsively returned to the swamp to search for "clues" or sit in silent vigil at the edge of the woods, sometimes remaining there through the night. This continued for a period of weeks before he finally sought psychiatric help. Sometimes officers who develop mental problems describe themselves as feeling "enveloped by a black cloud." They feel "bad," angry, depressed, "bummed out," "sick" though not with any specific disease—all symptoms of an extreme anxiety reaction. Marital tensions and sexual dysfunctions, including impotence and premature ejaculation, are not unusual. These may be hidden behind a facade of virile braggadocio. One officer belligerently asserted, "I'm the biggest fucker around. I can fuck anything that moves!" In fact, he'd been unable to get an erection since killing a suspect. He really wanted very tender lovemaking in which his wife held and comforted him, but he didn't know how to ask for it.

Some officers deal with their psychological wounds by resigning from law enforcement. Others manage to hold themselves together through one shooting experience, then "snap out" in spades the next time around. Some say, "All right, I shot someone once. I don't care what happens, I'm never going to pull this gun again." Such men are dangerous. They may try to be the hero who calms everything down with words during some future confrontation where shooting is the only sane survival option. For sure, you would not want someone with this attitude as your partner or your back-up.

In contrast to officers who deal poorly with after-burn, you *can* emerge from a shooting episode as a stronger person, if you shepherd yourself through the trauma in mentally healthy ways. A serious shooting tends to be a "watershed" experience; your life is changed one way or another, for better or for worse. No one invites a shooting, of course, as a means of self-improvement, but given that it has occurred, you need to be able to go on from it...to draw your gun again...to live normally— and you can. You can come away having gained a sobered feeling about the world...having grown up... having matured. You may emerge with a new and more realistic perspective of how serious police work really is. You may find yourself wanting to help fellow officers become aware of its dangers, difficulties and heavy responsibilities. All this reflects your ability to deal with one of your job's least pleasant demands in a positive emotional way.

Self-Help

Your recovery from a shooting experience properly begins with mental preconditioning. If you're like most officers, you naturally hope that using your gun will never be necessary. But to assume that such will be the case throughout your career is a risky mind-set. If it does happen, the shock waves afterwards will be all the more severe.

You'll be better prepared if you've spent some time seriously evaluating your job and its responsibilities. True, much of it is service oriented, not even involved with crime. Most of the criminal work, even, is accomplished without violence. But the possibility of deadly force is omnipresent and should be remembered.

In meditative, introspective moments, you should spend some time fantasizing about this. Rather than suppress thoughts that might be unpleasant to you, frankly confront the fact that as a law enforcement officer you are one of the few people in this country who have a legal right to take another human life. Try to picture yourself in that situation and face the pertinent question: could I do it? That's a question you need to resolve before the issue presents itself—not on the spot when the action is going down.

If you honestly feel the answer to that question is "No," then you probably should give serious consideration to getting out of police work. Your mental attitude makes you potentially dangerous to yourself, your fellow officers and the civilians you are sworn to protect.

If you believe you can kill in necessary and justified circumstances, then take more time to think about what the effect on yourself might be. Ask other officers who have been involved in shootings how they felt afterwards—and what they wish they'd known before the shooting occurred. Unless you are psychologically sick, you will be affected by the experience. You should realize ahead of time that not only will there be immediate psychological reactions, but you'll likely be visited by emotions of self-doubt, isolation, confusion and sadness that we've described. This is *perfectly normal*; indeed, they are a sign of your emotional health, because no matter how you slice it, taking a life is bound to be traumatic.

When these feelings come, acknowledge them— and try to find someone with whom you can honestly share them. Here again, other shooting survivors are a good resource. Get together and talk to them about how you feel. In their company you'll know you're with peers; these people have "been there." They're not likely to cater or condescend to you, but to talk frankly and supportively about their own reactions. They can look at what happened to you as no one else can, and the experience of sharing can be extremely helpful.

Your command personnel should be sensitive to your situation, too. Often it is not a good idea for them to transfer you to other duty or suspend you pending an investigation of the shooting, as is routinely done by some departments. By the same token, awards for your act may not be in your best interest, either. *Strong negative or positive responses to what you did may only add to your confusion and self-doubt.* Ideally, your supervisors should treat you as they do any other officer, allowing you to remain in the same assignment with the same expectations of performance as before.

Off-duty, make a concerted effort to maintain your normal routine. Look especially for opportunities to expend physical energy. This tends to reduce stress. Researchers at a number of universities have confirmed that such exercise as running, jogging, wrestling, swimming and cycling—but especially running, done thirty minutes a day, three times a week—is capable of significantly reducing depression and anxiety. Above all, *do not just sit at home by yourself*, artifically isolated and brooding. Be with people. Participate in activities. Life does go on.

Therapy

If your department has a psychologist or other therapist or you have access to one privately, it is recommended that you meet with him as soon after the shooting as possible. This does not mean you must undertake a long, psychiatric ordeal. Often, he can help you restore your emotional equilibrium in one or a few sessions.

Basically, a therapist is someone with whom you can fully "unpack" and sort out your feelings. In all probability, you'll have very mixed emotions about the shooting, yet you may believe that any ambivalence is "wrong or weak." He'll help you see that a hybrid reaction actually is normal, and he'll help you identify just what your feelings are so you can deal with them in an open, honest way, rather than let the churning inside destroy you.

Sometimes officers in therapy conduct a "dialog" with the suspect they've shot. Through this device, they're able to explain why they shot him...express their regret that his life turned out as it did...and bid him "goodbye" with an unburdened conscience.

The goal of therapy is not to make you forget the shooting. That's unrealistic. What you want is for it to recede into the background, so that your life does not become totally focused upon it. If you are cooperative and willing to talk about how you feel, a good therapist can help you free yourself of after-burn much faster than if you insist on remaining "blanked out" or uncommunicative in his presence.

If you have not contacted a therapist soon after the shooting, you may find that you need to do so later. Even with sympathetic supervisors and fellow officers, you may not be able to resolve your emotional turmoil on your own.

In some cases, the department may refer you for counseling. But if you're astute, you can detect on your own when your mental state is deteriorating and you need help. Among other clues, look for:

1. *hyperactivity*. Is your mood unusually elevated? Have you turned into a non-stop talker? Are you unnaturally happy-go-lucky?

2. *preoccupation*. Is it hard for people to get your attention? Have you become unfriendly and withdrawn?

3. *physical symptoms*. Is sickness, tardiness, forgetfulness affecting your work performance?

4. *personal care*. Have you become sloppy in your dress and grooming? Are you suddenly accident prone?

5. *disturbed sleep*. Do you have insomnia? Or nightmares that keep coming back again and again?

These and other disturbances in your normal pattern may indicate that you are denying reality...rejecting your work...feeling guilty—and need help. If you ignore the symptoms, your mental state is likely to get progressively worse.

Helping Others

If another officer is involved in a shooting, the best thing you can do for him is be a good listener. Let him know that if he wants to talk about his feelings or the experience itself, you're willing to hear him out—without passing judgment, trying to "correct" him or appearing either worshipful or repulsed. If he is your partner, say, try to reassure him. Point out that it might have been you, instead of him, who had to pull the trigger. Try, too, to reaffirm his value to you.

Once you've been in a shooting, you can help prepare other officers for the experience by sharing your reactions with them. Help them understand that in a moment of crisis, they *must* act—but they must also understand that afterwards there will be doubts that will take time and effort to resolve.

II. BASICS

...that Strengthen Tactics

PROTECTIVE EQUIPMENT 12

Winning an edge on the street, like getting ahead in the business world, is often easier if you know how to "dress for success." Out there, you're not concerned with pin stripe suits, Ivy League ties or "subtle but significant accents" of jewelry, as you might be in the corporate arena. For *your* professional wardrobe, what matters are items that can protect your body—and your gun—in a confrontation.

Of course, so-called "bulletproof" vests or, more correctly, "soft body armor," and the leather gear that carries your handgun and ammunition can't guarantee you immunity from attack. But armor, properly selected and worn, can significantly increase your odds of surviving if you are hit by one or more of an assailant's shots. And the right leather worn and cared for in the right way can help guard your gun against loss...assure its quick accessibility in the event of a threat...and, in an extended gunfight, readily make available adequate ammunition for fast reloading.

As with buying civilian garb, you have to know how to evaluate the many choices you're confronted with in order to be a shrewd consumer. The protective equipment of law enforcement, too, is subject to exaggerated commercial claims, fashion fads, myths and misuse—all of which can have a bearing on whether what you buy will give you the service you need.

The difference is this: if you make wrong choices regarding your civilian wardrobe, you may waste your money or be out of style. But *your decisions about armor and leather may very well determine whether you stay alive.*

In evaluating what you see in the market place and the word-of-mouth comments you hear from your fellow officers, you need to: keep in mind the patterns of encounter involved in most armed confrontations...understand the stresses to which you're likely to subject protective items...and know how to test them for quality or how they have fared in carefully controlled tests by others.

Location of fatal wounds sustained by officers during the last seven years. In this period, 378 officers out of a total of 761 died from wounds to the torso area.

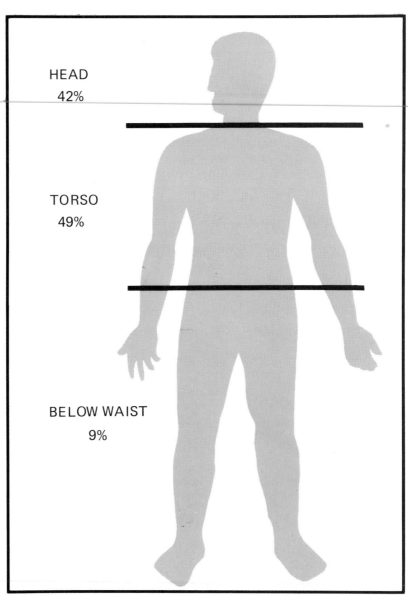

HEAD
42%

TORSO
49%

BELOW WAIST
9%

Body Armor

Contrary to their popular nickname, armored vests cannot be considered bulletproof; you won't make yourself an impenetrable force by strapping one on. Some suspects tote firearms and ammunition that can blast through anything, including armored cars and tanks. "And whatever protection you come up with," one armor expert says, "there'll always be some donkey in his basement making a round that'll take you."

What makes body armor make sense is percentages. Forty-nine per cent of the cases in which suspects fatally shoot officers, the bullets impact in the upper torso, the area most readily covered by body armor. Eighty-one per cent of the ammunition used in these assaults is .38 cal. or smaller, a "threat level" that good armor almost always can resist. That means, a little calculation reveals, that nearly 50 per cent of officer deaths from firearms could in all probability be prevented if body armor were worn. Put another way: if every defensive tactic you try fails and you are shot, you can be saved four out of ten times by the right armor alone. That's a survival factor hard to ignore!

Traditionally, modern body armor has incorporated ballistic nylon, ceramics, metal inserts and laminated glass fiber and was worn on the outside of clothing—fine for SWAT teams, but too cumbersome, hot, heavy and conspicuous for the ordinary officer. Within the last decade, however, armored vests have become available that are soft, lightweight, pliable and that you can easily and comfortably conceal under your uniform shirt.

Those that many experts consider best for law enforcement utilize a nylon-related fabric called Kevlar®, which pound for pound, is five times stronger than steel. Tests conducted by the U.S. Army show that just seven thin layers of this high tensile strength material can *consistently prevent* penetration by .38 cal. revolver bullets travelling at 800 feet per second and .22 cal. bullets travelling at 1,000 feet per second.

What this means in practical terms is illustrated by the experience of a young patrolman who was shot when he interrupted a burglary-in-progress. Two .38 cal. 158 grain lead bullets struck his vest-covered chest at a range of less than four feet. Normally, such a hit would at least have necessitated emergency surgery, assuming he had lived to reach a hospital. Yet with the vest on, he did not lose consciousness or even have to gasp for breath. To the surprise of his assailant, he was able to successfully chase and arrest him. Similarly, another officer who confronted a burglar with a handgun took a hit from a .22 cal., 40 grain slug fired from about 6 feet away. The shot smashed into his vest directly over his heart, clearly a mortal location, yet he experienced only slight, momentary discomfort and no immobility. In Indiana, a policeman was thrown violently backward, as sometimes happen, when he took a .45 cal. slug point-blank on his vest. But he still was able to draw and shoot his attacker five times, fatally.

Layers of Kevlar® peeled back.

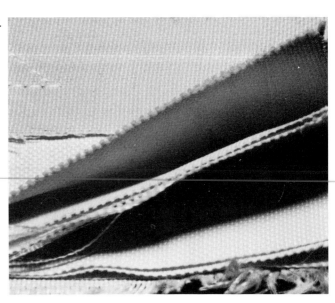

A .38 cal. 158 gr. bullet which was stopped in a soft armor vest.

Half a dozen manufacturers fabricate Kevlar® into soft armor vests with a variety of weaves and deniers. The strength depends in large part on the fabrication. In selecting soft body armor, you want to balance bullet resistance with comfort and wearability. For many officers, this balance is achieved with vests that incorporate protective panels of 8- to 10-ply Kevlar-29® of 1000 denier, plain weave. No ballistic nylon should be included. The garment should feature cotton enclosures from which the front and rear Kevlar® panels can be removed. (It's a good idea to buy several enclosures so they can be washed regularly.)

Well-balanced armor should protect you from the kinds of rounds you are most likely to encounter on the street—.357 Magnum, 9mm and all ammunition .38 cal. and smaller. There is body armor capable of withstanding higher threat level ammunition, including that fired from shoulder and military ball weapons and .44 and .41 Magnum handguns. But this armor may be rigid, cumbersome and uncomfortable to wear on normal duty. Such armor often winds up in the trunk of a patrol car rather than protecting an officer's body.

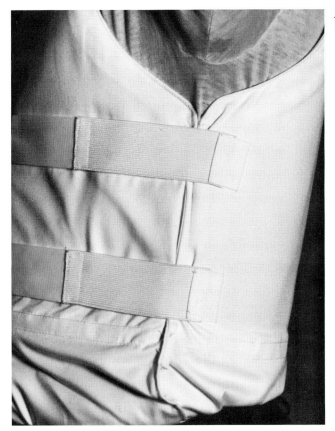

A properly worn vest should fit so that the side panels meet for a close fit.

For a workable balance between protection and comfort, you'll want to choose armor that:

1. *almost encircles your torso*, providing some defense to your sides, as well as front and back. Consider allowing for about a 1½-inch opening at each side for heat to dissipate. Excessive heat is the major complaint from officers about armor, and it's better to lose this slight protection on each side than to lose total protection because you don't wear the vest. You may hear the argument that fatal shots from the rear are so rare you don't need a double vest. But statistics on officer deaths show, in fact, that about 10 per cent are shot in the back. When lead is flying and possibly ricocheting erratically in a shoot-out, you can't depend on an assailant's bullets impacting only where they're "supposed" to.

2. *extends to about one inch above your belt level and has a V-neck.* If the vest is too long, you'll get the "turtle-shell effect"—that is, it will ride up under your chin—when you sit down. Without the V-neck, the top may rub your Adam's apple even when you're standing.

3. *resists water.* Moisture tends to lubricate the threads in vest fabric, weakening the weave and lowering its stopping power. Fabric that has been wet may part enough to allow certain slugs to pass through.

If you have a vest that isn't waterproof, check with the manufacturer about the advisability of applying water-repellent spray. Follow the manufacturer's instructions, explicitly. Don't use a vinyl cover. It won't allow heat or sweat to dissipate properly. (If the Kevlar® portion of your vest should get wet, immediately contact the manufacturer to find out if its bullet resistance has been compromised.)

Besides bullet resistance and comfort, you want to be certain that the armor you choose can be worn *inconspicuously*, under your clothing. A vest that's obvious can be self-defeating: if an assailant realizes your torso is protected, he can shoot at your head or below your waist. You won't get the right fit just by picking a vest that's the same as your coat size. It needs to be more *snug* than that. A good custom fit is a must. It may require 15 points or more of measurement, and for obvious reasons, additional special tailoring is usually necessary for women. Soft body armor makes a good Christmas or birthday gift from a spouse or close friend, but because of the fitting and other special requirements involved, you should have a hand in the selection.

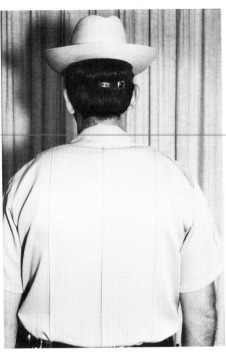

A properly fitted vest should not interfere with a professional, trim appearance.

SUPPORT POLICE VEST FUND

PBA

Even though a well-chosen vest allows you to withstand an assailant's first strike, you may still experience injury. When a slug impacts at high velocity, it drives the armor inward against your body as the shot's kinetic energy dissipates. This force may cause a shallow wound or lesion in your flesh and may, in addition, produce invisible blunt-trauma injuries to internal organs. There is *no* correlation between a seemingly innocent or severe skin lesion and possible internal injury beyond it. What looks innocent may, in fact, have produced damage that can have serious repercussions later.

Therefore, *any time you are hit*, even if the lesion below your body armor seems strictly superficial, *you should be hospitalized for observation*. Doctors will want to monitor you carefully for blunt trauma damage to your heart, lungs, liver, spleen, spine and/or abdominal wall.

The most important rule about body armor is to wear it. If you leave it at home, in your locker or in your patrol car, you are not planning ahead or anticipating danger, as a survival orientation necessitates. *Armor not worn is no armor at all.* Some officers have been discouraged from wearing armor by the claim that it may increase the chances of being attacked. An officer whose body is protected, this theory goes, will be more aggressive because he feels "superhuman" and, through his actions, will provoke shooting incidents.

This pernicious assertion has recently been soundly disproved. In a study of 4,500 officers in 15 U.S. cities, reserachers found that those wearing protective garments experienced no higher incidence of assault, where suspects wielding shotguns and rifles were concerned. Interestingly, for reasons not fully understood, there is some evidence to suggest that officers with vests actually experience fewer attacks with handguns. One factor might be that officers wearing armor tend to have a heightened awareness of danger. As a rule, they are more attuned to tactics and survival.

One of over 10,000 bumper stickers placed in New York City taxi cabs as part of Burger King's promotion to raise money for body armor. Burger King was the first major corporation to support the Patrolmen's Benevolent Association's drive to equip officers with vests. Similar campaigns could be started in any community.

Service Holsters

Late one spring night in Michigan, an officer searching a stopped car found a .38 cal. revolver lying partly under a seat and promptly arrested the driver for carrying a concealed weapon. At the station, the incident took a rather unexpected turn. A check of the serial number on the gun showed that it belonged not to the bewildered motorist, but to the arresting officer! During the search, it evidently had dropped from his holster unnoticed and landed where he "uncovered" it.

In this case, the failure of a holster to adequately retain an officer's gun proved only embarrassing. But imagine yourself having cornered an armed suspect after a foot chase, reaching for your gun...and discovering that it had bounced out somewhere along the way. Or as happens to officers year in and year out, a suspect starts to struggle while you are handcuffing him, manages with little effort to snatch your gun from its holster and uses it against you at point-blank range. You begin to appreciate that a holster is one of your most important pieces of survival equipment, a complement to the firearm it carries and worthy of equal attention in selection and maintenance to your gun itself.

There's no such thing, of course, as a loss-*proof* holster, just as there's no bullet*proof* vest. If a holster offered you perfect security, you probably wouldn't be able to draw your gun without a week's notice. What you can—and should—expect is a reasonable balance. The holster should fit your gun well enough to retain it without the safety strap snapped and without the gun moving and shifting inside it...yet still allow you to draw quickly and easily with either hand, from the front or rear, in event of a threat. In other words, you don't want a holster that's too heavy on security *or* a fast-draw competition type that overemphasizes availability. Some officers drastically reshape their holsters with metal-lined shanks to produce outlandish quick-draw angles. Such an unsightly configuration, like any other imbalance of features, heightens your risk.

You can performance test a holster for proper compromise with the following exercises:

1.   With your gun *unloaded* and your holster's flap or strap unsnapped, vigorously jump up and down at least six times without touching your gun or the holster, to simulate running. You should still be armed. (Perform this test over a soft surface, of course, in the event your holster fails and your gun falls to the ground.)

2.   On the range at the 7-yard line, with your gun strapped to the holster, draw and fire one round.

You should be able to hit center mass on a silhouette target in approximately 2 seconds.

Also:

1. With your sidearm unloaded, *secure* it in your holster.

2. Have your partner try to remove it by only grasping the stock, as an opponent might. Have him pull forward, backward, sideways and straight up, which are possibilities in any brawl.

3. If he removes it, look for a more secure holster. (If you drop your gun while running, you *may* be in trouble. If a suspect takes it away from you, you can bet that you *are* in trouble, perhaps fatal trouble.)

Throughout these tests, your holster should fit your belt tight enough to stay in place. You want always to know exactly where the butt of your gun is, so you can draw suddenly without having to look. Your gunbelt should be worn directly over your pants belt. Clamping devices called ''belt keepers'' can help you keep your gunbelt in place. Your sidearm should be at a pitch and angle that allow you the most comfortable, natural motion making the draw. For some officers, this means the gun should cant slightly forward of a vertical line. Others prefer a slightly backward cant which generally yields a faster draw. The holster should hide as much of your sidearm as possible, while still providing you accessibility, and carry your gun high at the belt line. Some officers carry their guns slung so low they look as if they're headed for the O.K. Corral with their pants falling down!

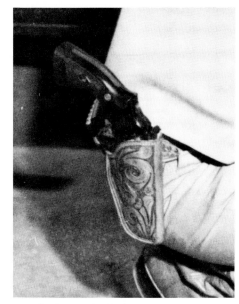

Any holster which does not contain a retention strap makes your sidearm an open invitation to any observant offender.

The ''gunslinger'' approach to law enforcement.

All the items on your gunbelt, including your holster, should blend into your uniform. You don't want the look of a dime store display rack, with keys, chains, knives and as much other glitter and sparkle as you can muster. When officers rig themselves that way, it's difficult to decide whether the officer is wearing the gun or the gun is wearing the officer! A display of this nature attracts unnecessary attention and may invite trouble from someone bent on obtaining your sidearm. Stick with neat, trim leather gear without unneeded paraphernalia.

Because faulty leather goods can be as unsafe as a faulty gun, don't look for bargains when you're holster-shopping. There are many brands and designs that are unsafe. *Buy quality.* The sharpest looking rig may not be the best made or the best for your needs. (If there are no gun shops or other outlets in your area where you can personally inspect a variety of leather, buy some gun magazines and send for catalogs from holster manufacturers who advertise there. These will give you an idea of the range of equipment available.)

The holster should be made of the best leather and stitched with nylon or other rot-resistant material. Naturally, it should be comfortable to wear for long periods of time, especially sitting in a patrol car. And the design should allow for leather to completely cover the trigger and trigger guard to lessen the chance of accidental discharge. Some individual features may enhance your survival capabilities. One model, for instance, uses a false snap on the front side of the holster, calculated to fool a suspect who grabs for your gun. This snap can't be unfastened. The real one is on the belt side near the hammer, where you can release it by thumb pressure. Another manufacturer offers a holster with a built-in track for the front sight blade that makes your gun difficult for anyone but you to get un-

Properly positioned leather accessories are critical to proper appearance and officer survival.

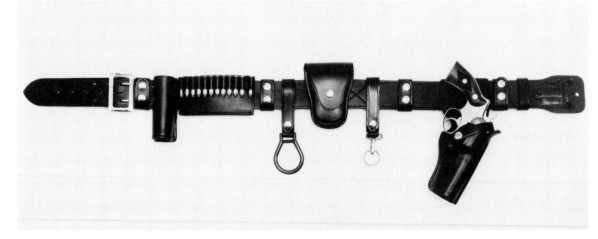

holstered; any unexpected tug from the side or rear will bind the barrel tightly enough to keep the gun in.

You want to be careful, though, that seemingly good features don't, in fact, constitute hazards. For example, some new "form-fit" holsters are so tight that the retentive, shaped leather may actually pull the trigger as you force the gun into place. Inside linings which offer soft, smooth protection for your gun at first, may wear through with use and hang the gun up on its front sight when you try to draw. And swivel holsters which allow your gun to move to comfortably accommodate your sitting down, can become dangerous with wear, because the holster may break loose at the swivel.

Be cautious, too, about holsters that depend on spring-loaded catches, hinges or similar mechanical devices. These may jam when you need your gun the most...or unexpectedly dump it out by accident. If, for example, in returning your gun to a button-released clamshell holster you happen to apply pressure at the top or bottom, the holster shell may lock incompletely and pop open under stress.

A quality holster is as important as the sidearm it protects. This particular holster epitomizes the look of security. It offers full grip clearance, trigger guard protection, and a thumb break with a one-way snap.

Being conscious of your holster is no different than being conscious of your wallet in your pocket.

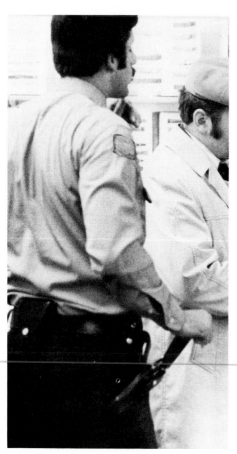

The "bench rest" approach to law enforcement.

You want to remember that claims for mechanical holsters may be exaggerated. The front-opening clamshell holster, which allows you to draw fast on target by bringing your gun forward and parting the tension-spring-controlled front seam rather than lifting it up and out, is often touted as "suspect-proof." This is because a special trigger-housing inside makes it difficult for anyone to snatch the gun out of the holster from the rear or side, even with the safety strap unfastened. However, in New Mexico, an officer with a so-called "breakfront" holster was successfully disarmed and shot with his own gun while struggling to subdue a robbery suspect. The assailant, face-down on the ground with the officer astride him, simply reached back and yanked the officer's service revolver forward. The holster parted...and suddenly the felon was armed. Similar incidents have occurred in other states.

Although a holster should be chosen with regard to what's most comfortable and serviceable for you, the best design is likely to be one that rides high and holds your gun securely, close to your body on your shooting-hand side. It should allow you to draw up and out with one smooth, fluid motion...and no hangups.

With any holster, you'll need to "work" the leather when it's new, like you would to break in a baseball glove. You also need to practice to perfect your draw and to get accustomed to the leather in realistic situations. Be sure your gun is empty to prevent accidental discharge. Practice with your gun strapped in the holster so you become adept at drawing through the security device. For a smoother, snappier draw, try spraying the inside of your holster periodically with silicone, available in aerosol cans at most hardware and automotive stores.

Cross-Draw Holsters

A cross-draw holster may look dramatic, but its use for an officer's primary weapon is discouraged by many law enforcement agencies because of safety and survival considerations. They concede one advantage: the cross-draw position makes your gun more accessible when you're sitting in a car. But they argue that the disadvantages heavily outweigh this. On the other hand, some major departments consider the disadvantages to be of little consequence and specify cross-draw holsters as part of their regulation uniform. Where given a choice, you will want to evaluate the arguments against the cross-draw and come to your own conclusions.

Faced with a gunfight that's imminent or already started, a cross-draw generally will take you longer to get on target to defend your life. When you're excited and moving fast, there's a greater tendency for the gun's hammer spur to snag on clothing. But even if you manage to draw smoothly, you have to reach across your body and pull the gun back through a 90-degree arc before you're pointing it straight ahead. In other words, your hand must travel farther to the holster, and your gun must travel farther to the assailant. While this is eating up valuable milliseconds, it's giving him good opportunity, if he's close enough, to restrict your hand or knock it into a missed shot since, in effect, it must travel in front of his body as well as your own in making the draw.

Through the entire swing back, your muzzle sweeps across a broad non-target area that may include fellow officers or innocent civilians. With your arm and hand moving sideways, it's hard to halt your gun in exactly the right spot. If you swing past the suspect, you lose even more time, further benefiting him...and expose an additional undesired area to possible premature or accidental fire.

Most officers conclude that in close situations particularly (which most armed confrontations are) you strengthen your direct-hit potential with a conventional ''punch-out'' or ''directional'' draw from a holster on your strong side. With this, you may be able to hit lower parts of your assailant's body even before your gun is in its final position, giving you more total target time than is possible with a cross-draw. In any case, you can keep your muzzle under control, pointing either safely at the ground or at your assailant from the instant it clears your leather until you shoot.

Back-Up/Off-Duty Holsters

Choosing supplementary leather has its special complications because in addition to a balance between security and availability, you probably want this holster to be concealable. Where that's the case, you'll have to be ready to accept some trade-offs, sacrificing some qualities you'd normally demand in exchange for keeping your gun hidden.

One common design for supplementary leather is the ankle holster, popular because suspects often tend to overlook it. An off-duty female officer in Detroit was entering her car in a parking lot one night when an armed robber suddenly accosted her, threatened her life and snatched her purse. At that instant, her badge, I.D. card and handcuffs all went into his hands. But not her gun. She was able to draw a .38 Colt Cobra from a holster on her left leg and defend herself. In other cases, by pretending to be shot and crumpling over, officers have been able to reach extra guns in ankle or boot holsters. And it's possible, if you ever were taken hostage, that you could save your life with the gun an undetected ankle holster could put in your hand at the right moment. That happened with an officer in New York who was being held hostage by a gunman. By pretending to scratch his leg, he was able to draw a revolver from an ankle holster and shoot the suspect fatally.

When you work undercover, avoid putting any firearm in your waistband unsecured. The risks of dropping or losing it are far too great.

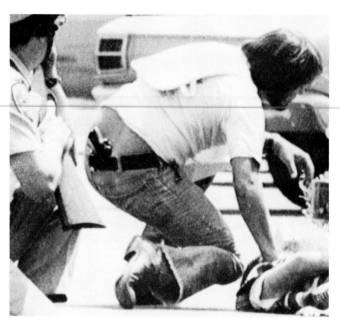

There are negative factors you should weigh, though. Ankle holsters usually have a minimum amount of leather to enclose your gun...an open trigger guard...and a snap-on security strap that is subject to strain when you walk or run. In numerous instances, the design for certain of these holsters has contributed to accidental discharges. Indeed, *some variety of "gimmick" holster*—ankle, shoulder, cross-draw, fast-draw—*is most often the equipment involved when a gun is lost or unintentionally shot off or an officer is disarmed.* Even when the ankle holster properly retains your gun, you have to reach down or raise your leg up to draw, either of which can put you in a bad position in close combat.

Similarly, belt clip-on holsters favored by some officers because of their convenience and relative concealability, also can present serious survival risks. On most models, the clip is easily dislodged when you run, are jostled in a crowd, get in or out of a vehicle or just walk naturally. When you try to draw, the whole holster may come along with your gun, and when you sit at a desk or in a car, the holster clip may ride up over your belt.

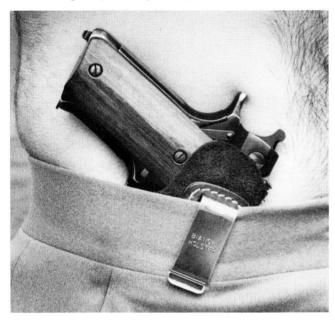

An important consideration behind any non-patrol holster is concealment. The clip-on type is most effective when clipped to a leather belt, rather than to a cloth surface.

Probably the *best* holster for off-duty use is a secure belt model, worn in the same place you wear your service sidearm when on duty. We are all creatures of habit, and you're most likely to reach there instinctively in case of danger. Perhaps next best for off-duty wear (and a good compromise for a back-up gun on duty) is a shoulder holster. It does put your gun in a cross-draw position, which is normally considered a strong disadvantage, but it is readily concealable under a coat or jacket, reasonably secure and comfortable and generally allows you to draw easily. A shoulder holster, if it must be used, should be of similar construction to a good belt holster and should allow the muzzle to point down rather than up.

A properly worn shoulder holster should stay close to your body. A belt strap is also a requirement for maintaining a secure, flat shape.

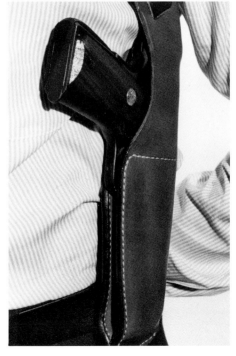

Cartridge Carriers

Although a shooting is likely to be over before you have to reload—remember, an officer fires only 2 or 3 shots in the average gunfight—you need to be prepared at all times for the exceptions. Multiple assailants with heavy firepower may force you to

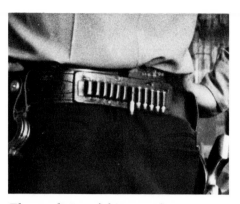

The condition of this cartridge carrier [stapled onto his belt] is an indication of this officer's concern for survival.

quickly expend what's in your gun. Or during an extended foot pursuit, you may squeeze off rounds at several points where you can stop and fire along the way without bringing your suspect down. Once your gun is empty, extra ammunition becomes critical to your survival. How fast you can get back on target and how well your ammunition works when you do may depend in large part on how you carry it.

For revolver ammunition, you have three basic possibilities: belt loops...dump pouches...or speed-loaders. Departmental regulations may give you little choice in the type of equipment you can use. But within each category there are guidelines that can help you provide the best possible protection for your extra rounds.

Belt loops offer perhaps the greatest security for your ammunition, but they expose your extra cartridges to the abuses of weather, seat-belts, restaurant table edges, et cetera...and they take considerable practice for quick loading. Good loops, like good holsters, balance retention and ease of extraction. If your loops are on a separate piece of leather that slides over your duty belt, it should fit with no slippage or loose play. You will probably want to carry two 6-round loops, worn on the same side near the front of your belt rather than at the rear. You want to be certain the design positions the cartridges where you can reach them quickly and comfortably and where they will not interfere with drawing your gun. The loops should be out a bit from the rest of the leather, rather than flat against it to ease withdrawal and high enough to allow you to "rock" the cartridges free. If the loops are too tight, you can stretch them slightly by working them with mink oil or saddle soap. They should be loose enough that the cartridges can easily be pushed up from below by your index finger, yet tight enough to provide safe retention. Double belt-loops can be dangerous, because the heads of the top row of bullets rest almost on the primers of the row below when the loops are full. With any style, you'll need to watch and maintain the leather carefully. As it ages, the loops tend to lose their retention, and under heavy stress, rounds may drop out.

Dump pouches need regular maintenance, too, because they tend to accumulate dirt and moisture. You want a pouch in which the leather has been dry-tanned. Oil tanning contributes to deposits building up on the rounds inside, and within a matter of months, you'll have green scum on your shell casings that may affect your ammunition's performance. Be sure your pouch has a metal or plastic insert to reinforce the leather and preserve its shape.

314

Otherwise, it can bend against your cartridges, holding them inside the pouch or dropping them erratically. Also, be sure it's well enough designed that it operates smoothly in cold weather (some jam when the temperature drops) and that it will not easily pop open during a scuffle, dumping your live rounds on the ground. Be aware of the maximum number of rounds that can be contained in your dump pouch. You don't want to cram it to the bursting point, but by the same token, you can often load seven or eight rounds, instead of just six. If you carry extras in the pouch, you'll be covered in the event you drop a couple when reloading under stress.

Speed-loaders, with extensive practice, probably allow the fastest reloading, but performance varies with different models, so you want to test several. Many officers find they get the best results with speed-loaders, as compared to ''speed strips,'' which hold cartridges in a narrow, flat piece of rubber. Any style you choose should be mechanically simple and reliable...should reload all chambers in your revolver simultaneously without being blocked by your left grip panel...should be the type designated for your ammunition...and should retain the cartridges it carries if you drop it or toss it to a fellow officer who's out of ammunition in a gunfight. Bear in mind that in approaching many potential confrontations, you want to be as unobtrusive as possible. Therefore, make sure your loader is designed to minimize cartridge rattle when you walk or run. This can be done by keeping styrofoam or rubber padding in the bottom of the case. In buying speed-loaders, consider getting sufficient leather gear for carrying two loaders on your belt. This will give you a total of 12 rounds for reloading.

In selecting a carrier for semi-automatic ammunition, you want a model that: 1) allows you to carry two extra magazines, so you have a total of three available, counting the one in your gun; 2) has individual pockets for each so you don't have to force both down into the same space, where they may bind; 3) protects the lips of the magazine against damage; 4) is sealed on the bottom and snaps over the top to provide good security and to prevent dust and dirt from entering the magazines. The carrier should hold the magazines snugly, but not so tightly they can't be easily drawn for reloading under fire.

When you are off-duty or on plainclothes assignment, take care to see that your spare ammunition stays concealed. In more than one case, an officer out of uniform has exposed ammunition on his belt by reaching into his front pocket for coins as he walks into a liquor store or drug store—

A quality, double magazine case for a semi-automatic.

unaware that an armed robbery is going down inside. One glimpse of your ammunition under those circumstances and the bad guys can "make" you as a threat to be swiftly shot and killed. When you're out of uniform, consider using a speed strip which can be carried in a shirt pocket (a round speed-loader is too bulky for concealed wear). Another option is an ammunition wallet similar to a cigaret case, which you can use to carry cartridges in strips or loose. If you wear extra ammunition in plainclothes, keep it on the side of the hand you load with for fastest use—that is, on your strong side if you use a revolver, your weak side if a semi-automatic. (This positioning is important if you're in uniform, too. Some officers wear their ammunition in places that are inaccessible to their loading hand.)

Leather Care

The care you give your leather will influence whether it provides the protection it should. Leather that is repeatedly exposed to the elements without cleaning or restoration may decay or become brittle. If you use your gun butt for an arm rest or a rack for hanging other equipment, you risk stretching the holster out of shape and making your gun less secure. If damage goes undetected, your leather may unexpectedly experience stress failure that leaves you vulnerable in a shooting situation.

Periodically, you want to examine all your leather, looking for worn stitching...ripped loops... evidence of stretching...cracked or punctured surfaces. Rub paste wax into the stitching to help keep it from drying out and snapping. Wipe the inside of your holster with a dry cloth, especially after exposure to rain, snow or other moisture. Also, clean out all lint, crumbs and other foreign particles. These can absorb and retain moisture and may have a corrosive effect on your gun, or they may work their way into its action. For a fast clean-out job, spray the inside of your holster with a service station air hose or use a vacuum cleaner.

Your holster should have a "weep hole" in the bottom. This will allow some foreign particles to fall on through and help keep condensation from building up inside. If yours lacks a hole, you can cut one. But then have the stitching reinforced at a shoe repair shop to keep the cut threads from loosening and weakening your holster.

To clean or to restore leather that has become dried out, follow this procedure:

Your leather gear should have that same "cared-for look" as your shoes and uniform. [Note the position of the handcuff case and belt keepers.]

This rig was actually worn by a police officer in this country.

1. After removing your gun, ammunition, all buckles and other items that snap or slide on, wash the leather with a sponge, strong soap and hot water. Allow it to dry at room temperature for about 30 minutes. *Do not* use cleaning fluid or any product containing alcohol or gasoline.

2. Apply warm neat's-foot oil. This can be done while the leather is still damp.

3. Apply leather dye of an appropriate color, also while damp. After it has dried about 20 minutes, rub off excess dye with a damp rag. *Do not* use liquid shoe polish or similar materials, because they eventually will crack or peel.

4. Apply harness dressing with a sheep's-wool swab. Rub briskly to assure good absorbency at first, then use long, even strokes. Several coats may be necessary to achieve a good shine, if you want one. Dry at room temperature for at least an hour.

Leather care, as well as the other attention you give your protective equipment, is more than spit-and-polish regimen. Well-chosen leather, sharply maintained, makes a psychological impact on you, as well as the public. But more important, it's part of being ready with a total weapon system. And readiness, down to even the smallest mundane detail, is the heart of survival.

Some officers fail to maintain their leather—or replace it when it's worn out—because they think that a scuffed, worn appearance gives them an "I've-been-there" look, distinctive from the rookies. Actually, besides making an officer look like a slob, this attitude is grossly unsafe and usually reflects a general laxity toward survival practices.

An officer who is too cheap or too lazy to buy replacement gear or who lacks self-respect in his appearance and grooming is inviting disrespect from his fellow officers and the public alike. Authority is founded on respect, and appearance is a large part of the battle.

FIREARMS CONTROL

Look in the files of firearms discharge reports for any law enforcement agency, and the cases are there in abundance: an officer pursuing a suspect on foot with his gun in hand trips and shoots himself... an officer demonstrating a quick draw with an "unloaded" gun shoots his partner...an officer fires a warning shot and the bullet hits someplace—or someone—he didn't expect...an officer cleaning his gun is killed when it suddenly discharges...an officer's youngster finds his father's handgun at home and fatally wounds himself...an officer fires at a fleeing vehicle, and the bullet ricochets into an innocent pedestrian...an officer under attack by an armed assailant fires back two shots that miss, and then his gun jams...or he shoots and the gun explodes, blowing away part of the cylinder or blowing off the barrel and threatening himself and bystanders with flying fragments.

Such incidents are usually tabulated as "accidental discharges" or "weapon malfunctions;" either the gun fired when its owner didn't want it to, or it failed to fire when he needed it to. Sometimes, "unintentional hits" are involved; the officer meant to shoot, but not for the bullet to impact where it did. What all this really boils down to is a *loss of control* over the firearm. And this loss almost always occurs through some negligence on the part of the officer responsible for the weapon.

There's a persistent myth, even among some veteran officers who've handled guns for years, that a firearm can just "go off" spontaneously,

through no one's fault. Actually, *guns don't fire themselves.* A loaded, cocked gun could lie on a table for centuries—forever—and if left alone, it would not shoot.

For your gun—any gun—to fire, it must be loaded and the trigger/hammer mechanism must be activated by someone's finger or another object, so that the firing pin detonates the primer on a live round. In short, human intervention is required to initiate the chain reaction that makes a gun shoot, and this is true whether the discharge is "accidental" or intentional. Most cases, the human factors responsible are such that unintentional discharges would more accurately be characterized as "careless" rather than "accidental."

Similarly, there's nearly always a human element involved with firearm malfunctions. On extremely rare occasions, a mechanical failure may occur because of some manufacturing error or the normal wear of working parts—but overwhelmingly the cause is more likely to be poor handling or poor maintenance of the weapon.

In cases of unintentional hits, negligent judgment is usually involved. An officer shoots without considering just where the bullet that speeds from his gun might end up.

Negligence that results in loss of control is one of the deadliest sins a person can commit in regard to firearms. And law enforcement officers are disproportionately guilty of it. Primarily because of carelessness, *police officers as a vocational group have a much higher rate of firearms mishap* than members of any other profession, including the military. That translates, of course, into higher rates of needless injuries and deaths.

Accidental discharges may be reported in a firearms discharge report. But rarely is that information related to other officers so they can avoid duplicating the same mistake.

321

The core of the problem is lack of familiarity with firearms and of respect for the procedures necessary to control them. At the time they come on the force, an estimated 70 per cent of new police officers have had *no* previous experience with guns. And contrary to the common public impression that most cops are "gun nuts," many officers remain basically uneducated about the most important tool of their trade. A survey in New Mexico, which likely reflects the country generally, reveals a staggering level of ignorance: in the average police department there are significant numbers of officers who are not sure of the brand name of their service revolver...its caliber...if it has fixed or adjustable sights...what type of ammunition they carry on duty, and so on. In a sample inspection, 1 out of 10 guns was found to be grossly unsafe. Officers were carrying *on duty* handguns that were jammed so the cylinder couldn't turn or that had been tampered with so that even slight pressure on a cocked hammer spur could cause a discharge. On the average, officers were firing their guns less than 2 times a year, evidently no more than the bare minimum for qualifying, and by no stretch of the imagination enough to assure competency.

This officer died because he was unfamiliar with a semi-automatic. When he tried to defend himself during a robbery, he forgot the safety was engaged.

The longer you're with the department, the greater your chances of experiencing an unintentional discharge or malfunction, and the greater your opportunities for firing shots that may hit where you don't intend. Part of this, of course, is a matter of exposure; your risk goes up simply because you handle more guns more often, in more situations. But more important where many officers are concerned is the tendency to become complacent and develop bad habits. With time, they stop thinking of a gun as a deadly weapon.

Consider the facts about "accidental" discharges. A survey of such shootings by police officers in Illinois indicates that nearly 1 out of 4 occurs when an officer is "playing" with his gun—while watching television, practicing fast draws, showing off, or just "daydreaming." In New York City, at least 30 per cent involve semi-automatic pistols that were "not safely handled or were improperly carried," and 35 per cent were linked to officers' use of "improper or gimmick" holsters. An estimated 15 to 20 per cent of accidental discharges occur while an officer is cleaning his gun—although it is impossible to shoot unintentionally then if you're cleaning properly. Careless discharges predominately involve on- and off-duty handguns, though about 30 per cent are with shotguns, usually weapons with which officers are even less familiar. The shootings take place in patrol cars, in police stations, in public places, occasionally at the range and frequently in officers' homes...they injure and kill persons doing the shooting, as well as fellow officers and civilians in the vicinity...and there is no identifiable correlation between the accident rate and the size of the department, an officer's age or his years of formal education. In one major west coast department, often heralded for its profes-

sionalism, nearly 30 per cent of the total number of shootings by officers are unintentional. And a study in New York City has shown, startlingly, that *officers involved in accidental discharges run a significantly higher risk of being injured than do those involved in armed confrontations!*

If there's a bright side to this dismal picture, it's this: because human error is the root cause of most accidental discharges, firearm malfunctions and unintentional hits, their number can be drastically reduced. Human error is *not* a fixed liability. You can eliminate it in yourself, and others can avoid it, too, by becoming thoroughly familiar with how your firearms operate and by following procedures that assure you maximum control over these weapons at all times, under all circumstances. The officers who have accidents and malfunctions by and large are the ones who either don't *know* what they're doing or they aren't *thinking* about it.

Remember, your gun is a mechanical device, a finely crafted tool; it has no heart, no brain, no conscience, no gift of reason, no forgiveness, no capacity for making allowances; it can function only as well as its inner workings and your judgment when you activate the trigger permit. *These variables are within your power—and responsibility—to control.*

Here are some pointers on what you can do— and should avoid doing—to guarantee a firearm's safe performance and thereby promote your survival.

Basic Safety

The *first* mistake with a firearm is the one to avoid. With many aspects of patrol and investigation, you can backtrack and correct errors made along the way. But a bullet fired can't be recalled. Mistakes with firearms tend to be violent and dramatic, the consequences irreversible, often permanent and potentially drastic.

Basically, the rules for maintaining control are nothing more than common sense. Like other survival techniques, they involve thinking ahead... continual mental alertness to your actions...and faithful practice that will make safe procedures habitual.

1. *Handle any gun, all the time, as if a bullet were going to blast out of the muzzle in the next instant.* Regard all guns as always loaded. That means you keep the muzzle pointed in a direction where a bullet will do no harm should the gun dis-

charge, whether you are indoors or out—unless, of course, you are in or approaching a potential confrontation situation. You never point a gun at anyone in jest...even if you "know" the gun is unloaded. Countless people have been shot by "unloaded" guns. If you see someone pointing a gun in your direction, get out of the way so the barrel can't line up with your body.

2. *When you take a handgun from its holster for any purpose other than defense or law enforcement, unload it.* Never give a loaded gun to someone else. But by the same token, always consider any firearm you handle—yours or someone else's—loaded until *you* determine otherwise, even if you've just seen the weapon unloaded. If you are handed a gun or draw it, eject the cartridges or magazine into your hand...check the cylinder holes or chamber and magazine well to be sure they're empty...and count the number of rounds in your hand to make sure all are accounted for. Don't take anyone's word for whether a gun is loaded or not; reliable as they may have been before, this could be the one time they're lax—and it only takes once. Check the gun yourself...then check it again; you look once to see if it's loaded, and twice to be sure you're right.

3. *Resist the temptation to show off your firearm.* One indication of your maturity, stability, and training is the *conservative* display of your gun. You don't practice quick draws in front of the locker room mirror...you don't flaunt your possession of the weapon in public places...you don't show your gun to every visitor, civilian or child who expresses interest in it...you don't allow it to be indiscriminately handled at family gatherings and parties. Many people are totally ignorant of firearms; yet few will admit to a lack of knowledge of firearms safety.

4. *Remember that a gun is not a toy;* don't play with it. Nervous habits like flexing the trigger, spinning the cylinder, swinging the cylinder open and closed should be avoided. They have no functional purpose and can only encourage careless discharges and/or malfunctions.

5. *Don't mix intoxicants and firearms.* Having a gun with you when you're drinking or using narcotics can be as disastrous as driving when you're under the influence. In a midwestern incident, an off-duty patrolman returned home early one morning from a night of drinking. He mistakenly went to the wrong apartment, and when his key didn't work, he kicked down the door. Startled awake inside, the occupant barricaded herself in her bedroom. In his drunken confusion, the officer drew his service revolver and fired a single shot through the door. It

entered the woman's back and exited through her stomach, puncturing her intestine enroute. She lived, but she incurred more than $30,000 in medical bills—and sued the officer. When you're drinking, your gun is safest left at home. If you lock it in your car, it could be stolen.

6. *Don't carry delicately tuned target-shooting arms on duty.* These guns may be accurate in range competition, but their unusually sensitive tolerances can result in jams and other malfunctions when subjected to the wear and tear of police work. Also, a trigger with a very light pull can result in an undesired discharge in times of stress.

7. *Never loan your gun to someone else.* You can never be certain to what use it will be put while out of your control nor what shape it will be in when returned.

8. *Always be conscious of your firearm.* Know where it is...what condition it's in (cocked? loaded?)...and don't leave it lying around unattended or locked in a car where someone else might pick it up or steal it. One off-duty patrolman, driving with his wife and four-year-old daughter on vacation, placed his loaded .38 Chief's Special on the seat between himself and his wife. His wife fell asleep, and the officer, absorbed in driving, failed to notice his daughter pick up the revolver to play with it. She accidentally discharged the gun, and the round lodged in the spine of the officer's wife, paralyzing her instantly.

Where firearms are concerned, it's prudent to be a bit pessimistic. You can best protect yourself and others if you remain cognizant of "Murphy's Law," the axiom that says: "If something can go wrong, it will; if several things can go wrong, the worst will at the worst possible time!"—unless you take the necessary actions to prevent it.

On the range, you are taught safe firearms handling so you won't shoot yourself or another trainee. On the street, safety is just as important. You don't want to shoot your partner, an innocent civilian or yourself because you ignored safety procedures.

Transporting Firearms

The way you carry a gun, whether it's in your hand or in a security device like a holster or shotgun rack, will help determine the amount of control you can exercise over it. During a tour of duty, you may have to transport a firearm under a variety of circumstances, and in each case you want effectively to balance safety and availability. The type of gun you have and exactly what you are doing with it will determine the proper handling.

To carry a handgun (including a back-up gun) while you're on patrol or in non-threat situations, you want it holstered—not stuck in your waistband, belt or pocket or stashed under the car seat or in the glove box. The holster should be positioned at the same place on your body at all times so you'll know instinctively where to reach for your gun if you need it. *A revolver should never be carried cocked*, because of the high risk of an accidental discharge. With a semi-automatic, though, you have other options. What's best for you in that case will depend in part on your gun.

If you have a double-action semi-automatic, such as the Smith & Wesson models 39 and 59, one means of carrying it in your holster on the street is with a round in the chamber, the hammer down and the safety on. As you draw, you can push the safety off. However, with the 39 and 59 this is often an imprecise move, and you may miss the safety, especially if you have small hands. On the other hand, one advantage of this carry is that suspects generally seem less familiar with semi-automatics than with revolvers, and there's the chance if you are disarmed that the suspect will not know how to kick off the safety to get the gun in action to use against you. Another version of this carry is with the safety off, so there's nothing to remember when you need the gun for instant use. Bear in mind, though, that without the safety on, the gun may fire if dropped on its muzzle with a round in the chamber. Still, most officers with double-action semi-automatics carry them this way.

Some officers who use a *single*-action semi-automatic, such as the Colt .45, carry the gun fully cocked with the safety on and a round in the chamber. They keep the holster security strap snapped into place over the hammer track between the cocked hammer and the rear of the slide to prevent an accidental discharge. This carry gives you a high state of firearms readiness, but some departments discourage this procedure, arguing that it's safer to carry the single-action semi-automatic with a loaded magazine and an empty chamber with the hammer down. When you draw, you then must activate the slide to cock the gun before you can fire. However, you'll need two hands to do this and if for some reason you have only one available, the lag time may be insurmountable.

Where semi-automatics are involved, you must know your department's policy.

As you exit your vehicle, unlatch your seat belt, then place your gun hand over the sidearm and holster.

A shotgun, while you're on patrol, is best carried in a *rack* in the front seat of your patrol car, so it stands vertically with the muzzle toward the roof. It should be within arm's reach of the driver, but more on the passenger side. It should *not* be locked in the trunk, where it's more likely to be subjected to moisture from rain or condensation and where you have a built-in delay in reaching it. The magazine should be fully loaded, but with no round chambered. All that's necessary then is to pump the gun, and it's ready for action.

If a live round is carried in the chamber—or left there after dealing with an emergency—there's a noteworthy risk of setting it off accidentally while the gun's in the car or being removed. In a number of cases, officers have blown holes in the roofs or doors of patrol cars that way. Also, with that method of carry, the gun is more likely to be used successfully against you if a suspect gets hold of it.

In most cases, it will be safest to draw your sidearm outside your vehicle while maintaining a grip on the door with your non-gun hand.

If a round is chambered, he needs only to pull the trigger to fire the gun.

Some officers carry the shotgun cocked, with a shell chambered but the trigger blocked by sliding the cross-bolt safety into position. This is risky, too, because a shotgun can discharge even with the safety on, if struck by a strong enough jolt. If you carry a shotgun with the safety on, be sure always to train with it that way so you don't forget to push the safety off under stress.

While the shotgun's in the rack, incidentally, you should *avoid manipulating* it in any way. Some officers play with the trigger, which, if enough pressure is applied, can eventually damage the safety—or fire the gun, if a round has been un-wittingly chambered.

When you exit from your patrol car, take care to protect your firearm. Many accidental discharges occur at this time, when a holstered handgun becomes wedged between the seat and other parts of the car or tangled in the seatbelt. By protecting your holster with your hand and keeping it close to your leg, you can shield your weapon as you exit. As you open the door, place your foot against the inside panel. Then, as you exit, place your non-gun hand on top of the door for support. If appropriate to draw your sidearm, do so *outside* your vehicle, from behind the door. Here, you're least likely to encounter obstructions to a smooth draw.

In exiting with a shotgun, remember to release the weapon from the rack *before* your patrol car's engine is turned off; some racks are electronically controlled and won't work otherwise. You're better able to keep an eye on the suspect or action you're heading toward if you get the gun out of the car

In exiting from your vehicle, take a firm grip on the shotgun, swing your legs out, then put the gun between them. You want the shotgun outside your vehicle pointing straight up and free of obstructions before you exit.

before you, rather than reach back in for it. Take a firm grip on the gun at the back of the steel receiver (not the muzzle), with your fingers away from the trigger. Put the stock between your legs...then swing your legs out so the shotgun is outside your vehicle, pointing straight up and free of obstructions before you emerge. Be sure the muzzle does not strike the roof of the car; keep it pointed away from your face and body as you exit. If you have a partner, whoever is the passenger officer should handle the shotgun to avoid interference from the steering wheel.

On foot, keep the security strap or safety snap of your holster fastened until you start to draw your handgun. Otherwise, the gun can easily be lost without your being aware of it if you run...climb... fall...or get into a physical struggle with a suspect.

If you draw your revolver or double-action semi-automatic for protection while moving forward, *do not cock it*. Cocked, these guns require only about one-third the normal trigger pressure to fire. Your chances of accidental discharge with the hammer back therefore are *much* greater. In addition, cocking your gun leaves less leeway for changing your mind and preventing a shot once you've begun to apply pressure on the trigger. This could result in tragic consequences where you realize at the last split-second that you've drawn down on the wrong person. Depending on your method of holster carry, your single-action semi-automatic may already be cocked with the safety on when you draw. If so, as you move forward, leave the safety *on*, with your thumb resting on it. If you need to shoot, simply wipe the safety off with your thumb and pull the trigger. If you don't carry the gun cocked, you'll need to activate the slide and release the safety before shooting.

In advancing, keep the muzzle of your handgun

When on foot with your sidearm drawn, keep the muzzle pointed downward, at an angle away from your legs.

pointed down at a slight angle away from your legs. The bend in your elbow will help prevent muscle strain, and from this position, you can easily swing the gun up into the isosceles instinct shooting stance. If you stumble or fall, the gun is angled so you're unlikely to shoot yourself in the leg. Such accidental discharges can also be avoided if you *keep your finger outside the trigger guard until you are ready to shoot.* As you approach your final location or anticipate danger, move into a two-hand hold, with your gun pointed slightly down in front of you. This readies the sidearm for swinging into the full instinct shooting position.

If you should fall with your gun, try to avoid jamming the muzzle down as a support to break your fall. Some officers do this to save getting their uniforms dirty, but your gun can wind up with a barrel full of dirt or mud, which later may cause a dangerous malfunction.

In carrying a police shotgun on foot, you may alter the gun's position to suit the situation, but you want always to know where the muzzle is. In a non-threat situation, one technique is to point the muzzle straight up, with the heel of the buttplate tucked into your belt against your hip. Here you grip the gun firmly around the "pistol grip," the neck of the stock just behind the receiver, taking care to keep your fingers away from the trigger.

When you're heading into a situation where you may need to *use* your shotgun, there are two basic carries: "guard" and "port arms."

For the guard position, you grasp the gun by the pistol grip in your strong hand and rest the butt on your hip. The barrel tilts out and up at about a 45-degree angle. This is a deliberately high profile carry, when you want to look menacing and alert anyone who sees that you have a shotgun. This is appropriate to use in situations such as roadblocks or when guarding prisoners.

Probably the *best* combination of safety and availability, though, is the port arms carry. Here the gun is positioned across your chest, with your strong hand gripping the pistol grip, your other hand under the slide, and the barrel up toward the shoulder of your non-shooting side at a 45-degree angle. Your trigger finger rests across the outside of the trigger guard until you are ready to shoot. This is the only practical carry to use when you have to run with a shotgun and the best for approaching a potential suspect. By swinging the butt of the gun up you can quickly convert it into a club to resolve a scuffle. Bear in mind, though, that like the guard position, this carry presents a menacing profile, which may be undesirable in certain sensitive situations.

One variation of the guard position with a shotgun.

The port arms carry. Also notice the officer's finger is outside the trigger guard until he is ready to shoot.

Of course, any time you're approaching *known danger* and the need to fire appears imminent, you should have the shotgun in position for instinct shooting.

Two situations require special handling to maintain proper control over your firearms: 1) when you're seated at a lunch counter where your holstered gun would be next to a civilian and 2) when you're in a toilet stall.

At a lunch counter, consider bringing your holster around so it is in your lap, if possible, keeping it within your reach and making it harder for the person next to you to grab.

In a toilet, remove your gun belt (with the holster attached)...buckle it...and drape it around your neck or diagonally across your chest from one shoulder. Or hang the entire gun belt over the crotch of your pulled-down trousers. This keeps you from forgetting your gun and lessens the chances of dropping it to the floor from your pants or from a cubicle hook. *Do not* lay the gun belt on the floor. Someone in the next stall could reach under the partition and grab your gun, with you in no condition to respond.

Wild Shots

Among the gravest hazards of high-stress situations are unintentional hits. Unlike accidental discharges, you mean to fire your gun, but the shots impact someplace—perhaps in someone—you did not intend. This is always a risk when shooting at a suspect some distance from you, but the danger is magnified in certain types of shooting; namely, rounds fired as warning shots...those fired at or from moving vehicles...those fired while you are running...and those fired when you are uncertain of the suspect's location or in a cross-fire situation.

Most police instructors insist that warning shots intended to scare a fleeing or reluctant suspect into surrendering don't work, that if anything, they only make a fleeing suspect run faster! Actually, it's not that warning shots never work, but that *they're rarely worth the risk involved.*

First of all, if an officer argues that from a legal standpoint warning shots are something less than use of deadly force, he's probably wrong. Any time you shoot your gun, in most jurisdictions, you're employing deadly force. Even if you intend to miss a suspect, you'd better be legally justified in killing him when you pull the trigger, or you could be on shaky ground.

In a suburb of Washington, D.C., for example, an officer fired one shot in an effort to stop a shoplifting suspect who bolted out of a police substation while being booked. "The thought that I might kill the guy never entered my mind," the officer said later. "I never thought he would die. Never." But to the officer's surprise, the intended "harmless" shot struck the fleeing suspect in the back of the head, and he died in a hospital two days later. The officer was fired from the police force after an administrative trial and at this writing is working as an auto parts salesman.

If you are justified and lethal force is necessary, it's probably safer from your standpoint and from that of fellow officers and innocent bystanders if you *aim directly at him*, rather than shoot at the ground or fire an uncontrolled shot into the air. Remember, *bullets don't vanish*; every round you shoot has to terminate *somewhere.* If you're in a passageway between high-rise apartment buildings in a crowded urban neighborhood, a shot you send into the air may crash through someone's window...or hit somebody leaning over a porch railing to watch the action...or simply by the pull of gravity land in an unpredictable—and undesirable—spot. When one officer shot into the floor of a suspect's apartment, the bullet penetrated the floor and came out through

A wild shot can impact almost anywhere.

the wall in an apartment below. By firing into the ground while running, some officers have shot themselves in the leg. In one case, an officer who came upon the scene of a chase-in-progress thought he was being fired at when he heard another officer's warning shot, and promptly killed the fleeing suspect—who, it turned out, had not committed a crime that warranted lethal action.

Whenever you shoot, you're responsible for where all your bullets impact, regardless of your intent at the time or the reasons you give later in filling out your shooting report of the incident. A young Connecticut patrolman found this out the hard way. Attempting to break up an argument between his partner and a suspect, this officer fired several warning shots into the air from his revolver. The bullets struck the canopy of a building and ricocheted down, wounding his partner in the foot and a civilian passerby in the head. Both sued the patrolman for an aggregate $45,000 damages, claiming his shooting was "willfully and maliciously" negligent.

In most circumstances, warning shots unnecessarily endanger other people, members of the public you are sworn to protect and whose safety should be your first consideration. They may also increase the jeopardy of your own life because sometimes, rather than halt a fleeing suspect, your warning shots will prompt him to return fire. You are then in the midst of a gunfight with at least a partially empty firearm.

Some of the same arguments apply regarding your shooting at or from moving vehicles.

A classic, old-time movie scene shows a roadster swerve to the curb of a darkened street. Several men inside roughly shove a sobbing young woman out onto the sidewalk, and the car speeds away. A patrolman walking his beat nearby witnesses this, immediately draws his revolver and empties a cylinder full of bullets at the fleeing car, before running to aid the damsel in distress....

This concept of "law enforcement" is as hoary as the scene itself. The officer shoots without knowing a) what crime (if any) has been committed; b) whether any of the men in the car committed it, and c) whether their actions justify the use of lethal force. Moreover, he shoots with little realistic hope that his shots will have any desirable effect.

In law enforcement, handguns are intended for use primarily against people, not vehicles. Shooting from a distance of more than 15 yards, you're unlikely to penetrate a vehicle body using a standard-velocity .38 Special cartridge or any other handgun round. What's probable, instead, is that your bullets will ricochet off the curved metal or safety glass—or most likely, miss the vehicle entirely—and fly into other cars or innocent pedestrians. Ricochets, as we've seen, can be as dangerous as bullets in their initial flight, and passersby can be just as dead from police bullets as from suspects'.

Suppose you *do* hit the vehicle. Slugs punching through the body won't stop the vehicle; bullets don't kill cars. If you destroy a tire or kill or wound the driver, the car may go out of control, sending a ton of steel careening down the street to the danger of everything and everyone in its path. In one case, a racketeer was shot dead at the wheel of his speeding limousine in a heavily populated area. The car kept going, killing one pedestrian and seriously injuring another before crashing into a wall.

In certain surroundings, an out-of-control car might be an acceptable risk. In Arizona, sheriff's deputies waiting at a roadside riddled both sides of a van whose occupants had earlier fired shotgun blasts at other officers while crashing through a roadblock. The driver was shot in the head. As he slumped over the steering wheel, the van sped on for several hundred feet, then veered crazily off the road before stopping. But this was on a remote desert highway, with nothing around to damage but mesquite and cactus. Similarly, Utah authorities recently pursuing a teenager who'd murdered a highway patrolman used shotguns to blow out front and back tires of his pickup truck, causing it to swerve off the road and crash through a fence. But this, too, was in an isolated rural area.

In other situations, courts have held that firing on a fleeing suspect vehicle is "a practice so wanton and so hazardous" that it should "not be tolerated in a civilized state." Remember, if someone in the car is killed as a result of your shooting, you must be justified in having used lethal force against him.

Shooting from a moving vehicle can be just as fraught with danger as shooting at one.

If you're driving and you're right-handed, you'll probably have to depend on your weak hand for aim and accuracy while you steer with your strong hand. Effective weak-hand shooting is difficult even if you are stationary. If you are moving and in pursuit of a suspect who's also moving, the difficulty is geometrically compounded. In shooting, you're just wasting ammunition and creating an unnecessary hazard.

Even if you're on the passenger side, distractions may divert your full attention from your aim and decision making...bumps or swerves may cause accidental or premature firing...and sudden changes in distance or direction may wipe out any hope of getting on target safely. Also if your gun is knocked or dropped from your hand during some jarring movement of your vehicle, you may not have a firearm available at the end of the chase when you'll need it in face-to-face confrontation.

As with other types of shooting that produce wild shots frequently, *you are responsible* for your gunfire from moving vehicles that causes accidents, injuries or deaths, regardless of the suspect's criminal actions.

The risk of unintentional hits is also high when you shoot while running. The physical and emotional stress caused by the exertion alone is likely to seriously affect your proficiency. Add the nettlesome dynamics of trying to hit a target that is moving while you yourself are moving, and the problem is magnified many fold. As the distance between you and the suspect you're chasing increases, your ability to shoot him while running decreases dramatically, to the point that a hit becomes pure chance.

Sometimes your best option is not to give chase but through communications to alert other officers to his path of flight so they can intercept him at another location. At the very least, you will want to call for back-up before beginning a chase. If you are alone and in a built-up area with many potential hiding places, going after an armed suspect on foot may verge on suicide.

Where you are involved in a foot chase and have both the need and legal justification for shooting at the suspect, your best option is to stop and shoot from a stationary position, using some support for your hands if appropriate. Support possibilities might include a car body, a tree, a mailbox or a fireplug. Use the instinct shooting crouch...grip... and aim. Provided that your own safety and that of others can be protected, the most opportune time to shoot is when some obstacle slows the suspect's flight; for example, when he stops to enter a car... go through a door...or scale a wall or fence. If you can anticipate his reduced mobility, you can find cover...get in position...and be ready to fire at the instant you have the best chance of hitting him. If there are no obstructions to slow him down but he is running in a fairly straight line, then you might be best off to angle your gun at the pavement and try to take him down by hitting his legs with ricochet shooting. This could be especially effective if you are armed with a shotgun.

Be prepared for him to shoot back in any case. If you miss him or if the obstacle he encounters is insurmountable, like a blind alley, high fence or locked doorway, he may turn sharply on you, committed to shooting it out.

(This also may happen even when he is not trapped or you are not shooting at him; your pursuit alone may be enough motivation. That's why, in a foot chase, it's important to utilize available cover along the way, trying to keep parked cars, trees and other barricades between you and the suspect. Where no cover is available, you're usually safest running in a line parallel to the suspect's line of flight, but not directly behind him. Change your course slightly from left to right to make yourself a harder target. Take advantage of shadows and darkness for concealment where possible. Quick-peek around corners, and use extreme caution when entering alleys, stairways, cellars, buildings or dimly lighted areas. If you lose sight of the suspect, he may seize that opportunity to shoot at you from ambush.)

One important safeguard against unintentional hits is to *ALWAYS be sure of your target before you shoot*. That means you don't shoot at muzzle flash...noise...or movement—even if you have been fired on—unless you are positive the suspect made it. What moves, makes noise, even shoots may not be the bad guy. It may be a fellow officer who has responded to your aid. Or it may be an innocent civilian who has happened to be on the scene of action or whose movements you are mistaking as threatening.

This problem of target identification is accentuated at night or in bad light, where it's hard for you to see. At three o'clock one morning officers in a California community answered a complaint from neighbors claiming that a young bartender and his girlfriend were fighting in his car and that she was being held against her will. As the officers approached the car, the girl jumped out of the passenger side and the bartender reached under the seat with his right hand, then raised it and pointed it at one of the officers. Both policemen, responding to what looked like a threatening move, fired into the car, killing the young man. Afterwards, they discovered that his hand had been empty; he was not armed. At this writing, the officers face a $2 million civil suit brought by the victim's family. In Wisconsin, an officer looking for a robbery suspect entered a house with his gun drawn. He was creeping upstairs when he was startled by the sudden appearance of a human figure. He fired and shot dead a teenage girl who lived in the house and was not a suspect at all.

Controlling your fire until you have good target identification may become unusually troublesome if you're at a scene with other officers. In one situation, several officers were on a rooftop across the street from a building where an armed assailant was barricaded. Only one of the officers was positioned where he could actually see the suspect. At an opportune moment, he shot. Hearing his gun go off, all the others cut loose with everything they had, too—although later they conceded they did *not* know where the suspect was located and were shooting toward various irrelevant locations in the building!

This Pavlovian response is called "the domino effect," because one shot touches off many in a chain reaction like falling dominoes. Wild shots resulting in unintentional hits are a frequent consequence of shooting just because you hear rounds going off or see someone else around you firing. *You want to hold your fire unless you know why you should shoot.* This is called firearms discipline.

Don't try to shoot a suspect you haven't located...
and *don't* shoot when you know you have no chance
of hitting him. Remember, every officer is responsible for his own actions. If you follow the lead of
 nother officer who has fired by mistake, out of
fear, as a result of stress or indecision or for any
number of other questionable reasons, you may find
yourself answering a criminal charge for gross
negligence.

Finally, watch the background toward which
you're shooting. Sometimes officers become so focused on the suspect they forget to notice what's
behind him. In an Ohio city, for example, an angry
suspect roared into the parking lot of a police
station, vowing to ''blow away'' every officer he
could find because of a grievance over a traffic
stop. Officers in the vicinity drew their guns and
completely surrounded his car—not realizing that if
any one of them started shooting, others would
be in the path of bullets that missed or passed
through the offender.

This cross-fire situation ended without casualty
because the suspect meekly surrendered. But that
was not the case with an episode in California,
which reflects a number of wild shot phenomena.

In that case, six vice officers had surrounded
the home of a narcotics dealer for the serving of a
search warrant, when a shoot-out suddenly erupted.
Scores of shots were fired into the dwelling from all
directions. Later it was established that the police
had positioned themselves around the building,
with guns inadvertently pointed at one another.
Some fired because they heard what they thought
were shots coming from the suspects inside. Others
fired because they saw a fellow officer fall back and
thought he had been shot. Actually, this officer fell
back from the recoil effect of his own gun. *No* shots
at any time came from the inside of the building or
from the suspect. The first bullet, like all the rest,
came from a *police gun*. An overeager officer at the
front of the building had fired blindly into the
interior as soon as the door was forced open. The
gun ''battle,'' complete with cross-fire and shooting
at unseen ''assailants,'' dominoed from that.

The drug dealer, by the way, escaped during
the furor. But an officer was wounded.

Ammunition Control

Understanding and controlling your ammunition is also an important part of firearms control.
A malfunction or improper discharge can be caused

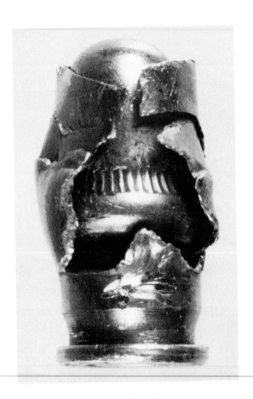

by the ammunition you use, as well as by the way you handle or maintain your gun.

Your first concern is *always* to use *only* the type of cartridge *meant* for your weapon. Even though two cartridges *look* similar or are of the *same caliber*, it is not ipso facto evidence that they are interchangeable.

Officers have been known to try to put rifle bullets into revolvers...to switch cartridges between revolvers and semi-automatics...to carry rim-fire ammunition sometimes used on ranges in duty guns designed for center-fire rounds...or to carry wadcutter rounds specifically designed for target practice instead of service ammunition. If the wrong ammunition is forced into a gun it may lock in the cylinder or hang up in the magazine. In other cases, inappropriate ammunition may *seem* to fit, but when you try to shoot the gun, even small differences can cause malfunctions. A semi-automatic round that's too short for the magazine in use may be forced into the chamber so hard that it won't seat properly. Revolver rounds, which uniquely have a protruding lip or rim on the shell cases to keep them from falling through the cylinder, will

The owner of this .25 cal. semi-automatic was a detective who reached into a bag full of various kinds of ammunition. On the range, he loaded a .22 cartridge in the magazine. The result was an internal explosion. The bullet was forced back into its own shell casing during the explosion.

A large variety of ammunition is manufactured in the U.S. On the right are a few of the rounds you may be familiar with.

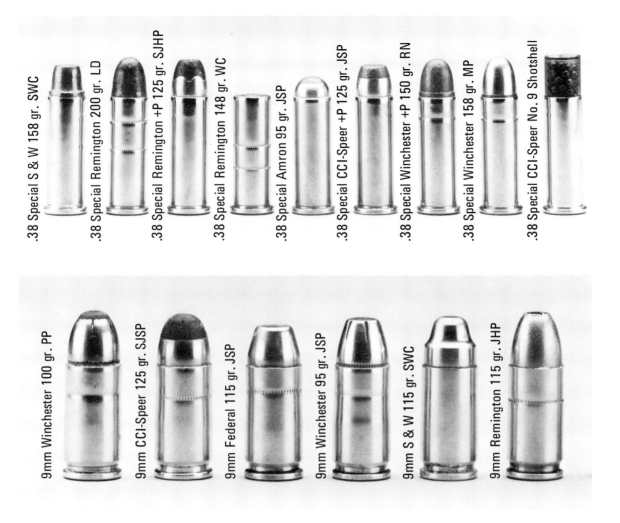

.38 Special S & W 158 gr. SWC
.38 Special Remington 200 gr. LD
.38 Special Remington +P 125 gr. SJHP
.38 Special Remington 148 gr. WC
.38 Special Amron 95 gr. JSP
.38 Special CCI-Speer +P 125 gr. JSP
.38 Special Winchester +P 150 gr. RN
.38 Special Winchester 158 gr. MP
.38 Special CCI-Speer No. 9 Shotshell

9mm Winchester 100 gr. PP
9mm CCI-Speer 125 gr. SJSP
9mm Federal 115 gr. JSP
9mm Winchester 95 gr. JSP
9mm S & W 115 gr. SWC
9mm Remington 115 gr. JHP

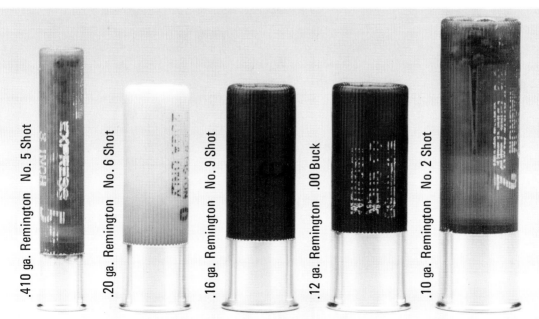

.410 ga. Remington No. 5 Shot
.20 ga. Remington No. 6 Shot
.16 ga. Remington No. 9 Shot
.12 ga. Remington .00 Buck
.10 ga. Remington No. 2 Shot

Know which ammunition goes into your firearms.

.38 S & W   .38 Auto   .38 Long Colt   .380 Auto   .38 Short Colt   .32 S & W Long   .41 Long Colt   .32-20   .357 Magnum

Numerous cartridge calibers may look like they are acceptable in a .38 Special revolver—but they aren't.

The result of reloads with too much charge: a blown-out top strap and cylinder. The risk to your hands and eyes in these kinds of accidents is staggering.

not chamber if loaded into a semi-automatic magazine. With a shotgun, if you load a .16 ga. or .20 ga. shell, then load a .12 ga. shell, the barrel could explode if fired.

This kind of carelessness with ammunition is a habit with bad guys, too. They're lazy; they figure if it fits, they'll use it. Often their ammunition tends to be old, too. But your professionalism demands higher standards than that. There's less chance of getting the wrong ammunition into the wrong gun, incidentally, if you coordinate your on- and off-duty firearms so that they require the same type of round. And remember, ammunition that *seems* similar isn't, necessarily. For instance, .38 cal. Smith & Wesson rounds won't work in .38 Special revolvers, and .357 Magnum rounds won't chamber in a .38 revolver.

Selecting the right ammunition involves getting it from a reliable source. Some officers like to manufacture their own rounds by reloading spent cases. If the reloader is experienced, knows what he's doing and is careful, reloads are okay for the range, but your department may insist on factory-loaded cartridges for use on the street. Even if it doesn't you <u>should</u>. Despite the best reloading equipment and most conscientious personal effort, quality control for reloads is generally far inferior to that maintained by most commercial manufacturers. When you reload ammunition yourself, you run a higher-than-normal risk of producing rounds with:

•*improper powder charges*. If a round gets too many grains of powder it may blow up the cylinder or touch off "sympathetic" discharges of other rounds, causing even more extensive damage to the gun—or you. If there's too little powder to produce enough energy for proper propulsion, the bullets may lodge in the barrel, causing a jam or explosion the next time you fire. Where semi-automatics are involved, weak loads can also cause spent cases to be rechambered or prevent the slide from being driven back far enough to pick a fresh round out of the magazine. Then when you pull the trigger, no shot will fire.

•*high primers*. In reconstructing the cartridge, the primer may not be seated deep enough. The defect may not be noticeable to the human eye, but loaded in, the primer may protrude enough to keep the round from chambering or the cylinder from turning.

•*poor crimping*. The bullet may be too loosely crimped into the shell, allowing it to move forward slightly from recoil until the tip projects out of the cylinder, keeping it from rotating into line with the barrel.

Four .357 Magnum bullets were lodged in this barrel as a result of reloads with an insufficient charge.

Factory-loaded ammunition can also
be defective. Notice the improper rim
area at the base of the two cartridges
on the left. The cartridge base on the
right is properly formed.

The .38 Special round on the left has
a casing crack due to continual reloading. The middle cartridge was reloaded while the shell casing was
squashed. The cartridge on the right
reinforces the need to examine reloads
before their use.

•*casing fatigue*. Each time a cartridge is fired, the shell expands and must be resized for reloading. If you reload the same cases over and over, they're susceptible eventually to splitting. A cracked casing won't fire reliably because it won't seat properly.

•*foreign matter*. Sometimes grease or small bits of cotton find their way into cartridge cases during reloading. If they lodge between the primer and powder, they may prevent the cartridge from discharging (called a "misfire"). Or, more dangerous, the foreign matter produces a "hang-fire;" you think you have a dud, but after a delay the round goes off. This can happen if the primer ignites the grease or cotton, which in turn ignites the propellant after an interval of several seconds.

Of course, reloads are less expensive than factory-made ammunition. But considering the possibilities for error, going the reload route is an economy that could cost you your life. Even serious competitive shooters insist on factory ammunition in a match, although they may practice with reloads. Foolish frugality can be just as threatening to good firearms control as thoughtlessness, laziness and immaturity.

Even with factory loads, however, a healthy skepticism promotes survival. What you buy should

The two .45 auto cartridges on the left contain corrosion and rust from storage in a damp garage for a number of years. The two .38 cartridges contain green deposits from an officer's dump pouch which hadn't been opened in four years.

be good and probably will be, but you're safest to *check every round you load or carry* to be sure that it is. First, visually examine all your duty ammunition and eliminate any cartridges that appear cracked, swollen or badly "bruised." Then, if you're using a revolver, load and close the cylinder, pull the hammer back slightly and rotate the cylinder with your fingers. Or if you're using a semi-automatic, cycle each round through the gun by working the slide back and forth manually, being sure to stand over a soft surface or to catch the cartridges as they eject to keep them from falling on hard surfaces. These tests on the range or in some other safe location will allow you to detect "high primers" which may protrude slightly from the cartridge because of manufacturing mistakes and cause binding or jamming when you try to shoot. If you've just opened a new box of cartridges or are trying a new specification of bullet for the first time, test-fire half a dozen or so as a means of sampling the run and satisfying yourself that what you're loading will prove dependable in a fight. With semi-automatics, especially, some cartridge styles feed more smoothly than others, and if you've got a "finicky eating" situation on your hands, you want to know it before you're in an emergency and it's too late to field test.

For a shotgun, too, all ammunition should be visually examined for burrs and gouges on the plastic or brass that may cause feeding problems. Samples from new batches should be test-fired to verify reliability. But cartridges should *not* be cycled through the gun by operating the action. The ejector/extractor on a shotgun may scar the rim of the shells in repeated cyclings, and plastic cartridges ejected onto the ground may develop burrs, which may later cause them to jam in the magazine.

You want to store ammunition in a place that's dry and cool. Moisture can cause corrosion. Direct heat from the sun or other sources can alter pressure in the cartridge and may also cause lubricant inside the shell to run into the powder, affecting firing qualities. Sharp shifts in temperature are undesirable because they can expand and contract cartridge cases and also produce condensation.

Theoretically, most ammunition has an "acceptable" shelf life of about 5 years, but consider replacing it every 4-6 months. Not to keep it fresh when your life is at stake is another foolish economy. You can take your old stuff to the range and shoot it off there, as a chance to test your firearm and to requalify. If you keep it in your gun or ammunition carrier, you're inviting a malfunction. On his way to work one day, one officer recognized a suspect wanted for armed robbery and approached to arrest him. Although the officer had his gun in hand, the robber managed to draw and shoot him fatally before the officer could get off a shot. Later, tests showed that the primers of two of the officer's cartridges had been struck by the firing pin of his gun; he'd tried to shoot, but his ammunition had failed to fire. It had deteriorated from age and improper maintenance. Of six rounds in his cylinder, four were so corroded they had to be forced free.

If you're using a semi-automatic, don't store ammunition for long periods in magazines, either. In time, this may promote corrosion, and the continual tension on the follower spring may weaken it. Magazines should be rotated in and out of service periodically and stored empty.

The revolver ammunition you take with you for active use should always be transported in a cartridge carrier, where it is better protected from dirt and other abuse. Carrying loose rounds in your pocket or purse can be dangerous, especially if they are able to come in contact with the power supply terminals of hand-held radio transceivers or spare radio batteries also carried there. In several states, officers have been injured under such circumstances when cartridges made electrical contact with the terminals and were detonated.

Customizing

Just as factory ammunition usually has the qualities that best contribute to your survival, your firearm, too, is generally in a condition you can't improve on as it comes from the factory. Some officers, especially those who fancy themselves gun aficionados, are tempted to make do-it-yourself modifications, but unless you're a *qualified* gunsmith, you're wisest to *avoid hot rodding or customizing any firearm you use on or off duty.* Even if you're competent for the task, any adjustments or modifications should be made *only* by official permission, with the okay of your department's armorer.

A revolver has more than 10 moving parts, a semi-automatic more than 15, a shotgun more than 20. All of a gun's components are carefully engineered to complement each other and to provide a certain balance to the action of the weapon. Manufacturers establish precise standards of adjustment and tolerance, based on intensive studies of how guns should perform under various temperature and climate conditions. By adding equipment...

tampering with factory adjustments...or making structural alterations, you can seriously interfere with a duty firearm's proper performance, causing a life-threatening malfunction during an armed confrontation. (You may also affect the way the gun fits into its holster, making it more susceptible to accidental discharge or to loss during vigorous activity.)

What tends to happen with customizing is that you change your gun with one *intent* in mind and wind up with quite a different *result* because you failed to understand how form affects function. As illustration, consider these modifications hot rodders commonly make on basic gun components and the unexpected dangerous consequences that frequently follow:

TRIGGER: By attaching a metal device called a "trigger shoe," some officers try to widen the trigger to facilitate a smoother squeeze. This may be acceptable for slow, single-action target shooting, the purpose for which the shoe was designed half a

The trigger on this Ruger Mini-14 was designed for a proper trigger squeeze. For duty use, a trigger shoe addition isn't worth the risk of a malfunction. The danger with a trigger shoe is the possibility that the holding screw will work loose and force the shoe to jam the trigger.

century ago, but on a duty weapon it creates several problems. Because it extends outside the trigger guard, the broad shoe is more likely to snag on clothing...it may catch on the lip of the leather and discharge when you shove your gun into its holster, shooting you in the leg. The added bulk makes it nearly impossible for you to properly position your finger for double-action shooting, unless you have exceptionally large hands...and, no matter how firmly it is placed, the set screw that holds the shoe in position may work loose so the device slips down and jams the trigger in a forward position, making the gun inoperative. Trigger shoes are dangerous on any firearm, whether a handgun or a long gun. This was learned the hard way by a California officer, who tried to employ a Ruger Mini-14 rifle in a firefight that erupted during a sniper incident. The rifle stopped firing because a loose trigger shoe was blocking the pull of the trigger.

SCREWS AND SPRINGS: On revolvers, officers trying to reduce trigger pull may loosen the strain screw which maintains pressure on the main-spring, and on some semi-automatics they often cut links off the recoil spring and hammer spring to make the slide easier to pull back and to give the gun a crisp ''snap.'' The strain screw is designed to be screwed all the way in tight. If you tamper with it or the hammer spring, you can cause mis-fires because the hammer will fall too lightly to detonate the cartridge. By altering the recoil spring you may weaken the tension so that the slide won't positively feed a live round into the chamber as it's supposed to when you need to shoot, or the slide will not completely close. There are at least 15 springs, screws and pins in the average handgun. Each has an important purpose regarding the control of the weapon. *The length and tension of springs and the tightness of screws should not be changed in any way from factory configuration.*

INTERNAL ACTION: Some officers try to modify the sear and locking mechanisms inside their guns to lighten trigger pull. But the engaging surfaces of a gun's action are surface-hardened only. If you scrape away or stone off even a small amount of surface metal, you expose soft metal underneath, rapidly accelerating wear and precipitating parts failure and replacement. Unless you are an experienced gunsmith, you should never remove the side plate from your revolver for access to the action for *any* reason.

HAMMER: Wide hammers are sometimes installed for easier cocking...or the hammer spur is ground down to keep the gun from snagging when drawn. In practice, an enlarged hammer, like a trigger shoe, can catch on your clothing or holster causing an accidental discharge. The need for cocking your gun on the street is virtually non-existent, anyway. In reducing the hammer spur, you risk lightening the weight of the hammer fall so that the firing pin fails to drive into the cartridge's primer with enough force to detonate it. You click the trigger...the hammer drops...nothing happens.

SAFETY: Sometimes officers may try to "tie down," grind off or otherwise disable safeties, arguing that they are "inconvenient" and may under stress be engaged when an officer needs to shoot. Tampering with the external safeties of a semi-automatic or the built-in safety of a revolver can make a gun as dangerous for the officer who holds it as for the suspect it's pointed at. If you remove the safety mechanism from a revolver, for example, you create a "push off" risk; that is, when the gun's cocked, a slight pressure on the hammer can cause it to fall forward and discharge a cartridge. Thus the gun is highly susceptible to firing if dropped or bumped. If you disable, say, the grip safety of a .45 cal. semi-automatic, the gun may double fire when you are recovering from the recoil. *Safeties help to assure that your gun does not fire accidentally*, and should be maintained as they are.

FRAME: Occasionally officers add chrome to a blue-finish hand gun to make it look "sharper." Or, if they're carrying a large caliber semi-automatic, they may substitute an alloy frame to lighten the weight. Although a chromed gun may wear better and be less susceptible to corrosion, it may also attract the kind of attention you don't want; because it's more visible, it makes you a better target. An alloy frame may not have the durability you need. The original heavy frame is designed to take the shock of the slide slamming back and forth, while the heavy recoil against the alloy will quickly loosen vital tolerances. Leave the frame —and the contour of the frame—as is; *don't replace fixed sights* with temperamental and fragile adjustable sights...*don't add a longer barrel*, which may reduce accuracy...*don't try to use an oversized magazine* in a semi-automatic to load extra rounds...*don't experiment* by interchanging parts and accessories to see what "suits" you best. Use your time and energy instead maintaining what you have, to keep it in the most reliable condition possible.

GRIPS: Sometimes the left grip panel on a revolver is changed or modified because it protrudes too far to accommodate the smooth, quick use of speed-loaders. This is an appropriate and necessary alteration. But more often, officers switch

Oversized grips like these are totally impractical for duty use.

As you attempt to eject rounds, the sixth cartridge cannot clear the grips. Under conditions of a shootout, attempting to reload quickly would be time consuming.

grips because they believe oversized or fancy ones add drama to the appearance of their handgun. That may be true, but substitutions frequently add hazards, too. Oversized grips on a revolver, for example, may interfere with unloading, unless they are specifically designed for combat use; when you plunge the ejector rod, five of your casings fall out, but the spent round closest to the grip hangs up. To get it out, you have to rotate the cylinder by hand. A midwestern officer was killed during a shoot-out because of the extra time this required. Some grip panels with built-in thumb and finger rests make a handgun hard to carry in a holster... make drawing more difficult...and also hamper effective weak-hand shooting. Grips made of bone or plastic sometimes chip off around the stock pin, causing the gun to jam if the chip works its way into the action. Also plastic tends to slip in your hand if you're sweating, as do smooth wooden grips, loosening your hold on the gun. Probably the best all-around grips are of checkered walnut. These can reduce slipping of your hand from sweat...allow evaporation of condensation...can be filed, sanded or smoothed with 00 steel wool to give you a custom fit for both weak- and strong-hand shooting. The right fit is extremely important. Incredibly, some officers install grips that are too big for them to handle well because they're embarrassed to admit that they have small hands! To determine your proper grip size, hold the gun in your weak hand... put your index finger on the trigger at the first knuckle...and try to assume a normal hold on the gun. If the grips are too large, the barrel will be pointed outward; that is, to the left in the case of a right-handed shooter. If the grips are too small, the barrel will angle inward.

What all the cautions about customizing add up to is this: if you have the tinkering urge, restrict it to firearms you use in target shooting competition, where all you have at stake are a few score points, not your life. The more the mechanism of a defense gun is left alone, the longer and better it's likely to perform its intended function.

That is not to say that guns are always perfect when they come from the factory. An officer in the midwest recently discovered that a new shotgun right out of the box would not rack in the first round. Mistakes can be and are made in manufacturing. Have any gun you acquire, especially a used gun, inspected and tested by a reliable, competent gunsmith or your department armorer—not "a friend who knows all about guns"—*before* you carry it on duty. If the gun is new, you want to be sure it meets the standards it should; if you've bought it used, you want to be sure it hasn't been worked on inside by some unqualified hobbyist.

When you get the gun back, draw and *test fire it thoroughly under all conditions before taking it out on the street.* You want to shoot at least one full magazine or cylinder of service-load ammunition, and possibly some practice ammunition as well. Some gunsmiths recommend firing at least 20 rounds on 2 separate occasions with a new gun to be sure it's functioning flawlessly. This testing should be done after you've had a gun repaired, too. There have been cases in which officers received a firearm back from a gunsmith and shoved it into the holster without checking—only to discover in a gunfight that the original malfunction had not been corrected or that a new defect had turned up since the gun was last in their possession.

Handling with Care

Any gun worth staking your life on is a masterpiece of precision engineering and manufacturing. It's durable enough to stand the ordinary wear and tear of duty work, but at the same time it has a fine edge of built-in accuracy that can be knocked out of whack forever by improper handling. When that happens, the gun you're depending on may no longer be dependable.

Revolvers, which most officers carry, are particularly vulnerable to damage from abuse, because so much of their mechanism is open. And it doesn't take much rough handling to affect performance. If the hammer spur is broken or bent, you may be prevented from firing...a bent trigger guard can interfere with your trigger pull...sights bent or broken off may hamper in shooting accurately at a distance...a bent ejector rod can keep you from unloading or stop the cylinder from rotating...and a bent barrel may result in the gun "blowing up" when you shoot. Needless to say, it is not advisable to follow the example of one eastern officer; when his son's baseball fell into a sewer, the officer raised the sewer lid by prying it up with the barrel of his revolver, which understandably bent. Semi-automatics may be even more susceptible to physical damage because they have more moving parts than revolvers. But any gun has vulnerable points where a relatively light blow can bend a part, jamming the action and making the gun unreliable or inoperative.

Excessive roughness often creeps in during loading or unloading. Some officers like to replace or check on the rounds they're carrying in a revolver by flicking the cylinder open and closed with a sharp twist of the wrist, like the tough guy cops on television or in the movies. This may look macho, but in real life it can cause many functional problems over a short period of time. Among them: it can warp or break the crane or yoke...spring the cylinder so it fails to lock in the proper position when closed...and throw it "out of time," so that it does

Exposure to snow, rain and continued lack of care finally caught up with the officer who abused this gun. He died holding a loaded revolver which couldn't fire.

This is one of the .38 rounds found in the officer's revolver. It's obviously loaded, but because the hammer fall was so light and off center, the primer couldn't detonate.

not line the cartridge up precisely with the barrel when you shoot the gun. This can affect both accuracy and safety. Any time you open the cylinder, you should ease it outward without undue thrust, and ease it back into place with the same care and deliberation.

Similarly, with semi-automatics, there's a tendency sometimes, especially under stress, to slam the magazine into place, possibly a carry-over from military training where this is standard procedure during inspection drills. A hard slam can bend the lips of the magazine so it won't seat properly and therefore may not feed cartridges into the chamber for firing. The proper loading method is to slide the magazine into the magazine well and snap it into battery with a firm tap or push with the heel of your weak hand to be sure it locks in place. Magazine lips can also be bent by the magazine dropping on a hard surface. If you drop a magazine or if you see that it is pitted, bent, cracked or has a loose floor plate, you're safest to throw it away and buy a new one. This is the most critical part of the gun.

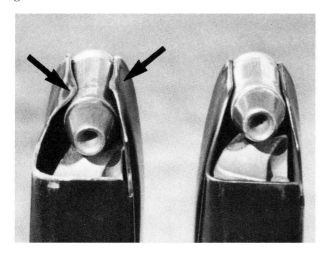

If you slam in a 9mm magazine or drop it, you run the risk of bending the lips. The result is a magazine which won't feed in new cartridges. The magazine on the right will function properly.

The result of a revolver which was dropped. A bent ejector may prevent rounds from ejecting from the cylinder.

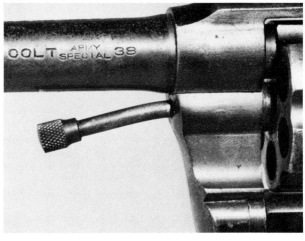

Dropping your gun itself can also cause damage that will make it inaccurate or inoperative. The front sight or hammer spur may be bent or broken off...a severe blow on the side may cause misalignment of the cylinder...the ejector rod may be bent...or the shock may spring, break or damage some other working part. This can happen even if the gun is dropped while in its holster, as sometimes happens when officers are tossing a firearm from one to another. If your gun is dropped, examine it carefully for damage:

1. *Open the cylinder* and move it back and forth to see that it swings freely;

2. *Work the ejector rod* up and down while turning the cylinder to see that the rod operates straight and without binding, wherever the cylinder is positioned;

3. *Check the clearance space between trigger guard and trigger* by dry firing with double action;

4. *Check all screws* on the gun to be certain they have not been loosened by the sudden jar.

Because hard blows can foul a gun's functioning and may cause accidental discharge, it's advisable *not* to use your gun as a club in trying to subdue struggling suspects. Even with the relatively well-protected semi-automatic, you risk breaking the magazine catch or knocking off the floor plate, so the gun can't be reloaded. Moreover, most guns make pretty poor bludgeons; their sharp corners tend to cut rather than stun. And if you swing and miss, you could hit the suspect with your wrist rather than your gun. This could knock the gun from your hand, leaving you unarmed.

Disregarding your firearm has resulted in many officers losing a finger, an eye or the respect of fellow officers.

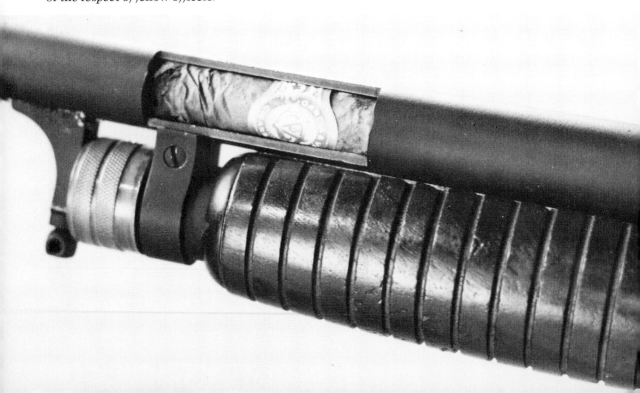

Careful handling, of course, includes protecting your firearm against dirt and other foreign matter. Dirt in working parts or even in the barrel can produce serious malfunctions. Yet some officers are incredibly negligent in this regard. One eastern officer was chasing a psycho at a botanical garden when he slipped and fell into a pond. He cleaned himself up afterwards—but "forgot" to do anything about his gun. Later he happened to notice that the barrel was full of mud. If he'd needed to fire the gun, this obstruction could have severely damaged the weapon and may have injured the officer himself.

Anytime the muzzle of your firearm touches the ground, check the barrel to insure no obstruction is lodged there. And of course, you don't want to deliberately create one. Hard as it is to believe, this is a frequent problem where shotguns are concerned. While on patrol, some officers reach for the shotgun barrel as the most convenient receptacle for ashes, cigaret butts, candy wrappers, even chicken bones. Some use it for storage. One female officer kept her Tampax there, and a male patrolman in California thought it made a great humidor—until he needed to "smoke" something besides a cigar; then the obstruction caused the barrel to blow apart when he pulled the trigger. If you ever have a shotgun in your hands when the barrel explodes, you'll find out fast that you're exposed to one hell of a risk!

Survival always hinges on respect for weapons. With firearms, respect is grounded in careful handling and thorough maintenance. If you were aboard a ship, you would not unnecessarily abuse the life preservers, particularly when faced with navigating treacherous waters. On the street, you are in treacherous waters all the time—and your life preserver is your gun.

Correcting Malfunctions

Among the nightmarish fantasies you experience in relation to the street may be the common one in which you confront an armed suspect, need urgently to shoot to save your life—but your gun jams. For some officers, each year, this fantasy turns into reality. When that happens, the loss of firearms control can mean disaster, unless the victim officer is able to respond quickly and get himself and his weapon back into action.

To lessen the chances of mechanical hitches in the first place, the most important procedures are to 1) always handle your firearm protectively, and 2) keep it clean through proper maintenance. even if you've been conscientious with care, though, guns will still occasionally fail to fire in stress situations. In those circumstances, most officers have no idea what to do. They may peer quizzically into the muzzles of their guns...or play around with them hoping by luck to get them going again... or simply panic and lose the fight.

Usually there is some simple way out of this problem, if you can apply what is called "immediate action." As the name implies, you're not going to take time to do any elaborate gunsmithing. With an assailant's bullets flying at you, you want to reduce the stoppage as fast as possible and get back into the action to save your life, without investigating the cause of the malfunction at that time.

The kinds of malfunctions you might encounter with a well-maintained weapon and the immediate-action tactics you can use to correct them on the spot vary with the type of gun you have in your hands.

REVOLVER: When in the course of using a revolver you squeeze the trigger and the gun fails to fire, your first immediate action should be to take your finger off the trigger and let it fly all the way forward (making sure, of course, that the muzzle is pointing in a safe direction). In the heat of firing rapid shots, you may unconsciously have failed to let the trigger go completely forward between rounds; in that case, when you try to fire again, the trigger becomes "frozen" and won't pull or it won't advance the cylinder fully to a fresh chamber. If you follow your natural instinct and pull all the harder, you'll only prolong the problem. But if you release the trigger, you'll free the mechanism and likely get your gun working again on the next shot.

If that doesn't do the trick, eject everything in your cylinder and immediately reload. Chances are overwhelming that you've shot your gun dry of ammunition. Indeed, the most common cause of failure to fire in a well-maintained revolver is that the gun is empty, without the shooter realizing it. If that is not the case, you may have some ammunition that's bad; your next load may be better.

SEMI-AUTOMATIC: As a rule, a semi-automatic is more susceptible to malfunction or "jamming" than a revolver, largely because of the way it's designed to fire. While a revolver depends on manual mechanics to advance each new round, most semi-automatics depend on recoil impulse from a fired round to move the slide and cause the

360

next cartridge to feed and chamber. With this more sophisticated mechanism, there's more opportunity for things to go wrong.

Ninety per cent of the time, though, jamming of semi-automatics is caused by poor maintenance and cleaning, poor ammunition (either the charge of a reload is too weak or the configuration of the bullet inhibits good feeding) or by a problem with the magazine (such as improper seating, which fails to position cartridges where they can feed properly).

If your semi-automatic fails to fire and you're sure it's still loaded, check first for the most obvious malfunction.

Occasionally, a semi-automatic may fail to eject spent shell casings.

Sometimes because of a weak charge, a bad primer, a dirty chamber or a defective ejecting mechanism, a "stove-pipe jam" will occur. Instead of ejecting cleanly, the spent case pops up and locks standing vertically in the side ejection port. You'll be able to see the shell sticking out. Here for your immediate action, tilt the gun sideways so the ejection port is down. Then *vigorously* pull the slide to the rear. The used shell should be released and fall free from gravity. You can make certain it gets out by placing your weak hand so it covers the casing as you activate the slide. You can "wipe away" the shell between two fingers or in the web of your hand as you pull the slide back. As your hand glides off the rear of the slide, the slide returns, chambering a new round. The gun should now fire. This maneuver takes about half a second, if practiced thoroughly.

If there's no obvious reason for your semi-automatic failing to fire, then apply your first immediate action to the magazine. With the palm of your weak hand, slap the magazine butt up to be certain it is firmly locked into place. Then grab the slide with your weak hand behind the ejection port and pull it smartly to the rear to chamber another round. Release and attempt to fire.

If your semi-automatic still doesn't work, you may have a round jammed in the action. To apply immediate action, remove the magazine...pull back the slide...release it...insert a fresh magazine... pull back the slide again...release...and attempt to fire. If the round isn't dislodged by this procedure, then lock the slide to the rear, drop the magazine and shake out the round. Then insert a magazine, release the slide and fire. Obviously, because of the extended time it can take, this maneuver is best handled behind cover.

In all cases when applying immediate action, keep the gun in the firing position. Don't bring it down to your stomach to work on. Should the gun fire while in that position, your chances of injury are much higher.

This malfunction may be corrected by pulling the slide to the rear, then tilting the semi-automatic on its side, which allows the shell casing to eject.

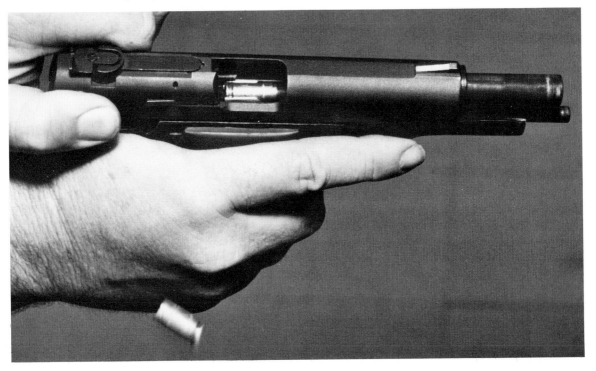

Note: In some cases, the failure of a semi-automatic to fire is not a "malfunction" at all. The officer, in his excitement, has simply forgotten to kick off the safety. To prevent this dangerous oversight under stress, you need to practice drawing and shooting under simulated combat conditions until disengaging the safety becomes an instinctive part of your shooting dynamics. (You probably won't want to carry a double-action semi-automatic in your holster with the safety off because of the risk of unintentional discharge.)

SHOTGUN: With a shotgun, the most frequent malfunction is the slide hanging up half way back, having failed to eject a spent shell or chamber a new one because of the gun's sometimes-tempermental rearming mechanism. Your immediate action begins with the slide.

First, pull it to the rear as hard as you can and as far as it will go. Then run the slide forward. If that's not effective, then run the slide to the rear, turn the gun over and shake it. The old round may fall out...or you can probe your finger in and get it out. Obviously, you should be behind cover when doing this.

Once the receiver and chamber are clear, then run the slide forward and to the rear, then forward again. You should be able to fire.

The next step will be to release the slide forward to activate a live round in the chamber. Remember to keep the muzzle aimed down range during this process.

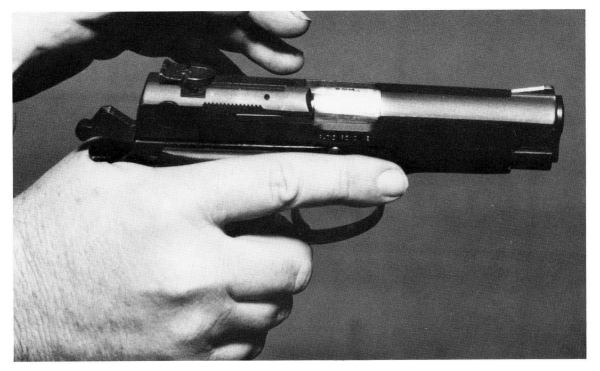

The cartridge fired from this spent shell casing detonated with such force, metal fragments blew out the side of the cylinder.

If you can't, take the next most practical course: lay the shotgun down and get into action with your handgun.

AMMUNITION: When ammunition malfunctions, it may: 1) fire so weakly that the bullet does not exit the barrel (excessive smoke, reduced recoil and a subdued "pop" may be clues to this mishap); 2) "misfire," that is, not shoot at all, or 3) "hang-fire," appear to be misfiring but then shoot after a delay of a few seconds, usually because of a defect in the primer or powder.

On the range when you experience an ammunition malfunction, you're instructed to keep your gun pointed at the target for at least 10 seconds to prevent injury in case you have a hang-fire situation. And you are told not to fire again until you have unloaded and checked the barrel for obstructions and hunted for the cause of the malfunction.

On the street, this is not practical advice. It is true that if you immediately fire again after ammunition has malfunctioned, you may injure yourself, damage your gun or both. But with your life already in jeopardy, there usually is no reasonable alternative but to take that risk. Your immediate action for malfunctioning ammunition is to keep firing or to totally reload and hope for the best. As we'll see later, though, there are ways you can minimize your chances of experiencing ammunition malfunction *before* you are caught in an armed encounter.

Home Security

Control over firearms must necessarily extend to any you bring into your home. Nearly 40 per cent of the time that officers' guns discharge "accidentally," the firings occur at home—an extremely high rate, considering that one would normally expect a police gun to have the least amount of use there. If, like many officers, you store your off-duty gun at home while you're at work and keep your service handgun there when you're off, at least one gun is in your house around the clock, increasing the possibility of a mishap.

Educating your immediate family about your gun is *mandatory*, of course. But even assuming they are all mature enough to absorb and obey instructions on avoiding or properly handling your firearm, you'll quite likely have visitors who know nothing about guns. These can include neighborhood children, baby sitters, friends, relatives, deliverymen and repairmen. If they happen across your firearm, they may be intrigued and have a strong urge to handle it; while some people are repelled by guns, many more are fascinated, especially kids. And we know that *people unfamiliar with guns almost always handle them in the most dangerous way possible*; by immediately putting a finger on the trigger and pointing the muzzle in an unsafe direction.

Nobody should be considered "too young" to shoot a firearm. One Los Angeles police officer's three-year-old climbed up on a dresser, took a handgun from the drawer, and by using both hands, pulled the trigger, critically wounding himself. In Michigan, an officer's son who was only *22 months old* found his dad's loaded revolver and fatally shot his mother.

If the combination of curiosity and ignorance doesn't produce a tragedy, it may at least provoke a serious scare. A Minneapolis detective who was involved in investigating a teenage prostitution network returned home from running errands with

Unload your sidearm when you come home, and place your ammunition in a separate location that's cool and dry.

his wife and small daughter one afternoon to find a bullet had been shot into his pillow. Assuming that this was a "warning" from prostitution racketeers, his wife became hysterical. After a frantic evening, the detective finally determined that the slug had been fired by a carpet layer who, working in the house alone, had discovered one of the officer's weapons and shot it off accidentally.

For maximum security, you want to make your gun inoperative and inaccessible. As soon as you arrive home, you unload it in private so that live rounds can be stored separately. By placing your handcuffs or a padlock behind the trigger or around the top strap of a revolver with the cylinder open, you make firing impossible. With a semi-automatic, you can lock the slide open, run a length of small-link chain through the barrel from the muzzle to the breech and magazine well and then secure both ends with a padlock. If you're afraid of scratching your gun, trigger or cylinder locks with protective padding are available. For inaccessibility, you can lock the gun inside a substantial metal storage box that is up high, like on a closet shelf, and bolted into place. The ammunition can then be put in a soft container, like a chamois bag, and kept in some other hard-to-reach place that's cool and dry.

....Then make your sidearm inaccessible by locking it in a metal storage box, and place it up high.

Some officers prefer to find clever hiding places. One puts his gun under the sink in an empty detergent box; one weekend while he was away, a burglar ransacked the place, but the gun was not discovered. Another unloads his gun, locks the cylinder open with his handcuffs, then locks the cuffs around the bar of a hanger in his closet; he drapes a scarf over the bar and gun, puts clothes on the hanger, then buttons a raincoat over the whole works, keeping the gun both secure and out of sight. Others handcuff their guns to water pipes in the basement or bury them under clothes on a closet shelf. For too many officers, however, "hiding" a gun consists of hanging it in its holster from the back of a bathroom door or from a hook in a closet—or tucked into a dresser drawer, a place a burglar or curious child will surely look. They delude themselves that no one would dare touch it even if they saw it, reflecting a rather poor understanding of human nature and ignoring the numerous documented cases in which injuries and deaths have resulted from guns kept in just those locations.

Obviously, while a gun that's inoperative and inaccessible is safest, it is probably *not* easily put into action if you need to defend yourself or your family at home. Indeed, a gun that's perfectly safe is perfectly useless. If that concerns you, you may want to consider a compromise; try keeping the gun loaded in an old holster tacked to the back of the headboard of your bed. It's out of sight...hard enough to reach that you won't grab it when you shouldn't...yet convenient enough that it can be reached in an emergency.

Do not keep your gun under your pillow or on a bedside table. If you have nightmares or are awakened by noise, you may shoot yourself or members of your family before you are fully awake. One officer woke up, grabbed his revolver and fired a shot into his closet and through all his clothes while still half asleep. Later, he could not explain why he did it—but he never kept a gun at bedside any more, either.

However you deal with your gun and ammunition at home, be consistent. If you follow the same routine every time, you're less likely to forget something important—like reloading your gun before returning to duty. One Ohio officer wisely unloaded his gun every night at home because he was afraid his kids would get it—but unwisely forgot to load back up one morning. He spent the day on the street with an empty gun. In Illinois an officer was shot in a gun battle because he'd forgotten to reload and went to work with an empty gun.

The ultimate hurt is knowing firearm accidents occur in moments which are usually in your power to control.

One option here is to place your ammunition at the time you unload into the pocket of the pants you intend to wear the next day. You'll know by weight that it's there when you put the pants on. Or, place the rounds in your holster, in a secure place.

Of course, any officer who's survival conscious will check his gun thoroughly before going on duty, performing the recommended serviceability tests. This precaution will reveal if you're missing ammunition, plus alert you to other factors that might otherwise unexpectedly affect your firearms control and throw your life into jeopardy. Where there is the slightest question about the reliability of a firearm, it should be brought to your department's firearms instructor or other competent gunsmith for inspection.

For some, good habits are never important enough until it's too late. Like this officer who forgot to load his sidearm before leaving home...and died because of an empty gun.

14 | CLEANING

Some officers consider cleaning to be just an onerous chore of housekeeping. But if you think of it in terms of survival, you can view it in an altogether different light.

Your firearm is your most important piece of equipment. It can keep you alive when all else has failed. But for that to happen, *you* not only have to know how to use the gun—it has to be able *to be used.* When you squeeze the trigger, with perhaps only one chance to neutralize an adversary, your gun must not jam...misfire...explode or shoot crooked if it is to save you. And yet some officers who lose armed confrontations realize in their final flash of consciousness that that is exactly what has happened.

Without doubt, *the single greatest cause of such firearm malfunctions is poor maintenance.* With reasonable care, guns seldom wear out or are shot out. But a dirty and neglected gun quickly becomes undependable; when you pull the trigger, you can't be sure what will happen.

There's no way to keep your gun from being exposed to elements that promote deterioration. Dust, dirt, lint, food crumbs and a variety of other foreign materials inevitably sift through your holster and over your firearm in the course of a working week. If you're working in rain, mist or snow or even going in and out during extremes in temperature, your gun is subjected to moisture or condensation. In seacoast cities, salt from the air can attach to its metal surfaces. When you handle your gun, you leave behind deposits of salt and body acids, particularly if you've been sweating. And anytime you shoot, the detonation of the cartridge and exit of the bullet leave residues of burnt powder, lead and various airborne impurities.

Singly and in combination, these elements can rapidly and seriously affect performance. To cite only a few of the consequences of a neglected gun: Powder particles or debris under the ejector star of a revolver can make the cylinder hard or impossible to latch into place...An accumulation of lint in the channel in which the firing pin travels may affect its contact with cartridge primers and cause hangfires or misfires...Dirt, rust and corrosion on the surfaces of working parts can cause binding or unnatural friction and may penetrate into the action... Lead building up in the bore can ruin accuracy...And other foreign matter allowed to accumulate there can cause blow-ups or promote rust and pitting.

Harmful effects can prey on a gun with a stainless steel finish as well as one that's blue-steel; semi-automatics and shotguns are as susceptible to damage from neglect as revolvers. *Any* gun requires that you take care of it if you expect it to take care of you.

Some maintenance is necessary on a *daily* basis to keep your gun in good shape. After your tour of duty, especially if you've handled your firearm or it has been exposed to inclement weather, wipe off the outside surfaces with a dry, silicone-treated or slightly oily cotton cloth. This will remove salt, moisture and other corrosive residues and coat the surfaces with a light protective film. Wipe your ammunition dry, too, if it has been exposed to moisture. If your leather is wet, allow it to dry thoroughly before you return your gun and ammunition to it.

Every day that you fire your gun—or twice a month as a matter of course, even if you haven't shot—you want to clean your firearm thoroughly. Even if it doesn't look dirty, it still may be, because some residual materials that can lead to damage are not visible; a buildup of residue as slight as .006 inches can alter tolerances of some key firearm components. Gun cleaning needn't be a big job. It's not quite as easy as one Illinois rookie thought; he's reported to have put his service revolver into a washing machine for cleaning! But with the steps we'll outline here, you can do everything that needs doing simply, quickly and inexpensively. You should be able to clean extensively enough to eliminate the risk of most malfunctions and maintain your gun's proficiency in about the same time it takes to shine your shoes. Not a bad investment of time, considering the potential payoff.

You can be the most capable, intelligent and dedicated officer in the world, but if you carry a poorly-cared-for gun, you're defeating your own purpose and that of law enforcement generally. On the other hand, a clean weapon is likely to help you gain an edge over the bad guys. They often neglect cleaning their guns, just as they neglect other aspects of a sensible life.

Preliminaries

You'll probably do most of your gun cleaning at home, except, perhaps for the shotgun, which you may be required to clean at the range or in the station. If you're a homeowner, you're probably safest cleaning your handgun in your basement or a shop area; if you're an apartment dweller, the kitchen may be your best place. You want a clean, lint-free surface where you can spread out your equipment. And you want to be able to work *alone in private*, ideally at a time when you can finish the job without distraction or interruption.

Your equipment will include:

—a cleaning rod, complete with knob-end and slotted-end attachments;
—plenty of cleaning patches;
—a bore brush with nylon or phosphor bronze bristles, appropriate to the caliber of the gun you're cleaning;
—a good grade gun-cleaning solvent;
—a good grade gun oil that can protect against rust and that is not affected by temperature (some lubricants will cause a gun to freeze solid in cold weather);
—a toothbrush;
—a dentist's probe;
—clean rags or towels;
—a silicone-treated cloth;
—a screwdriver whose blade will snugly fit the screw slot on your gun.

You can buy these materials at most gun or sporting goods stores as individual items or in kit form. Be sure you use equipment *designed* for the job, not makeshift tools. Using a screwdriver or fine steel wool instead of a brush to remove lead deposits, for example, can mar the gun and may affect its accuracy. In general, your cleaning materials and implements should not be harder than the steel surfaces to be cleaned.

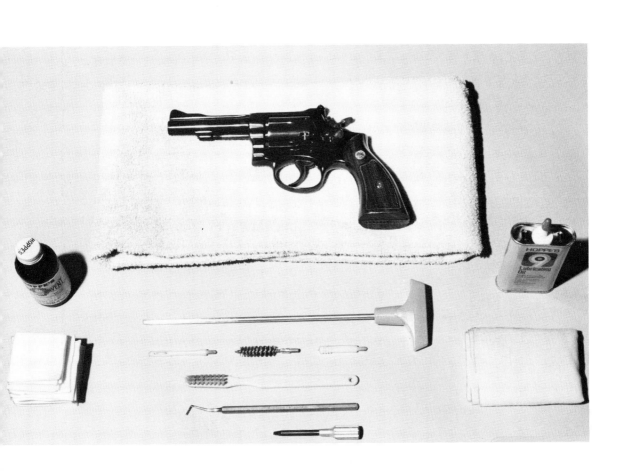

During your preparation, you want to lay the groundwork for a *safe* cleaning. To eliminate the risk of an accidental discharge:

1. *Unload your gun.*

2. *Secure the ammunition in another room,* so the firearm and its cartridges are nowhere near each other.

3. *Work with the muzzle pointed away from yourself,* toward an outside backyard wall, if possible. Accidental discharges from "empty" guns have killed persons sleeping in bedrooms adjoining the cleaning area.

4. *Do not leave your gun unattended at any time,* even for a few moments to answer the phone or doorbell. If you must interrupt the cleaning, secure your gun so no one can handle it.

Even short of inflicting serious injury or death, violating these basic safety rules can carry a heavy price, as one midwestern officer learned while cleaning his service revolver on a kitchen countertop. Mistakenly believing the gun was empty, he pulled its trigger, and a round fired into his kitchen sink. It ricocheted off the porcelain, then off the ceiling and cut through his ear lobe before striking the floor. Bleeding profusely, he ran to his car and drove off toward the nearest hospital. Meantime, a neighbor who'd heard the shot flagged a patrol car and excitedly reported the officer's wife "finally took all she could and shot him." Actually, the wife was at the grocery store. Believing themselves responding to an "officer down" call, more than a dozen officers swarmed to the scene. Entry was made, the blood discovered all over the floor, but no victim and no assailant could be located. An APB was issued for the wife, a search launched for the missing victim. Soon the wife drove up with her groceries, only to be surrounded by policemen who accused her of shooting her husband. When she saw the blood in the kitchen, she became hysterical. Fortunately, the wounded officer arrived before long and straightened everything out. But he says he has been living in "total embarrassment" ever since. "I'm the station house joke."

Besides observing basic safety while cleaning, select an area to work where the pungent smell of the solvent will not be offensive to others in your household. Spread out an absorbent cloth or towel underneath where you're going to work to protect the gun and soak up any solvent, lubricant or debris that might drip out. (Note: *Don't* use newspapers. Solvent and oil will readily filter through them to the surface underneath.) You may want to put on an old shirt and pants so you don't ruin good ones. Then you're ready to begin.

Revolver

The key during cleaning will be to hold the weapon down flat against your work surface, with the muzzle pointing off to the side, away from you. Concentrate first on the interior surfaces. To loosen dirt, powder deposits and other debris left there from firing your gun:

1. Unload your revolver and place ammunition in a separate place.

2. Fold patch in half. Insert corner into slot in your rod's slotted-end attachment. Pull halfway through.

3. Dip patch in solvent so it's well saturated, but not dripping wet; carefully extract patch to avoid splattering.

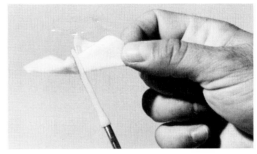

4. Insert rod into barrel and move it back and forth several times to get bore wet.

5. Push rod through so patch fully exits forcing cone, but don't crash it against firing pin access hole.

6. Repeat in each cylinder hole. Change patches often so dirt isn't moved from one surface to another.

7. Move clockwise around cylinder. Scrub each area until solvent-soaked patch comes out clean.

8. Remove rod tip. Screw on bore brush—[a wire brush for stubborn deposits, nylon for normal cleaning].

9. Work brush back and forth in barrel until all sediment is loose. Fully clear barrel ends to avoid binding.

10. Repeat process in each cylinder hole. Brushing will push out residue the solvent has dissolved.

11. Give special attention to spots where lead, powder and other deposits are difficult to loosen with a patch.

12. Dampen toothbrush with solvent. Brush front and back of cylinder...

13. behind erector star...

14. on nose of hammer...

376

15. around firing pin hole and hammer groove...

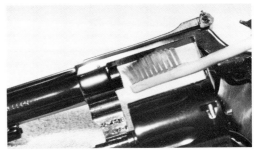

16. underneath top strap and above forcing core, and...

17. around end of barrel.

18. With dentist's probe, clean hard-to-reach areas, like top strap corners and above forcing cone.

19. Using knob-end accessory, clear residual moisture from bore and cylinder holes with clean, dry patches.

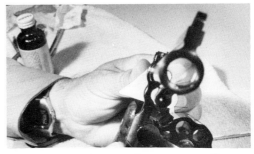

20. Hold thumb or patch against recoil plate to reflect light into barrel for final inspection.

21. Now use dry patches to wipe moisture and dirt from all other surfaces you've scrubbed.

22. Clean outside of barrel, cylinder and other exterior surfaces with solvent and patches. Dry with fresh patches.

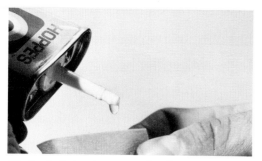

23. For lubrication, use oil only. Grease can cause your action to lock up like glue.

24. Only 3 moving parts need oil: ONE drop around base of hammer. Then work action so it gets inside...

25. ONE drop on ejector rod in front of cylinder. Then plunge rod up and down to spread oil...

26. ONE drop on crane hinge.

27. With one drop of oil on clean patch, apply thin coat as rust preventer inside barrel and cylinder chambers.

28. Check that screws on side plate and grip panels are tightly secured.

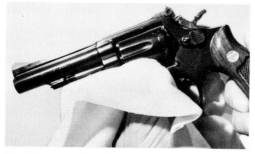

29. Wipe revolver dry with silicone-treated cloth.

Semi-Automatic

In cleaning a semi-automatic, your objective is still to remove dirt, lint, lead, powder, metal particles and other residue that can cause malfunctions. The semi-automatic contains more moving parts than the revolver, so you need to break it down farther. When you start to work, lay out each component part in the order in which you field strip it. That way there's no confusion about what goes where when you want to reassemble.

For a .45 cal. semi-automatic, disassembly begins with the plug just below the muzzle. You push it in while simultaneously turning the barrel bushing 90 degrees in a clockwise direction. Keep your finger on the plug and release the tension on the recoil spring slowly to keep it from popping out. Ease the plug out of the spring by turning it clockwise. From that point on, follow essentially the same steps appropriate to S&W models 39 and 59 and other semi-automatics. Follow these procedures:

1. Remove and unload magazine.

2. Pull back slide until slide stop enters disassembly notch. Check chamber to make sure gun is unloaded.

379

3. With weak hand, push in slide stop pin section from opposite side of receiver and remove stop.

4. Move slide forward and disengage from receiver.

5. Remove barrel, recoil spring, recoil spring guide. You now have eight basic components.

6. Apply solvent inside barrel with patches attached to cleaning rod.

7. Use wire brush to lift out stubborn lead deposits. Then clean and dry with fresh patches.

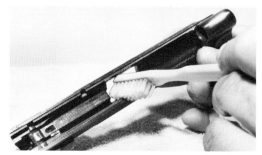

8. With toothbrush dipped in solvent, scrub every exposed surface, including slide rails and ramp...

9. and receiver and magazine well.

10. Clean barrel bushing, recoil spring, slide stop and recoil spring guide with solvent-soaked toothbrush.

11. Now rub all these surfaces with clean, dry patches to soak up moisture and remaining dirt.

12. Place ONE drop of oil inside hammer area...

13. and along all sliding surfaces—except magazine and magazine well.

14. Wipe off excess with dry patches or clean, dry cloth.

15. Reassemble your gun, reload magazine.

16. Wipe all external surfaces with silicone cloth.

Note: As with the revolver, any disassembly further than that described here should be done by a competent gunsmith. When cleaning a semiautomatic, the magazine can be broken down further, but generally this is not necessary.

Shotgun

If you're like most officers, your department probably will not authorize you to break down and clean a long gun completely. But you can clean the barrel periodically, and since that's where so many shotgun malfunctions originate, it's well worth the few minutes it takes to do it properly. Follow these procedures, which apply to most .12 ga. police shotguns:

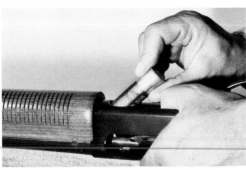

1. Inspect bottom loading port to make certain shotgun is empty. Place shells in separate location.

2. Unscrew magazine tube cap, keeping gun pointed away from your face.

3. Gently grasp end of barrel and pull it straight out to separate it from receiver held in other hand.

4. Lay the barrel aside. Replace magazine cap so magazine spring and retainer won't fly out.

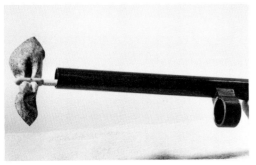

5. Run several, solvent-soaked shotgun patches through barrel from receiver end out the muzzle end.

6. Scrub inside of barrel with .12 ga. bore brush soaked in solvent to loosen stubborn particles.

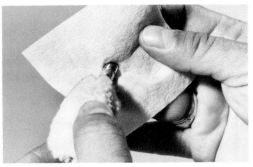

7. *Attach solvent-soaked patch to screw end of dry swab. Run rod without tip attachment through barrel from muzzle end.*

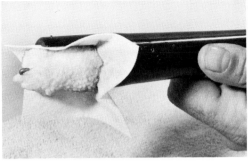

8. *Attach swab to rod. Run it through barrel, out muzzle end. Patch somewhat protects swab from dirt.*

9. *Repeat with fresh, solvent-soaked patches until a patch emerges clean. Then, use dry patches until they exit clean.*

10. *Rub the exterior of barrel with solvent-soaked patches.*

11. *Dry barrel outside with patches.*

12. *Apply light oil coating to inhibit rust. Wipe off excess with clean cloth.*

13. *Reassemble shotgun. Check that barrel is seated properly before screwing on magazine cap.*

14. *Wipe off all metal surfaces with silicone cloth.*

Ammunition Precautions

As part of your cleaning process, you want to wipe off ammunition with a dry, untreated cloth to retard corrosion. Shotgun patches are good for this job. But be sure you keep all your cartridges away from any solvent or oil. Wipe any excess liquid off all surfaces of your firearm, especially inside the cylinder holes of a revolver, *before* reloading. And don't spray the gun with an aerosol lubricant *after* you've loaded up.

Spray lubricants or solvents are super penetrating, and the liquid from them, as well as from other solvents, can work its way around and into the primer by capillary action and dampen the powder charge, fostering misfires. Such liquids may also loosen the bullets in cartridges so that when you fire one shot, the recoil will force the remaining bullets to thrust forward in their cases, causing your cylinder to jam. In either event, you can end up with a useless load of ammunition. *Oil or solvent can adversely affect ammunition even faster than water*. Within a matter of days, fresh ammunition exposed to these liquids can become deactivated.

The risk was probably first identified in Seattle, where an officer drew his service revolver to ward off an armed assailant and discovered the gun would not fire. Subsequent lab analysis revealed that the powder in each of his cartridges had been contaminated by oil that had soaked in from aerosol lubicant sprayed on his gun. The powder was caked together and its flashpoint greatly retarded, so that when the primer ignited, the charge only smoldered, then died out before lighting and discharging the round.

That's why your gun needs to be dried thoroughly after cleaning, before you reload. For certain, you want to avoid what some officers do. They simply remove a gun from its holster occasionally, spray it with aerosol solvent with the ammunition in place, shake it off and reholster, considering that this constitutes "cleaning" the weapon. *This is a deadly form of laziness*. Improper gun and ammunition cleaning can be as dangerous to your life as no cleaning at all.

With both your gun and ammunition properly clean, your firearm should now be ready for the street. First, however, check to be sure that it is functioning as it should by performing the recommended "serviceability checks," but be certain to perform these tests with the gun *empty*. The temptation after cleaning is to reload and then check the action. Such absentmindedness has resulted in numerous accidental discharges—and deaths.

SERVICEABILITY CHECK LIST | 15

After each cleaning and daily before putting your gun in its holster to start your tour of duty, a quick serviceability check can assure you that your firearm is functioning correctly and will perform if you need it. Some departments designate specific areas for conducting serviceability tests. Some locker rooms, for example, are equipped with "bullet traps," such as oil drums filled with sand; you point your gun into the trap so that any rounds fired inadvertently are safely stopped. If such an area is available, you may want to tape the serviceability check lists nearby for ready reference. If there is no designated area, you can perform these tests on the range, in a safe place outdoors or before you leave home.

Always be certain the muzzle is pointed in a safe direction away from yourself and other people and that your gun is *unloaded*. Check twice to be sure it is. Count your cartridges—twice—and separate them from your firearm by putting them in your pocket or in some other safe location. The risk of doing otherwise is graphically illustrated by the experience of a young patrolman in a Detroit suburb. He was performing serviceability checks on his .38 cal. revolver while sitting on the edge of his bed, with the gun fully loaded, the muzzle pointed toward the inside of his leg. As he pulled back the hammer to test cylinder rotation, his thumb accidentally slipped off and the hammer flew forward. A bullet shot through his thigh, almost shattering his knee cap.

Safely and properly conducted, the checks will take less than a minute. By making them a habit, you can catch life-threatening problems *before* they surprise you on duty. After all, if your gun fails to operate properly during a gunfight, you can't stop the action while you fix it.

Revolver

With your gun empty and the ammunition placed safely aside:

- examine the barrel. Is is straight...free of bulges... tight in the frame? Is the bore clean and free of pitting, rust or obstructions?
- check the sights. Are they firmly attached? Is the front sight and the rear sight, if there is one, straight?
- inspect the crane. Is it free of warping?
- work the ejector rod several times, while turning the cylinder. Is the rod straight? Is the movement free? Is the tip screwed on tight? (If the tip works loose, you may be unable to open or close the cylinder.)
- examine the cylinder. Are the chambers free of dirt and obstructions? Is the cylinder free of rust, burrs or pitting? (Pitting on the front of the cylinder may indicate it is improperly rubbing against the rear of the barrel.)
- dry fire double action, while closely watching the space between the firing pin hole and the cylinder. Is the hammer nose driven through the recoil plate far enough to detonate a cartridge? Is the firing pin secure...not battered or scuffed? (If the pin appears damaged, your hammer may be misfitted or your recoil plate faulty.)
- without touching the trigger, pull back the hammer until it is almost cocked and release it. Is the pin blocked from coming through the recoil plate? (If not, the internal safety is faulty. The pin could hit a cartridge primer if the hammer is struck or slips during cocking, causing an unintentional discharge.) Note: to perform this test on a Smith & Wesson, you must hold the cylinder thumb latch to the rear while pulling back the hammer.
- close the cylinder and dry fire each chamber. Does the cylinder rotate smoothly without skipping? Does the hammer release properly and fall smartly without binding or hesitation?
- try gently to rotate the cylinder, with the hammer down and your finger off the trigger. Does the cylinder lock without any pronounced movement? When you look down the barrel, is it

properly aligned with a chamber? (If you detect more than about 1/64-inch play in the cylinder, you have a faulty cylinder stop, which may cause misalignment. If the chambers are out of line with the barrel, the firing pin won't hit the centers of primers. This exposes you to the risks of possible misfires. Also, the bullet may shave lead as it enters the barrel, affecting accuracy.)

- cock the hammer and lay your thumb along the top of the butt strap and against the hammer spur. When you apply reasonable pressure to the arc the hammer normally travels, does it remain securely in place? (Don't *force* the hammer forward, as you may *create* damage.)
- check the screws holding the grips and the two screws on the sideplate. Are they firmly in place? Are your grips tight and unbroken?
- carefully reload your ammunition, with a safe surface below to catch any falling rounds. With the cylinder full and closed, rotate the cylinder until it clicks into place and all play is eliminated.

Semi-Automatic

Engage the safety, remove the magazine and pull the slide back until it engages the slide stop. Inspect the magazine well and chamber to be certain the gun is empty.

- as you pull back the slide, does it move smoothly? Does the stop work?
- check the action of the safety. Does it click into position properly?
- inspect the ejection port and the magazine well. Are there any obstructions? (If so, your gun may fail to feed or eject rounds.)
- with the safety off, let the slide spring forward. Does it return smoothly all the way to the front? Does the hammer remain cocked? (If not, an internal part is worn. You may be able to shoot, but you will have trouble firing fast, double-action shots.)
- engage the safety so the hammer is released and falls forward. Very gently squeeze the trigger. Is the trigger blocked?
- cock the hammer and press your thumb with reasonable force against the hammer spur from the rear. Does the hammer remain in place?
- examine the magazine. Is it free of pitting, burrs, rust, dents? (Pay particular attention to the lips.) Is the spring resilient enough to push rounds up to the chamber?

- insert the loaded magazine. Does it click and lock into position? (If not, it may fail to feed.)
- place the safety in the "on" position.

Note: If your semi-automatic is a .45 cal. single-action model, you also want to test the grip safety. With the gun EMPTY, cock the hammer, push the thumb safety off and then press the trigger while holding the gun by the frame so as not to depress the grip safety. *The hammer should not fall.* If it does, the grip safety is not functioning properly, and you should not carry the gun on duty.

Now cock it again. Be sure the thumb safety is off and pull the trigger with the gun in a normal shooting hold, while depressing the grip safety. This time the *hammer should fall.* If it does not, the safety is jammed and you won't be able to fire.

Shotgun

Carefully extract each live round from the magazine loading port, rather than from the side ejection port, if possible. With your gun empty:

- inspect the barrel. Is it free from cracks...bulges...rust...pitting...leading...obstructions? Is it tightly fitted into the receiver? (Bulges are usually indicated by a shadowy depression or a dark ring in the bore or by a bubble or raised ring on the barrel's outside surface. If you detect bulges or cracks or the barrel is loose, turn the gun over to your armorer. It is dangerous for you to use.)
- push the safety on and very gently attempt to pull the trigger. Does it move? (In this position, dry firing should not be possible.)
- cock the shotgun again. Take the safety off and squeeze the trigger twice to assure that the trigger mechanism is functioning correctly.
- with the safety on, remove the magazine cap and the barrel and test your firing pin. To do so, put a penny against the firing pin hole. Place two fingers flat across the top of the opening to prevent the penny from flying out. Now release the safety, cock the gun and pull the trigger. Does the pin hit the penny with enough force to dent it slightly? (If not, it won't detonate the primers of shells and the gun won't fire when you need it.) CAUTION: Never substitute your finger for a penny because of the strong striking force of a properly functioning firing pin.
- examine the magazine, inside and out. Is it clean...free of dents? (If the magazine is dirty or damaged, it may not feed the shells into the chamber.)

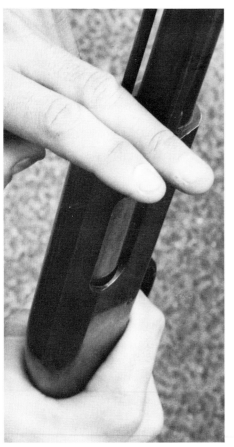

To conduct the firing pin test on the shotgun, empty the weapon first, then cock it. Use two fingers to keep the penny secure as you pull the trigger.

A properly functioning firing pin in your shotgun should strike the penny with enough force to dent it. [Here the dent is under the word "unum"].

- visually examine shells before reloading. Are there any cracks, gouges or other flaws that could affect feeding?
- reassemble the shotgun. Make certain that the barrel fits snugly into the receiver and that the magazine cap is screwed on tightly.
- reload, making sure that a live round is not in the chamber.

A Note on Dry Firing

With the exception of the shotgun, your firearms will benefit from dry firing. It tends to improve trigger pull and smooth up the internal action, as well as increase your familiarity with how your gun feels when it is functioning properly.

However, you should dry fire *only* after confirming that your gun is *empty*. As an extra precaution, you should never point the gun at people, interior walls, windows or in any other direction where the damage that might result from discharging an overlooked live round could not be lived with.

In the case of the shotgun, extensive dry firing can damage the firing pin and its channel. It is better to have the pin strike something about the same hardness as a primer when you pull the trigger. That's why the penny is recommended for the serviceability check.

16 | PHYSICAL FITNESS

Anyone can be an armchair survivor, like anyone can be an armchair traveler. You can sit for hours with a book like this and review the tactics that can help keep you safe before...during...and after an armed confrontation. But can you transfer them to the street, actually perform them wherever and whenever you need to? That's really the only question that's pertinent at this point.

Two factors will determine your answer: 1) the extent to which you are willing to practice the procedures and physical maneuvers we've outlined as necessary for survival skill, and 2) the degree of your physical fitness.

Let's face an unfortunate truth: most officers are in terrible physical shape. The longer they've been away from the academy, the worse condition they're likely to be in. In most departments, physical training is strictly voluntary and little is ever said about poor condition. Officers may tell themselves they're fit and toned, but many, faced with the necessity of exiting their units and running half a block in pursuit of a suspect, would fall flat on their faces before they got around to the front of their patrol car!

Like their disinterest in thoroughly familiarizing themselves with the firearms they carry, their physical negligence reflects laziness, complacency—and a failure to perceive the relevance to survival.

Physical fitness *is* relevant to staying alive in law enforcement. Effective defense maneuvers require dexterity, strength, agility, suppleness. For the physical exertion under stress that's common to armed encounters, you need a well-tuned cardio-vascular system. Quick reflexes and good eye-hand coordination are mandatory for the use of surprise and for accurate shooting.

As we said at the beginning, survival prepared-ness is a system that combines tactical knowledge, shooting skill, mental attitude— *and* physical con-ditioning. Eliminate or neglect any of these com-ponents and you have a system with a hole in it big enough to drive a bullet through.

Just practicing the survival techniques des-cribed in the previous chapters to the point that you can perform them efficiently will help keep you in good physical shape. By the same token, adding regular conditioning exercises and games that relate specifically to survival fitness will help you master the tactical techniques you are practicing. The more you do of each, the more proficient you be-come at both—and the better your chances of successfully handling challenges that threaten your life.

Exercises

The forms of exercise that can give you the best all-around conditioning for tactical readiness probably are running and swimming. These activi-ties can dramatically improve your cardiovascular system so that your heart and lungs can better accommodate sudden exertion. If you're *not* in shape and need to chase and then shoot a suspect, you'll have a tough time doing so, because your heart will be racing and your lungs heaving to the point that getting steadily on target becomes all but impossible. You'll experience some physiologi-cal effects from stress alone, of course. But if you've exercised so that your endurance is length-ened, your lung capacity expanded and your heart rate controlled, overexertion will not be complicating the problem. Consequently, your shooting accuracy will be far greater and your prob-ability for surviving improved considerably.

Some calisthenics, including those performed with a simple hand apparatus, can help strengthen and tone your shoulders, arms and hands, which are important in shooting and most other maneuvers. Good shooters tend to have well-developed fore-arms and shoulders. Push-ups help, of course. And arm curls, with dumbbells. These are exercises you can do while watching television. They'll help

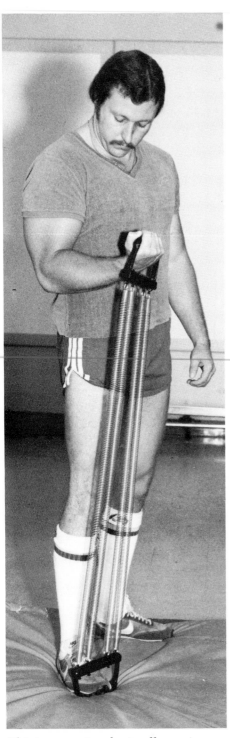

This inexpensive chest pull exerciser can be used 11 different ways to improve arm, chest, shoulder and upper back muscle tone.

quicken your draw by developing the muscles involved...give you extra strength in holding and controlling your gun to compensate for the *weakening* effects of stress during a confrontation...and also develop muscle mass to help absorb the recoil of your gun. By repeatedly squeezing a rubber ball in your palm or working a spring-loaded hand exerciser, either of which you can carry with you on duty, you can build up the strength of your grip. With the spring exerciser, squeeze only with your middle, ring and little fingers, slowly and deliberately, making sure that your trigger finger does not react at the same time. This helps train it to operate independently when shooting. To improve your endurance, put a nickel between the handles of your exerciser and see how long you can hold it in place by squeezing the handles.

Some officers hang a rubber ''squeeze block'' on the handle of their spotlight and ''work out'' their hands and wrists as they drive on patrol. Another patrol car option is to fill a Coke bottle with sand, cap it and hold it straight out to your side over the seat as you drive. This develops the muscles across the top of your arm and in your chest and will make it easier for you to hold your gun steady at arm's length, as in the instinct shooting position. To develop finger dexterity and grip, hold a full sheet of newspaper by one corner, using only one hand. Try to crush it into a little ball in the palm of your hand.

Isometric exercises, which pit your muscles against resistance to develop their strength, can also be performed in your patrol car. Press the very tip of your finger against the dashboard as hard as you can for increasingly long periods, for example. This will help strengthen your trigger finger and reduce the effort of shooting. When you're parked, put both hands on the steering wheel at three and nine o'clock positions and squeeze together as hard as you can with your hands and forearms. Keep your hands in that position and now pull outward. Now hold the wheel solid with one hand and wrist and try to turn it with the other. Switch both hands to the top of the wheel. Force them downward with all your strength, trying to lift yourself up with the strength of your arms and shoulders. Then with your hands at the bottom of the wheel, palms up, reverse your effort. Push up with your hands, trying to force your body down deeper into the seat. Start with 10 seconds of maximum effort for each exercise and build up gradually to 20 and 30. These exercises will strengthen your hand and arm muscles that relate to grip steadiness and endurance, tighten your stomach muscles and expand your lung capacity.

Other exercises will improve your reflexes and eye-hand coordination, which affect your ability to react to danger and to get on target quickly and accurately. One conditioner is to hold a dollar bill up between your thumb and trigger finger...drop it...and then try to catch it right away. This helps you reduce lag time; it's a lot harder than it sounds, and you've got to be well-tuned to do it. Another option, with your partner or a member of your family, is to have him stand with his hands about shoulder width apart and suddenly move to clap them together without warning you. You want to raise your hand from your side and get it between his hands before they can come together. Try this while watching his *eyes*, rather than his hands, and see if you can learn to detect the subtle "telegraph" messages that most people send subconsciously before they take offensive action.

While on patrol, you can exercise your eye-hand movements by quickly pointing at objects (unobtrusively) with your index finger, without looking at it. Check your alignment to see if you would have been "on target," had your finger been your gun. Considering that your gun is regarded as an extension of your hand in instinct shooting, this exercise can help sharpen your aim. At night you can make this exercise harder by first looking at lights, then looking away and abruptly pointing at something. You'll be surprised how far off you'll be—until, with practice, you learn to recognize and compensate for the way bright lights can alter your

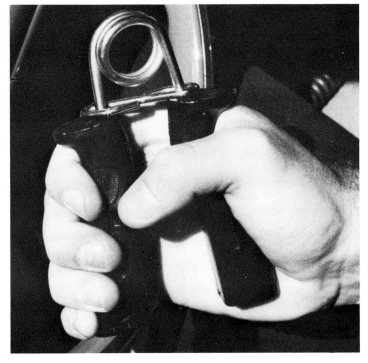

A $6 investment in improving hand strength, even during patrol. Squeeze until the handles touch, then release. Now turn the Hand Grips® with your thumb at the open end of the handles. Squeeze and release and repeat up to 30 counts each way. Practice with each hand as well.

An effective exercise which requires no gym or expense. The purpose is to strengthen the shoulders and arms, especially the tricep muscles. The result is improved coordination in using a firearm.

vision. Another eye sharpener is to try to read license plates coming toward you—not to detect wanted cars necessarily, but to quicken your reactions and observations.

Of course, by eliminating or reducing your intake of nicotine, alcohol, caffeine and other chemicals, you can improve your physical fitness in myriad ways—and your likelihood not only of surviving gunfights but extending your life in general.

If, despite conscientious practice, exercise and "clean" living, you find you still have trouble shooting swiftly and accurately, consider having yourself tested by a physician or therapist who specializes in detecting and treating dyslexia. This is an in-born disturbance of the relationship between the eyes and the brain which can cause perceptual distortions ranging from mild to severe. Some police trainers have found as high as 30 per cent of their students suffering from some form of dyslexic difficulty. A clue to this often is trouble in learning to read as a child. Such disorders frequently can be treated and either corrected fully or compensated for. But if you're unaware of the situation, it may be a factor in your missing your assailant in a combat encounter.

Sports

Certain popular games that people play for recreation, plus ones you can devise with a tactical purpose in mind, can also heighten your survival readiness. Ping-pong, racquetball, baseball, handball, indoor badminton—these fast-moving sports can help develop your eye-hand coordination and get you accustomed to manipulating effectively an object in your hands without having to look at what they're doing. This can work to improve your manipulation of your gun in a close combat situation. Hunting, too, is good. Or skeet- or trap-shooting. Any activity that demands quick shooting or hitting of a moving target.

With some imagination, you can turn the practice of survival techniques into a sport or game. One officer practices reloading his semi-automatic (using an empty magazine, of course) by turning off the lights in his living room and seeing if he can reload by touch before his wife can tag him. Using cap pistols, others practice disarming tactics with their wives, who try to come up with new ways of grabbing or holding a gun that can't be quickly defeated. Keep in mind that the longer you have to think about how to disarm an assailant, the greater likelihood you'll be killed if it were real life. In San Francisco, ex-convicts in a rehabilitation program meet with police officers to stage impromptu, realistic incidents like those they formerly experienced on the street, so the officers can become more familiar with adversary tactics and how to deal with them.

On patrol, you can turn "routine" observation into a survival-oriented game. As you watch people in a crowd or on the sidewalk, pick out certain ones at random and assume that they are armed suspects. How would you deploy to approach them? What cover might you use? How could you best protect yourself and/or shoot back if they suddenly displayed aggressive behavior?

With your partner or other officers, you may be able to set up your own "assault course" for target practice. With scrap you can get free from most dumps, you can erect moveable obstacles, barricades and "suspects" and practice firing under various scenarios that involve time and stress conditions. If you use duty rounds, rather than light loads or blanks, you'll get accustomed to just how your gun feels when it goes off. Naturally, you'll want to practice in a safe, isolated area where there's a good backstop, like a dirt embankment. Mix some empty cases in with your live rounds so you'll have a "malfunction" that will give you an opportunity to practice "immediate action" procedures. Working out there a few times a month, in all kinds of weather, will probably go a lot farther toward keeping you fit for the street than firing on a conventional range.

Another practice possibility with your partner is a sophisticated version of hide-and-seek. Using a building, an alley or other appropriate location, assume a given call, such as "prowler," "man-with-a-gun" or "burglary-in-progress." Take turns being the officer who plots a tactical approach and a suspect who tries to hide and outwit the police to get off the first shot. Obviously, live ammunition shoudn't be used in this exercise and even blanks might be disturbing to other people. Water guns, though, can add a little zest to the game, which can be played both by daylight and at night when you might need to consider light control. Afterwards, always critique the "officer's" movements and how they could have been better.

To add a strong dose of reality to your role-playing exercises, consider recreating in as much detail as possible the exact circumstances of incidents in which officers have been wounded or killed. With your partner and other officers, experiment with various tactics in an effort to discover how the officer injury might have been prevented. In this way, you'll realize how easily fatal mistakes can be made but also become aware of the tactical options available in most armed encounters.

With exercises and rehearsals, as with other components of survival, the core factor is *instinct*. Your goal is to develop your tactical engineering and your mental and physical fitness to the point that you can *plan, move and shoot instinctively*, in ways that keep you alive.

The challenge is never over, really. There are always new problems to consider...new tactics to develop...new skills to master in your effort to gain the edge over potential armed assailants. But the ways in which you see yourself improving, your survival senses sharpening, can keep you going. You need *determination, persistence, and willingness* to work hard.

You are like an athlete in training. But when *you* work out, you are training for the *ultimate* competition.

ADDITIONAL READING

Various other books and articles can provide useful supplementary information about some of the subjects we've covered, particularly in helping you understand, evaluate and maintain your firearms, ammunition and protective equipment. Some also provide additional data on what to expect in armed confrontations and examples of military combat procedures and techniques that can be adapted to street situations. Among those you may find helpful are:

BOOKS and MANUALS

Agosta, Roy, *Manual of Basic Police Firearms Instructions and Safe Handling Practices*, Springfield, Illinois: Charles C Thomas Publisher, 1978.

_____, *Ambush Attacks, A Risk Reduction Manual for Police*, Gaithersburg, Maryland: International Association of Chiefs of Police, 1974.

Bellah, Kent, *Book of Pistols and Revolvers*, New York, New York: Castle Books, 1975.

Brooks, Pierce, *Officer Down, Code Three*, Schiller Park, Illinois: Motorola Teleprograms, Inc., 1975.

Cooper, Jeff, *Principles of Personal Defense*, Boulder, Colorado: Paladin Press, 1972.

Daley, Robert, *Target Blue*, New York, New York: Delacorte Press, 1971.

_____, *Defensive Tactics, A Manual for Law Enforcement Officers*, Washington, D.C.: Federal Bureau of Investigation, 1970.

Fairbairn, Capt. W. E., and Sykes, Capt. E. A., *Shooting to Live*, Houston, Texas: Lancer Militaria, 1971.

Fyfe, James Joseph, *Shots Fired: An Examination of New York City Police Firearms Discharges*, Ann Arbor, Michigan: University Microfilms, International, 1978.

Grennell, Dean A., *Law Enforcement Handgun Digest*, Northfield, Illinois: DBI Books, Inc., 1976.

Jordan, Bill, *No Second Place Winner*, Shreveport, Louisiana: Bill Jordan, 1965.

Josserand, Michel H., and Stevenson, Jan, *Pistols, Revolvers and Ammunition*, New York, New York: Crown Publishers, Inc., 1968.

_____, *Law Enforcement Officers Killed Summary*, Washington, D.C.: Federal Bureau of Investigation Uniform Crime Reports, Annual.

Mason, James D., *Combat Handgun Shooting*, Springfield, Illinois: Charles C Thomas Publisher, 1976.

Milton, Catherine, et al., *Police Use of Deadly Force*, Washington, D.C.: Police Foundation, 1977.

Moyer, Sgt. Frank A., and Scroggie, Robert J., *Special Forces Combat Firing Techniques*, Houston, Texas: Lancer Militaria, 1971.

_____, *NRA Illustrated Firearms Handling Handbook*, Washington, D.C.: National Rifle Association, 1964.

_____, *NRA Illustrated Shooting Handbook*, Washington, D.C.: National Rifle Association, 1971.

_____, *Report of Police Body Armor Testing*, Gaithersburg, Maryland: International Association of Chiefs of Police, 1978.

Rexer, Fred L., Jr., *Dead or Alive*, Houston, Texas: IDAC, Inc., 1977.

Rice, F. Philip, *Gun Data Book*, New York, New York: Harper & Row, 1975.

Roberts, Duke, and Bristow, Allen P., *Introduction to Modern Police Firearms*, Beverly Hills, California: Glencoe Press, 1969.

Robinson, Robin H., *The Police Shotgun Manual*, Springfield, Illinois: Charles C Thomas Publisher, 1973.

Rubinstein, Jonathan, *City Police*, New York, New York: Farrar, Straus and Giroux, 1973.

Scanlon, Det. Robert A., editor, *The Law Enforcement Bible*, South Hackensack, New Jersey: Stoeger Publishing Company, 1978.

Skillen, C.R., and Williams, M., *American Police Handgun Training*, Springfield, Illinois: Charles C Thomas Publisher, 1977.

Sonderstrom, Dr. Carl A., et al., *Medical Assessment of a New Soft Body Armor*, Aberdeen, Maryland: U.S. Army Armament Research and Development Command, 1978.

Terry, Roger, *Flatfoot, Fuzz, Pig & Screw*, Chicago, Illinois: Roger Terry, 1978.

Van Heltebrake, Jerry, *Basic Combat Pistol Marksmanship*, Northbrook, Illinois: Budda Associates, 1973.

Van Kirk, Marvin L., and Lindell, James W., *Revolver Retention for Law Enforcement Officers*, Kansas City, Missouri: Kansas City Police Department, 1976.

Whittemore, L. H., *The Super Cops*, New York, New York: Bantam Books, Inc., 1973.

Wilber, Charles G., *Ballistic Science for the Law Enforcement Officer*, Springfield, Illinois: Charles C Thomas Publisher, 1977.

Williams, Mason, *The Law Enforcement Book of Weapons, Ammunition and Training Procedures*, Springfield, Illinois: Charles C Thomas Publisher, 1977.

Wood, J.B., *Troubleshooting Your Handgun*, Northfield, Illinois: DBI Books, Inc., 1978.

JOURNAL and MAGAZINE ARTICLES

Ayoob, Massad F., "Ambush," *Law & Order*, pp. 62-68, October, 1974.

Ayoob, Massad F., "When the Officer Faces an Armored Felon," *Law & Order*, pp. 74-79, October, 1977.

_____, "Bouncing Bullets," *FBI Law Enforcement Bulletin*, pp. 2-5, October, 1969.

Chambers, Herbert C., "The Police Handgun and Ammunition — Today," *Police Officers Association of Nebraska Journal*, pp. 23-29, 1976.

Chamblis, Lucy, "Does Combat Shooting Cost Cops' Lives?" pp. 88-92, 124-125, *Guns & Ammo*, September, 1976.

Christy, John, "Body Armor and the Endangered Executive," pp. 30-33, *Assets Protection*, vol. 3, no. 2, 1978.

_____, "Combat Stances for Police," *American Handgunner*, pp. 18-19, May-June 1978.

Cory, Bruce, "Deadly Force," *Police Magazine*, pp. 5-14, November, 1978.

Davidson, John, "Exercises to Improve Your Shooting," *National Marksman*, pp. 14-15, January-February, 1979.

DiMaio, Dr. Vincent J.M., et al., "A Comparison of the Wounding Effects of Commercially Available Handgun Ammunition Suitable for Police Use," *FBI Law Enforcement Bulletin*, pp. 3-8, December, 1974.

Dragland, Sgt. Don, "Soft Body Armor, Some Basics," *FBI Law Enforcement Bulletin*, pp. 15-17, February, 1979.

Green, Sgt. James J., "Plainclothed Police Personnel: An Identification Problem," *FBI Law Enforcement Bulletin*, pp. 16-21, April, 1975.

Guiffrida, Louis O., et al., "Service Sidearm Retention," *The Police Chief*, pp. 50-52, October, 1978.

Hashway, Robert M., and Nuttall, Ronald L., "The Effect of Wearing Protective Garments and the Aggressive Behavior of Police Officers," *The Police Chief*, p. 289-291, October, 1978.

Johnson, Norman E., "The Hows and Whys of Proper Gun Care," *Guns & Ammo*, pp. 62-63 88, December, 1978.

Lindell, James W., "Officer Disarmings—A Response," *FBI Law Enforcement Bulletin*, pp. 8-13, March, 1978.

Lovette, Ed, "Carrying Duty Ammo for Revolvers," *New Mexico Lawman*, pp. 10-11, January, 1977.

Lovette, Ed, "Firearm Training: Nuisance or Necessity," *New Mexico Lawman*, pp. 10-11, June, 1977.

Muirhead, J. C., "Some Comments on the Hostage Situation," *The Police Chief*, pp. 46-48, February, 1978.

O'Neill, Lieutenant Michael T., "Gun Retention," *FBI Law Enforcement Bulletin*, pp. 20-23, September, 1979.

Parsons, Kevin, "Revolver Speed Loading Devices: A Test Report," *Law & Order*, pp. 52-56, November, 1976.

_____, "Revolver Training and Night Firing," pp. 1-4, *FBI Law Enforcement Bulletin*, November, 1960.

Rummel, Bartlett, "Police Firearms Training: An Inquiry into the Governmental Duty to Provide Adequate Training," *The National Rifleman*, pp. 17-22, August, 1963.

Scacco, Dr. Anthony M., Jr., "Catch '22', the Continuing Bullet Proof Vest Controversy," p.22, *Law & Order*, August, 1979.

Salazar, I.E., and Lovette, Ed, "Another Look at the Practical Pistol Course," *The Police Chief*, pp. 24-25, October, 1977.

Simmons, Donald M., Jr., "Practical Guide to Complete Disassembly of the .45 Auto Pistol," *American Handgunner*, pp. 42-45, September-October, 1977.

_____, "Some Thoughts on Handgun Accuracy," *American Handgunner*, pp. 20-23, November-December, 1978.

_____, "Speed Loaders: Help or Hindrance?" *PWC Bulletin*, p. 2, 1977.

Spitz, Dr. Werner U., et al., "Physical Activity until Collapse Following Fatal Injury by Firearms and Sharp Pointed Weapons," *Journal of Forensic Sciences*, pp. 290-300, July, 1961.

Warter, Donald V., "Realistic Shotgun Training," *FBI Law Enforcement Bulletin*, pp. 3-9, December, 1976.

Williams, Mason, "The Combat Course, A Rational Firearms Course," *American Handgunner*, pp. 11-13, September-October, 1976.

Yount, August M., Jr., "Which Bullet is Best," *Illinois Law Enforcement News*, p. 4, Fall, 1977.

Yount, August M., Jr., et al., "Ammo Misfires," *Illinois Police Officer*, pp. 13-15, 51, Spring, 1974.

Yount, August M., Jr., and O'Rourke, Thomas W., "Breaking the Ice: A Study of Accidental Discharges," *The Police Chief*, pp. 70-76, April, 1978.

PHOTO CREDITS

Dennis Anderson, one of the nation's foremost directors of motion pictures for law enforcement training, supervised the unique visual content of this book. From hundreds of possibilities, he selected the documentary news photos used herein for their special instructional relevance. Also, except where otherwise indicated, he was personally responsible for all original photography, working with officers from a variety of municipal, county and state departments. Anderson, president of Bravo Productions, Inc., of Arlington Heights, Illinois, has been an active participant in the officer survival movement. He has helped conduct survival training sessions in several states and has directed a variety of realistic films oriented to survival methods, including: **Hostage Negotiation for Police, High-Risk Patrol Tactics** and **Shooting Decisions.**

Aurora (CO) Police Department—36; Bianchi Gunleather —75, 308, 313; Tony Bulaski—321; Burger King Corp.— 305; Chicago Tribune—258, 280, 368; Bob East III—56; Ernie Cox Jr./Chicago Tribune—192, 282; Bob Fila/ Chicago Tribune—55; Gustav Freedman/Evanston (IL) Review—34; Jim Frost/Chicago Sun-Times—310; Don Gruben/Evanston (IL) Review—34; Roy Hall/Chicago Tribune—77; Frank Hanes/Chicago Tribune—239; Bill Kesler/St. Louis Post-Dispatch—193; Arthur Kleist Jr.— 389; Walt Lemmon—320; Jack Lenahan/Chicago Tribune —6; Ron Lentz—62, 211; Marty Levin—317, 343, 344,

346, 347, 356, 364, 400; Library of Congress—191; Bill Mayer—8, 48, 60, 67, 89, 90, 102, 105, 130, 131, 132, 135, 186, 300; Marc Miller—Front Cover, 14-20, 22, 28, 41, 110, 141, 143, 161, 165, 169, 173, 176, 177, 185, 188, 189, 208, 245, 248, 249, 336, 345, 356, 358; New Orleans States-Item—99; Providence (RI) Journal Bulletin—73; Art Shay—33, 36, 233, 277, 344, 353, 373-383; UPI—24, 27, 34, 38, 50, 65, 113, 117, 157, 246, 267, 279, 307, 312, 333, 369; Bill Valerie/Los Angeles Times—4; Linda Warren—207; The Wichita Eagle—285; Wide World Photos—Title Page, Dedication, 3, 5, 10, 44, 53, 78, 155, 163, 176, 182, 191, 209, 247, 283, 284; Jim Young—100.

Photographs not identified were obtained with the request that their sources be kept confidential.

ABOUT THE AUTHORS

Special Agent Ronald J. Adams has been a prolific innovator of survival tactics since he joined the Riverside, California, Police Department in 1969. He is a graduate of numerous tactical training courses, including those sponsored by the California Specialized Training Institute, the FBI and the U.S. Marine Corps. He played a major role in developing one of the most unusual and realistic officer survival schools in the nation, located at Fort Irwin Military Base in the Mojave Desert. His on-going street experience has included assignments as a patrol officer and with the Riverside tactical unit. He has served as technical advisor on several award-winning instructional motion pictures and manuals produced by MTI Teleprograms Inc., including **High-Risk Patrol Tactics, Survival Shooting Techniques, Handling Firearms** and **Shooting Decisions**. He has also served as technical consultant to CBS *60 Minutes* on the subject of officer survival.

Lieutenant Thomas M. McTernan has helped train thousands of law enforcement personnel in survival procedures as a firearms and tactics trainer and instructor supervisor for the New York City Police Department. A police officer since 1963, with training in emergency management at New York University, he has served as guest instructor for the National Rifle Association's Police Firearms Instructor School, the firearms training program of the U.S. Customs Service and other outstanding courses concerned with tactical firearms use. His street experience has included patrol duties in the high-risk South Bronx Precinct and assignments with the Bronx Task Force. He has appeared in federal courts as an expert witness on what firearms training programs for law enforcement officers should encompass.

Charles Remsberg is a journalist whose twenty-year career has encompassed works on a variety of law enforcement topics. Author of more than 800 magazine articles and several books, he was won the prestigious Sidney Hillman Foundation and Penney-Missouri Journalism awards for his reportage. Throughout his career, he has specialized in writing about violence, crime and law enforcement for a variety of publications, including **True, Playboy, Reader's Digest** and **the World Book Year Book.** He researched and wrote the scripts for the motion pictures **Survival Shooting Techniques** and **Handling Firearms** and is the author of the widely used instructional manuals, **Hostage Negotiation for Police, Courtroom Performance** and **The Executive Survival Handbook** (for kidnap victims). During the 1960s, he served as a special consultant, on political disorders, to the President's Commission on the Causes and Prevention of Violence.